WHERE TO W

Ireland

SECOND EDITION

PAUL MILNE AND CLIVE HUTCHINSON

Christopher Helm

A & C Black • London

Second edition published 2009 by Christopher Helm,
an imprint of A & C Black Publishers Ltd,
36 Soho Square, London W1D 3QY

www.acblack.com

First edition published 1994

Copyright © 2009 text by Paul Milne and Clive Hutchinson
Copyright © 2009 illustrations by David Daly

ISBN 978-1-4081-05214

A CIP catalogue record for this book is available from the British Library

This book is produced using paper that is made from wood grown in managed
sustainable forests. It is natural, renewable and recyclable. The logging and
manufacturing processes conform to the environmental regulations of the
country of origin.

Commissioning Editor: Nigel Redman
Project Editor: Julie Bailey
Layout by New Leaf Design, Scarborough, North Yorkshire
Maps by Brian Southern

Printed in China by WKT Company Ltd

10 9 8 7 6 5 4 3 2 1

CONTENTS

CONNACHT   119

PREFACE TO THE
SECOND EDITION

It has been over 15 years since Clive conceived this invaluable guide to birding in Ireland and in that time many changes have taken place to the birds of Ireland and, indeed, to the practice of birding in Ireland. Sadly, many species are in rapid decline and one, Corn Bunting, has now become extinct as a breeding species. On the other hand, few birders in Clive's day would have envisaged the establishment of the Little Egret as a breeding species which is now ubiquitous on south and east coast estuaries.

Although many bird populations have declined, birding as a pursuit has flourished. Interest in twitching is steadfast among a hard-core of about 100 birders, but a general interest in birding for pleasure is much more widespread and concern for bird conservation has grown among the public and the authorities alike. More importantly, research in the field of Irish ornithology is now pervasive with many of the problems facing particular species under intense scrutiny and there is hope that the effort invested in Corncrakes and Roseate Terns, for example, will pay off in terms of breeding success and population expansion.

Climate change is playing a huge part in bird distribution compared to Clive's day. Apart from the expansion northward of Little Egret, there is evidence that Reed Warbler is spreading north and west. The tendency towards milder winters, on the other hand, has reduced Ireland's attraction as a winter refuge for large numbers of wildfowl, to the extent that Bewick's Swan is a real rarity away from traditional haunts in South Wexford. While the discovery of several breeding pairs of Great Spotted Woodpecker at east coast sites illustrates how other factors may be at play and just how unpredictable birds can be.

Given these changes to our avifauna, together with local changes to once favoured habitats and the emergence of new birding 'hotspots', it is opportune to revise *Where to Watch Birds in Ireland* with updated information on species diversity and populations as well as mentioning a number of new sites which have proved productive for resident and visiting birders alike.

I hope that readers will continue to enjoy Ireland's birdlife whatever future changes will hold, and to reserve special recognition for Clive's pioneering work in originating this guide.

ACKNOWLEDGEMENTS

This book has benefited from the assistance of a great many people all over Ireland, who have helped over the years with the provision of data for bird surveys and censuses, counting their own local site and ensuring that the results of their work appears in bird reports and survey papers. My own knowledge of the country's birdwatching sites originates from the early 1970s when I organised wildfowl and wader counts. My first car – a little Fiat – was used in 30 of the 32 counties of Ireland in search of birds, and while subsequent cars were not quite so widely travelled, I have tried to visit all the major wetlands, seabird colonies and migration watchpoints whenever away from my home base in Cork.

It is really impossible to list all the people who have helped me visit sites over the years or those who have accompanied me. They include many birdwatchers from all parts of Ireland, and if I list some I will certainly exclude others, so to all those who have watched and discussed Irish birds with me I express my sincere thanks for sharing your knowledge.

I must, however, single out those who responded to requests for information for this book and who kindly read sections of the text in draft and examined the maps. None of them is responsible for any errors which have slipped through the checking process, but they all helped to reduce the level of mistakes. Advice and helpful literature on reserves in Northern Ireland was received from Dave Allen (RSPB reserves in Northern Ireland), Sarah Anderson (Dundrum Bay), Shaun D'ArcyBurt (Quoile Pondage), Phil Davidson (Oxford Island), Uam McFaul (Rathlin Island) and James Orr (Castle Espie). Jane Coman provided information on the Birdwatch Ireland hide at the Little Brosna.

Texts were read and commented on by Declan McGrath and Paul Walsh (Waterford), Jim Wilson (Cork), Pat Smiddy (Ballymacoda, Ballycotton and Cork Harbour), Terry Carruthers and Peter McDermot (Kerry), Tony Mee (Limerick and Clare), Tony Whilde and Marianne ten Cate (Clare, Galway, Mayo, Sligo and Roscommon), Don Cotton (Sligo), Tom Cooney (Louth, Dublin, Meath, Wicklow), David Daly and Oran O'Sullivan (Wexford), Chris Wilson (North Slob), Oscar Merne (Offaly), Bruce Carrick (Westmeath), Dave Allen (Ulster), Ralph Sheppard (Donegal), Liam McFaul (Rathlin Island), David Thompson (Strangford Lough), James Orr (Strangford Lough and Castle Espie in particular), Shaun D'Arcy-Burt and Stephen Foster (Strangford Lough and Quoile Pondage in particular), Sarah Anderson (Dundrum Bay) and Phil Davidson, Bob Davidson and Brian Nelson (Lough Neagh sites).

Many of those who commented on earlier drafts suggested the inclusion of additional sites, but space has not permitted this. There remains an obvious demand, however, for detailed site guides covering many more sites in individual counties and I hope that some publications will appear shortly.

David Daly produced the line drawings which so enhance the text. I hope that the wider exposure that this book will give his work may lead readers to seek out more of his art. The stunning mural he has painted within the observation tower at the North Slob in Wexford should be seen by all visitors to that site.

The preparation of so many maps was a forbidding task but I received computing advice from Willie Kelly and technical suggestions on presentation from Tom Cooney, which removed a lot of the pain from the process.

Robert Kirk at Christopher Helm was a tolerant editor, always receptive to proposals on layout and quick to respond to queries.

Long evenings before a word processor could have a disruptive effect on some families. I have been fortunate in that much of the writing of the book was done while my sons were studying in the evening, so family activities did not suffer unduly. Indeed, I am grateful for the encouragement I have always had from Rachel, Andrew and Mark, and for the good company when seeking out new or little-known sites in the course of research.

In preparation for the Second Edition, much thanks is due to the Editor, Julie Bailey, who kept my efforts focussed and aligned to the new format, Brian Southern, the cartographer who drew the many new maps and to Marianne Taylor, the copy editor for deciphering my almost illegible scrawls.

Thanks is also due to the local recorders and compilers of local reports and websites which have now become a common feature of birders' information exchange. Such an amount of data was unavailable in Clive's day and the means to disseminate it had not yet been developed but it is gratifying that such collaboration by amateurs still thrives among the birding community – long may it continue.

INTRODUCTION

Ireland has a very distinct bird fauna, in some respects rather impoverished when compared with other European countries, but in other ways extraordinarily interesting. Compare Ireland to the neighbouring island to the east, and consider that only four-fifths of the species recorded in Britain have been recorded here; that only two-thirds of the number of breeding birds occur; up until 2009, there were no woodpecker species; that some migrant birds, which pass through each spring and autumn and nest as close as west Wales, do not stay to breed.

Yet, on the other hand, Ireland has a small human population, a relatively unspoiled environment and a rather small number of birdwatchers, so there are great opportunities for exploring places with potential for birds where other birdwatchers will not be found. Because of the location of the island right on the western fringe of Europe projecting far out into the Atlantic, the opportunities for seeking out migratory seabirds, waders and passerine vagrants from America are immense. The small size of the island, its climate and topography all contribute to the type of bird community it has.

SEABIRDS

There is an abundance of seabirds: Ireland projects into the Atlantic and is surrounded by rich and relatively shallow seas stretching to the edge of the Continental Shelf. Throughout much of the year, large numbers of shearwaters, auks and petrels are recorded on all coasts. These movements were first reported at Cape Clear, Co Cork, where birdwatchers were amazed in the early 1960s at the vast numbers of passing seabirds in summer and autumn and at the presence among the common species of rarer skuas from the north and of shearwaters from the south, including Great Shearwaters and Sooty Shearwaters from south of the equator and Cory's Shearwaters from the Mediterranean, the Canaries, Madeira or the Azores.

Since the discoveries at Cape Clear were made, birdwatchers have visited headlands and islands all around the coast and spent many hours in wet and windy weather measuring the extent of seabird passage. We now know that most south and west coast headlands can attract large number of seabirds in the right conditions. Passage on the south coast is predominantly westerly, on the west coast most birds pass south; on the north coast more pass west than east; on the east coast passage is largely southerly. Many of the movements observed involve feeding birds. For example, the late summer passage of Manx Shearwaters at Cape Clear clearly consists mainly of birds from the Kerry island breeding colonies. But the most remarkable movements, those in which southern shearwaters, northern skuas and rarities such as Sabine's Gulls and Leach's Storm-petrels are sometimes seen, appear to result from weather conditions driving birds which are normally out of sight of land inshore. At Cape Clear, south-westerly winds and rain, usually associated with the passage of a front, provide the best conditions as the birds are presumably pushed eastwards. At Brandon Point and Loop Head, westerlies and north-westerlies are optimal, funnelling the birds into Tralee Bay and Galway Bay. Seabirds moving back out to sea appear to follow leading lines when they encounter barriers to their movement, so those species which are normally not visible from the mainland can be observed temporarily as they pass headlands or islands.

There are clearly large numbers of seabirds feeding well out to sea, only to be seen from the land in exceptional weather conditions. Several trips have been made in small boats to observe seabirds at sea, and these have located high densities off south-west Ireland – higher than off much of the British coast –including many Great and Sooty Shearwaters, smaller numbers of Cory's Shearwaters and a few Wilson's Storm-petrels.

WINTER VISITORS

Wintering birds come from a wide geographical range of breeding areas. Being on the western fringe of Europe, Ireland provides winter quarters for birds from as far west as Arctic Canada, for a number of species breeding in Greenland and Iceland and for birds which breed in northern Europe east to Siberia. Brent Geese from northern Canada winter in Ireland. The wintering numbers of Great Northern Divers are far greater than the Icelandic population can account for, and may well include Canadian birds as well as Greenland breeders. From Greenland alone come Barnacle and White-fronted Geese and several wader species. Ireland is the principal wintering area for a number of Icelandic species, particularly Whooper Swans, European Golden Plovers, Black-tailed Godwits and Redshanks. From Scandinavia and the Baltic come many ducks, waders and finches and from as far east as Siberia come wintering Bewick's Swans, Grey Plovers and Bar-tailed Godwits.

VAGRANTS

Ireland's location is also the principal explanation for its pattern of vagrancy. Being on the western edge of Europe, Ireland is the first landfall for many vagrants from North America, but birds from as far east as Siberia such as Yellow-browed Warblers also occur every autumn. However, Ireland receives far fewer eastern or southern vagrants than Britain, which of course is not surprising, given the extra distance such birds have to travel.

ISLAND SIZE

The area of Ireland is 84,421 km^2; the adjoining island of Great Britain is 2.8 times as large. There is little doubt from island biogeography theory that the smaller size of Ireland is the principal reason why it has only two-thirds of the number of breeding species found in Britain.

A small island is likely to be landed on by a scarce bird than a large island, purely because the chances of the bird finding the larger island are greater. A smaller island is also likely to have lower habitat diversity than a large island. There are some habitats in Britain which are not represented in Ireland: the lowland heath and chalk downland of southern England and the high mountains and Caledonian Scots pine woodland of Scotland have no Irish equivalent. The absence of these habitats may explain why Woodlarks, Dartford Warblers, Stone-curlews, Dotterels, Greenshanks and Crested Tits do not nest in Ireland.

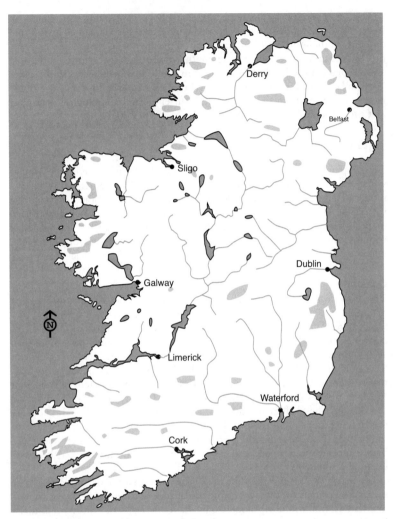

Land over 300 metres and river systems

CLIMATE

The mild but extremely moist Irish climate also affects bird distribution, both indirectly and directly. The high Irish rainfall, for example, produces winter flooding which provides refuge for wildfowl. Ireland's climate does, however, affect bird distribution directly when the milder winter temperatures keep the ground soft and the lakes free of ice, thus ensuring their availability for feeding birds, when extreme winter conditions over Europe drive many birds west-wards. In these circumstances, Teals, 'Northern' Lapwings and Redwings, to name just three species, flood into Ireland seeking exposed water or soft ground.

The onset of global climate change is likely to have unforeseen effects on Ireland. Climate models predict elevated temperatures accompanied by summer droughts in the south-east and winter floods in the north-west. In recent years, the Little Egret has colonised the southern and eastern counties and Reed Warbler has consolidated its bridgehead in south coast reedbeds. On the other hand upland breeding waders such as European Golden Plover and Curlew have collapsed in numbers, while Ring Ouzel is barely holding on. It is clear that the future holds many changes.

TOPOGRAPHY

Topography, like climate, affects bird distribution by its influence on the habitats which cover the landscape. Geological history has formed the basis of the modern landscape, but climate, the effect of erosion by wind and water, and the pattern of plant and animal colonisation after the Ice Age, have all played parts in producing the habitats which cover the island nowadays. The principal habitats can conveniently be divided up into the broad categories of coast, inland wetlands, mountain and bog, farmland, woodland and urban areas.

Coastline

The Irish coastline is varied. The cliffs support large populations of breeding seabirds while the estuaries and coastal lagoons hold many wintering and passage wildfowl and waders. More than 85% of the coast consists or rocky shore, but much of it is low-lying. Only about nine seabird colonies have more than 10,000 breeding pairs. Of these, only Lambay Island off the Dublin coast, Great Saltee off the south Wexford coast and Rathlin Island, Antrim, are away from the west coast. The largest colonies are in Kerry, where some tens of thousands of Manx Shearwaters, European Storm-petrels, Gannets and Puffins breed on the Blaskets, the Skelligs and the appropriately named Puffin Island. These are the largest European Storm-petrel colonies in the world. The colonies close to the Irish Sea have large numbers of Razorbills, Common Guillemots and gulls. Those species which feed farther out to sea are concentrated on the more exposed coasts.

Less than 15% of the coastline is sandy beach, mudflat or saltmarsh. These shores, however, incorporate a large intertidal zone and are important for wintering waders and wildfowl, though only six estuaries – the Shannon Estuary, Lough Foyle, Strangford Lough, Dundalk Bay, the North Bull and Cork Harbour – hold more than 20,000 waders regularly. These estuaries, as would be expected, have the largest areas of intertidal mudflat.

The sandy shores on the west coast are known to support quite large winter populations of Ringed Plovers and Sanderlings but their extent is not known. The sandy beaches are numerous and long and a coordinated count is not feasible at present.

As well as winter waders, sandy shores also support some breeding terns, though the colonies tend to be small and widely dispersed.

On the west coast, grassy islands are the main wintering ground for Barnacle Geese breeding in west Greenland. The Inishkea Islands, Mayo, hold nearly half the Irish winter population. Many of these islands also provide secure nesting sites for Arctic, Common and Sandwich Terns.

There is a small amount of sand dune machair in the west. Machair comprises stable dune grassland with sands enriched by calcareous shell fragments. It is heavily grazed and frequently includes wet pools and marshes. This habitat is thinly distributed in Donegal, Sligo, Mayo and Galway.

Inland Wetlands

In winter the open waters of the inland wetlands provide feeding and relative security from predation for ducks and geese, mainly from breeding areas to the north-west and north-east. The damp edges provide grazing for the wildfowl and also attract Northern Lapwings, European Golden Plovers and Curlews, which can locate food more easily on soft ground. In summer ducks and grebes nest on the larger waters, Little Grebes, Moorhens and Grey Wagtails on the rivers, and ducks and Common Snipes on the marshes.

The largest Irish lake is Lough Neagh which has a surface area or 387 km^2. In summer it holds well over 750 pairs of Great Crested Grebes, much the largest breeding concentration in the country, but in winter it is of European importance for the huge numbers or wintering waterfowl it holds. Lough Corrib, Galway, is the second largest lake with an area of some 170 km^2, and it too is shallow, with a large diving duck population in winter. These two lakes are much the most important for birds, principally because they are so shallow. The other large lakes – Lough Derg, Lower Lough Erne and Lough Conn – are deeper and of less importance in winter. However, a number of the midland lakes, especially Loughs Iron, Owel and Derravaragh, have sizeable winter duck populations.

In summer most of the lakes have breeding Great Crested Grebes, Mallards and Tufted Ducks. Common Scoters nest in decreasing numbers on Lough Corrib, Lough Ree and in very small numbers on other lakes. The principal inland gull colonies are on the western lakes and Lough Neagh, and Common Terns breed on islands on a number of lakes as well. Arctic and Sandwich Terns also nest on islands away from the sea, though in small numbers.

The water table in the west of Ireland rises with winter rain, the slower flowing rivers flood and the few remaining turloughs fill with water. This flooding produces large areas of water where ducks, geese and swans can graze, relatively safe from predators. It also drives invertebrates up to the surface, where Northern Lapwings, European Golden Plovers and Curlews search in the soft ground for prey; and it covers such large tracts of country that birds disturbed while feeding can find suitable ground again after a short flight.

The callows or flood meadows on both sides of the River Shannon between Athlone and Portumna, on either side of the River Suck in Roscommon and on either side of the Little Brosna in Offaly and Tipperary, are the finest examples, though the Blackwater callows in Waterford are also superb. Here Wigeons graze on the edge of the water in great flocks of several thousand birds, Whooper Swans graze out in the middle of the flood and large flocks of European Golden Plovers wheel about. Black-tailed Godwits probe in the soft alluvium, while the more common Curlews and Northern Lapwings can be seen in most fields. At some of these sites, White-fronted Geese winter in small numbers, feeding on the callows and usually roosting on the surrounding bogs. The feeding appears to be very rich in spring, for numbers of Wigeons and Black-tailed Godwits normally reach a peak in March on the Little Brosna, apparently because many birds of Icelandic origin assemble here before departing to their breeding grounds.

Because the central plain is so flat, most Irish rivers are slow and sluggish in their upper courses, but they tend to run much more rapidly as they come close to the sea. Moorhens are common on almost all rivers and Kingfishers, Dippers, Grey Wagtails and Reed Buntings breed on most. In recent years the spread of Mink on rivers has been seen as the cause of some reduction in bird numbers.

Mountains

The birds of high ground are little known. European Golden Plovers once nested on high ground in the south, east and midlands but now only remain as breeding birds in the north and west. Ring Ouzels continue to nest in small numbers in mountain ranges in the south-west and north-west of the country, though they are difficult to track down. Ravens were once true montane birds but have increased and spread into the lowlands. The principal birds of high ground are Meadow Pipits and, in winter, the highest hills hold Snow Buntings.

Woodland

About 5% of the land surface of Ireland consists of forest, most of which is planted coniferous woodland, but some oak woods remain and these tend to be rather richer in bird species. The most numerous species in oak woods are Chaffinch, Robin, Goldcrest, Blue Tit, Coal Tit and Wren, these six comprising 75–85% of the breeding bird communities in studies carried out to date. Comparison with results from Welsh and Scottish oak woods which had a somewhat similar history of management and utilisation shows that Willow Warblers, Garden Warblers and Blackcaps, all of which breed in Welsh and Scottish woods, were absent from the Irish plots, though they breed in other parts of Ireland. It may be that the absence of Willow Warblers was due to the occupation of their niche by Goldcrests, or that the absence of pioneer growth in the Irish census plots, especially of birch, excluded Willow Warblers. Both explanations have been proposed.

The birdwatcher going into mature planted coniferous woodland in summer will be impressed by the high density of Goldcrests. Studies of Norway spruce and Sitka spruce woods found up to 180 pairs of birds in total per 10 ha in the Norway spruce, of which 59 were Goldcrests. This is much the highest recorded density of Goldcrests in any habitat in Britain or Ireland, but unfortunately only 14 species in total were found. The Sitka spruce wood had fewer birds and only eight species were found. Again, Goldcrests were the most numerous species, with Chaffinch and Robin in second and third place as in Norway spruce.

Urban Areas

The features of Irish towns that have drawn most attention in the ornithological literature have been the roosts of Pied Wagtails and the increase in urban Magpies. On the other hand, the decline in House Sparrows mirrors that in Britain although there is now some evidence that this has reversed.

THE IRISH AVIFAUNA

The reasons for the differences between the Irish avifauna and that of Britain or other parts of Europe are obviously complex. Ecological factors arising from the small size of the island have been of great importance as have the location and climate of the country. The various habitats, which have evolved or been modified by man, have provided the conditions within which those bird communities which occupy the country must survive. Modification of these habitats can have a marked effect on their bird populations and man's activities are the principal cause of changes to the landscape or its vegetation. Conservation is mainly about the careful planning of the landscape, and the future of the Irish avifauna depends on the influence of conservationists in the years to come.

GENERAL NOTES
FOR THE VISITOR

POLITICAL SYSTEMS

The Republic of Ireland is an independent Republic with its own legislature and administration. Northern Ireland is part of the United Kingdom of Great Britain and Northern Ireland and is administered by a locally elected Assembly.

ACCESS TO IRELAND

As Ireland is an island, the visitor to the country must come by air or sea. The following airports have daily connections.

Dublin: major UK cities, most European capitals and some US cities
Shannon: major UK cities and some European, US and Canadian cities
Cork: London and other UK cities, and some European cities
Belfast: major UK cities and some European capitals

Services change from season to season, so a check should be made with a local travel agent for up-to-date schedules. In addition, there are regional airports at Derry, Galway, Sligo, Waterford, Knock in Mayo, Carrickfinn in Donegal and Farranfore in Kerry. These airports are serviced mainly from Dublin (others) but some flights are direct from the UK and the Continent.

Ferries bring passengers by sea to the following ports.

Dublin: daily from Holyhead with Irish Ferries and Stena Line; daily from Liverpool with P & O Ferries and Norfolk Line
Dun Laoghaire: daily from Holyhead with Stena Line
Rosslare: daily from Pembroke with Irish Ferries and Stena Line; several sailings per week from Roscoff and Cherbourg with Irish Ferries
Cork: several sailings per week from Swansea in summer with Swansea Cork Ferries, several sailings per week in summer from Roscoff with Brittany Ferries
Belfast: daily from Stranraer with Stena Line, daily from Liverpool via Norfolk Line
Lame: several sailings daily from Cairnryan with P & O European Ferries, daily from Fleetwood via Stena Line

PUBLIC TRANSPORT WITHIN IRELAND

The railway system links the major towns and cities: Dublin to Waterford, Cork, Tralee, Limerick, Westport, Ballina, Sligo and Belfast, and Belfast to Bangor, Lame, Portrush and Derry.

There is an express bus system covering the other large towns. Local services operate throughout the country, north and south. Details of routes and times are available from bus offices in the large towns, and on the bus company website www.buseireann.ie

DRIVING IN IRELAND

Driving is on the left-hand side in both Northern Ireland and the Republic. Cars can be brought on the car ferries or hired at the international airports.

CURRENCY

The currency in the Republic of Ireland is the Euro, in Northern Ireland the pound sterling. Most currencies can be changed readily at banks, of which there are several in every major town.

ACCOMMODATION

There is an enormous variety of accommodation in the country, ranging from high quality, and very expensive, hotels through modest hotels, guest-houses and hostels to camp sites. The tourist boards can provide current lists of available accommodation in all areas. Booking is essential for the months of July and August but outside this season accommodation is usually available to the caller at the door. Some camp sites and hotels close for the winter.

MAPS AND GUIDES

A number of road maps are available at various scales, but the standard Ordnance Survey 'Discovery' series is produced at a scale of 1:50,000. The Ordnance Survey of Ireland (OSI) publishes 71 Discovery Series maps covering the Republic of Ireland and adjacent counties of Northern Ireland. The Ordnance Survey of Northern Ireland (OSNI) publishes 17 Discovery Series maps covering the six counties of Northern Ireland and substantial parts of the adjoining counties in the Republic. Many maps of Northern Ireland have replaced the six county boundaries with the 26 District Council boundaries. However since many ornithological publications, including bird reports, continue to record on the basis of the county boundaries, they are retained in this book.

In addition, there are ten Specific Area maps which map these areas, which are mainly of tourist interest, to a scale of 1:25,000.

TELEPHONE SYSTEM

The telephone systems in Northern Ireland and the Republic are different. From the Republic dial 00 44 followed by the local code but omit the first digit 0 from the local code. From Northern Ireland or Britain use the prefix 00 353 before numbers in the Republic and drop the first digit 0 of the local code.

CONSERVATION

In Northern Ireland, the Department of the Environment (DoE) is responsible for conservation, the establishment of nature reserves and the protection of Areas of Special Scientific Interest (ASSIs).

In the Republic, the National Parks and Wildlife Service of the Office of Public Works has this responsibility, except that there is as yet no statutory protection of Natural Heritage Areas, the new term for Areas of Scientific Interest, though legislation has been promised.

Voluntary bird conservation in Northern Ireland is spearheaded by the Royal Society for the Protection of Birds (RSPB) which has its own headquarters at Belvoir Park Forest, Belfast BT8 4QT, full-time staff, reserves and a number of wardens. Its telephone number is 028 9049 1547. BirdWatch Ireland (BWI) performs a similar function in the Republic. Its address is P.O. Box 12, Greystones, Co Wicklow and its telephone number is 01 2819878.

The National Trust for Northern Ireland, Rowallane House, Saintfield, Ballynahinch, Co Down (telephone 028 9751 0721) operates the Strangford Lough Wildlife Scheme and Murlough Nature Reserve and employs its own wardens. The Wildfowl and Wetlands Trust (telephone 028 9187 4146) operates a reserve at Castle Espie on Strangford Lough. The Department of the Environment operates several reserves and Craigavon Borough Council runs Oxford Island Nature Reserve.

BIRDWATCHING

BirdWatch Ireland has a network of branches throughout the Republic. These organise both indoor meetings and organised outings each month in winter. Members receive *Wings*, a quarterly newsletter.

In Northern Ireland, the RSPB has members' groups in the major towns, which have a similar programme. Members receive the RSPB magazine *Birds* and, in addition, a Northern Ireland newsletter.

The British Trust for Ornithology has a network of regional representatives in Northern Ireland who organise survey work. BWI runs similar surveys in the Republic.

Up to date news of rare birds throughout Ireland is available to callers of telephone numbers in both Northern Ireland and Republic. The system in the Republic is charged at premium rates. The Northern Ireland number can be phoned from within Northern Ireland by dialling 028 9146 7408, from the Republic by the number 0044 289146 7408. The Republic of Ireland number, only available from within the Republic, is 1550 111 700.

JOURNALS, REPORTS AND MAGAZINES

The major Irish ornithological journal is *Irish Birds*, an annual journal available from BirdWatch Ireland, P.O. Box 12, Greystones, Co Wicklow. It incorporates the Irish Rare Bird Report, the Rare Breeding Birds in Ireland Report, the Scarce Migrants in Ireland Report and the Irish Ringing Report.

The Northern Ireland Birdwatchers' Association publishes the *Northern Ireland Bird Report*, which appears at intervals of several years. The report may be purchased from the RSPB, Belvoir Park Forest, Belfast BT8 4QT (telephone 028 9049 1547)

Annual bird reports are listed at the back of this book and all may be purchased from BirdWatch Ireland online shop.

BIRD OBSERVATORIES

There are two bird observatories. Visitors are welcome to stay at both.

Cape Clear Bird Observatory, Skibbereen, Co Cork, has accommodation for ten people in addition to the warden, who is in residence from March to the end of October. The observatory is open all year. The island is reached by daily mailboat from Baltimore. Bookings to BirdWatch Ireland, P.O. Box 12, Greystones, Co Wicklow or book online at www.birdwatchireland.ie.

Copeland Bird Observatory, Donaghadee, Co Down, has accommodation for up to 20. The island is reached by chartered boat from Donaghadee and the observatory is open most weekends and some weeks from April to October. Bookings to Neville McKee (telephone 028 9443 3068), email at neville. mckee@btinternet.com

BIRD RECORDING

After your birdwatching trip, please send your records to the local bird recorder. Bird recorders tend to change so no addresses are given in this book. Records for Northern Ireland are best sent to the RSPB and, for the Republic, to BirdWatch Ireland. Both organisations will forward records to the relevant recorders.

SUGGESTED ONE-WEEK AND TWO-WEEK TRIPS

Visitors from outside Ireland, or Irish birders willing to travel around the country in search of diversity of species, frequently look for suggestions for brief trips. The following is a list of the more popular areas for visiting at different seasons. It is based largely on records of rarer birds over the past two decades and is biased towards the autumn when most rarities turn up, but it should not be followed too rigidly. There are lots of good birding sites waiting to be found.

Suggested hotspots for short trips, especially in autumn

AUTUMN

Wexford and Cork

Week-long trips to the south coast in August, September and October can be built around visits to headlands and islands for passage seabirds and migrant passerines and to estuaries and coastal lagoons for American waders and the possibility of other vagrants.

August is the peak month for passage seabirds. In Cork, the headlands which have recorded the largest movements have been Galley Head, Cape Clear and Mizen Head. Expect Sooty Shearwaters and Great Shearwaters in conditions of south-westerly wind and rain, but Greats are erratic and not always seen in these conditions. Cory's Shearwaters are even more erratic, but these headlands are among the best places in Europe to see Great and Cory's side by side. Manx Shearwaters, Fulmars, Kittiwakes and auks are abundant and Great, Pomarine and Arctic Skuas can all be seen on a good August day. Fea's Petrel and other rare species are less regular, but remember that almost everything from Black-browed Albatross to frigatebirds have appeared off these headlands.

An August trip along the south coast in search of seabirds can be mixed with visits to the estuaries and lagoons to look for waders and terns. Lady's Island Lake and Tacumshin in Wexford and Ballycotton, Clonakilty and Lissagriffin in Cork are all well worth covering daily. They have attracted rarities such as Pacific Golden Plover, Least Sandpiper and Caspian Tern at this time. Migrant passerines tend to be fewer, though Cape Clear has a good list of species recorded during the month. Melodious Warbler and Red-backed Shrike are almost August specialities.

September sees reduced numbers of seabirds, though Great Shearwaters have appeared in thousands, but it is the best period for American waders. Any American species can occur on the coast, and not just the hot-spots listed in this book turn them up. Many small lagoons and patches of mud at the head of estuaries produce Pectoral, White-rumped and Baird's Sandpipers. These estuaries are all easily accessible, and a three-day run from Wexford Harbour to Mizen Head will give sufficient time for adequate coverage.

September is also good for passerines. Cape Clear has received far more coverage than anywhere else but, in recent years, Dursey Island and the nearby mainland on the Beara peninsula have been watched for several weeks at a time. Rarities have been prolific: Dursey has had Ovenbird and Cape Clear has had Northern Waterthrush at this time. Other headlands such as Hook Head in Wexford and Brownstown Head in Waterford are also worth visiting.

October is the month when most rarities are seen. A few late American waders turn up, and Sabine's Gulls can still be seen off the promontories, but the real action is in the little gardens, along the hedges and stone walls and in the small fields of the coastal headlands. Vagrants from Siberia can be seen in the same field of view as passerines which have just dropped from the sky after crossing the Atlantic. At Cape Clear, for example, Pallas's Grasshopper Warbler and Grey-cheeked Thrush were found within minutes of each other in the same garden. Working from east to west along this coast, Hook Head has had Radde's Warbler and Bobolink; the Old Head of Kinsale has held Grey-cheeked Thrush and Siberian Stonechat; Galley Head has had Paddyfield Warbler and Philadelphia Vireo; Mizen Head and Crookhaven have had Isabelline Wheatear and Buff-bellied Pipit; Dursey has had Northern Parula and Eastern Olivaceous Warbler.

A one- or two-week trip along this coast could take the form of a leisurely drive from site to site or, alternatively, choosing one place as a base. If driving about, one could take Wexford, Cork city or west Cork as a base. If spending a week or more in one location, there are several obvious options. Tacumshin has a sufficient turnover of birds to justify an extended stay and there are several other sites nearby which could be checked daily. Ballycotton has similar advantages and was once run as an observatory, with results that showed considerable turnover of birds. Galley Head and Mizen Head can be very exciting when the winds are right, but when quiet they can appear virtually birdless. Cape Clear is the obvious choice for a week's stay. The Observatory has excellent facilities and, if it is full, there are a number of guest houses, a Youth Hostel and a camp site. More importantly, there is excellent company from other birders. Allihies, on the mainland opposite Dursey, is another place to spend a few days and it can be very rewarding.

Great Saltee

A stay on Great Saltee Island for a week in autumn can be very exciting, but it does require permission from the owner and some organisation as all food and cooking equipment must be brought out to the island. The island is not particularly good for seawatching, but it can be outstanding for passerine migration. In recent years it has not been covered regularly in autumn – many modern twitchers fear uninhabited islands because they present logistic challenges to vacating them promptly when bird news breaks. Some of us, however, might find this a very good reason for spending a week on Saltee looking for our own birds. Rarities seen in autumn include Siberian Stonechat, Western Bonelli's Warbler and Olive-backed Pipit. The island has been overshadowed by other sites to the west in recent autumns, but there is no reason why it should not be a very exciting place when the winds are from the south-east in October.

Kerry

The corner of Kerry that runs from Lough Gill east to Tralee and north to Akeragh Lough, is where it was first discovered that many American waders are annual visitors to Ireland. Frank King, who put Akeragh Lough on the map in the late 1950s and 1960s, still watches the area regularly. Among his more remarkable records are flocks of 13 American Wigeons and 14 Pectoral Sandpipers as well as a list which includes the first Irish records of Least, Baird's, Stilt and Solitary Sandpipers and many other waders on the Irish list.

Drainage has led to deterioration in habitat at Akeragh Lough in recent years, but the adjacent Blackrock Strand attracts American waders. Tralee would be an excellent base for a stay in the area. When the wind turns north-westerly and rain comes, head immediately for Brandon Point at the west end of Tralee Bay. Some of the finest seawatching anywhere has been enjoyed from here: Sabine's Gull is a particular speciality.

Kerry has possibilities for passerine migrants which have only been explored in the last few years. The tip of the Dingle peninsula has been shown to have similar species to the west Cork headlands, though in smaller numbers, and there must be further potential on Valencia Island and around Ballinskelligs.

Loop Head and Bridges of Ross

The western tip of the Clare coastline has very little cover as it runs out to the lighthouse at Loop Head. Yet an informal bird observatory and ringing station has operated here with great success for several years. Several guesthouses in the area provide an excellent base for a week's holiday in September or October.

September tends to be the best time for seawatching, and north-westerly winds are essential. But, in these conditions, virtually anything can occur. Parties of Long-tailed Skuas and Sabine's Gulls and good numbers of Leach's Storm-petrels and Grey Phalaropes are the main feature, but both Wilson's Storm-petrels and Fea's Petrels are regularly recorded and there has been a record of Swinhoe's Petrel.

Passerine migration depends on quite different weather conditions of course, and numbers of birds are low, but the quality of birds seen is extraordinary: Rock Thrush, Siberian Thrush, Pied Wheatear and Canada Warbler are among the highlights. Each year produces some new and exciting bird.

The area is thinly watched in autumn. Rarely are there more than four bird-watchers present, except when seawatching is good, and then the nearby Bridges of Ross can have 20 or more people on the cliff.

The Mullet

Many birdwatchers have looked at the map of Ireland, noticed the westerly projection at the north-west corner of Mayo and realised that it has to be attractive to migrants in autumn. The area is a long drive from any of the major centres of population, and bird numbers and diversity can be low when weather conditions are unattractive for migrants.

There was a Bird Observatory here for a few years in the 1960s, and the activities of a resident warden at Termoncarragh Reserve has exposed the real potential of the area. Rare wildfowl, waders, seabirds and passerines from East and West have been recorded in recent years.

Other west coast sites

A number of other sites on the coast of Galway, Mayo and Donegal might repay an autumn stay. The island of Inishbofin off the Galway coast has had Mourning Dove in November and has excellent accommodation; Tory Island off the Donegal coast has produced some excellent birds and has a hotel and guest-houses. Also in Donegal, Arranmore Island and Rocky Point have repaid sustained efforts by dedicated birders but, in general, the west coast north of Loop Head remains very much virgin territory and there are many new finds to be made.

WINTER

Wexford

Early in January, if the weather is crisp and dry, there are few better places to spend a few days birdwatching than the south-east corner of Ireland. The climate in general is milder than elsewhere in the country and the concentration of geese on the Slobs provides a focal point. There are always lots of birds to see.

Accommodation is widely available in Wexford and a week's holiday, or even a long weekend, could be well filled by visiting the Slobs for geese, the shore at Curracloe for diving ducks and grebes, the lagoons at Lady's Island Lake and Tacumshin for ducks and the unexpected, and the harbour at Wexford and the coast at Kilmore Quay for gulls and other strays (Forster's Tern and Brünnich's Guillemot have both occurred).

The Slobs have nearly 7,000 Greenland White-fronted Geese, but they also hold Brent Geese and a few Canada (usually of one of the small races) and Pink-footed Geese. A white or blue-phase Snow Goose is present in most winters and other goose species may occur. There are modest numbers of Bewick's Swans (Whistling Swan has been seen among them) and most of the common duck species can be found.

On the coast, just north of the North Slob, the beach at Curracloe has long lines of Common Scoters offshore. Around the edges of the flocks are divers and grebes, and among the scoters are a few Velvet Scoters and, in some years, Surf Scoters. A telescope is essential to view the birds, but the sand dunes behind the strand provide a good vantage point. The strand is long and well worth working very thoroughly.

Wexford Harbour might seem rather unexciting from the town but birders have found Bonaparte's Gull and Forster's Tern just off the bridge, and there are lots of waders beside the road.

Lady's Island and Tacumshin are both well watched in autumn, but in January and February birders are far fewer and the chances of finding interesting birds for oneself increases.

Lough Neagh and Lough Beg

Lough Neagh is so enormous that it requires several days to cover it any way adequately, and Lough Beg requires a day to itself. Winter is one of the best times in the entire area, for then diving ducks are at their peak. One of the great unanswered bird survey questions is whether the wildfowl counts, which are carried out from the shoreline, are comprehensive, or whether there are large flocks of ducks in the middle of the lake which cannot be seen from the edge and are missed. Whatever the truth of the matter, the numbers which can be seen are absolutely immense and provide one of the great ornithological sights of the country.

A visit in December, January or February should catch the birds at their peak. At least two days should be spent in the south-east corner visiting Oxford Island and the smaller lakes nearby. Large numbers of wild swans and ducks can be found at Oxford Island, but there is considerable movement between this site and Lurgan Park Lake and the Craigavon Lakes. The rare ducks, which turn up regularly in this area, include Ferruginous Duck, Red-crested Pochard, Ring-necked Duck, Lesser Scaup, Ruddy Duck, Goosander and Smew. This really is a very exciting place for the duck enthusiast to spend a few days.

This corner of Northern Ireland is close to Belfast Lough and Strangford Lough to the east, where large flocks of Brent Geese winter together with divers, grebes, wild swans, ducks and waders. It is also close to Lough Beg, a smaller lough at the north-west corner of Lough Neagh, where rare ducks and waders turn up with regularity.

SPRING

Great Saltee

Without any question the prime place in Ireland for watching spring passerine migration is Great Saltee Island off the Wexford coast. Its location at the south-east corner of the country is right on the track which many migrants take on returning from Africa, and it has a lighthouse nearby at Tuskar Rock which is known to attract birds.

In late April and May, the best times on Saltee, falls of warblers can number hundreds of birds. Willow Warblers are usually the most numerous, but in the right conditions they are accompanied by Cuckoos, Turtle Doves, Common Redstarts, Grasshopper Warblers and Whinchats, and rarities such as Hoopoe, Golden Oriole, Woodchat Shrike and Tawny Pipit sometimes occur as well. Extreme rarities seen in spring include Lesser Grey Shrike, Dusky Warbler and Subalpine Warbler.

A trip for more than a day requires prior permission from the owner and considerable organisation as the island is uninhabited, but there are usually expeditions of ringers in May. The warden at the Wexford Wildfowl Reserve can usually provide information on whether there are birdwatchers on the island.

Cape Clear

Many birdwatchers find it difficult to organise a trip to Saltee and are wary of the very real risk of being stranded there for an extra few days if the weather turns foul. Cape Clear, which does not attract anything like as many spring migrants as Saltee, has the advantages of ready accessibility, social life in the island's bars and the facilities of a Bird Observatory.

The birdwatching on Cape Clear in late April and May is much more dependent on weather than is the case on Saltee where migrants trickle through in spring in most conditions. Cape Clear requires a period of south-easterly winds if it is to have a successful spring, and even then the numbers of migrants are small. Quality, however, can rival Saltee. Rarities at this time have included Stone-curlew, Red-footed Falcon, Scops Owl, Bluethroat and Black-eared Wheatear. Even when the passerine movement is slow, there is reasonable seabird passage with parties of Pomarine Skuas perhaps the highlight.

SUMMER

Great Saltee

It is already evident that Saltee is a great place to spend a few days in spring and autumn. It is also a wonderful place in summer with its huge numbers of breeding seabirds. The Gannet colony is not the largest off the Irish coast but it is one of the most accessible and the Puffins, Common Guillemots and Razorbills provide a wonderful sight. There are few better ways of spending a sunny summer day than sitting on the edge of the seabird colony on Saltee, watching the adult birds return from the sea with food for their young.

Bird photographers find the island irresistible and some visit it every summer. Not just seabirds can be approached closely, but also Oystercatchers and late migrant passerines.

A day trip is much easier than a visit for several days but the longer visit does provide better opportunities for close observation.

Shannon

This account of places to visit for a week or so has emphasised coastal sites with the single exception of Lough Neagh in winter. One site, the River Shannon, provides unrivalled opportunities for mixing a leisurely holiday with good birdwatching, and hiring a boat is far and away the best way to enjoy it.

The stretch of river between Athlone and Portumna is surrounded by callows, which flood in winter and hold great hordes of wildfowl. In summer they have one of the few concentrations of breeding Corncrakes left in Ireland and lots of breeding waders. Mute Swan, Common Teal, Mallard and Shoveler also nest, though the birds are hard to see from a boat. A boat provides access to several moorings, where the calls of Corncrakes still reverberate at night. Even from the town of Banagher, Comcrakes can be heard from a boat after the restaurants and pubs close.

Farther north, on Lough Ree, there are breeding Common Scoters, gulls and terns. North again, there are lots of nesting ducks, but the river north of Lough Ree is surrounded by reedbeds where birds are very difficult to see.

Boats of various sizes can be hired at Killaloe, Williamstown, Portumna, Banagher and Carrick-on-Shannon. Rates are highest in July and August, but the overall cost appears more reasonable if a party of five or six share the boat.

HOW TO USE THIS BOOK

THE COUNTRY

This book covers sites of importance for birds throughout the entire island of Ireland. Although the island is divided politically into the Republic of Ireland and Northern Ireland, the birds recognise no boundaries and birdwatchers from both parts see the island as a biogeographical unity. The text of the book is divided into sections, corresponding with the four provinces, and within these sections the site accounts are arranged within counties.

CRITERIA FOR SITE INCLUSION

As the country is quite large and a number of potentially exciting sites for birds have been little watched, the selection of sites for this book has been difficult. Firstly, those sites known to have a wide diversity of species, and to be attractive for uncommoner birds, have been included. Secondly, sites have been chosen which hold certain specialised birds (e.g. geese). Finally, care has been taken to ensure that most parts of the country are represented.

The authors of some of the companion volumes in this series have stressed that the listed sites are all open to the public. Not many of the sites in this book are nature reserves and very few have resident wardens, so the position is somewhat different. A number are on private land and, while most landowners do not mind birdwatching on their property, it is essential that permission be sought in advance before entering gardens or crossing fields.

A total of 154 sites has been included, a small number of which have been subdivided into smaller sites for separate treatment where appropriate. As some of the sites fall within Gaeltacht areas, placenames are given in Irish in order to be consistent with signposting in these localities.

BIRD SPECIES NAMES

The species names used in this guide are in accordance with those in the recently published (2008) checklist of the birds of Britain – *Birds of Britain: the Complete Checklist*, compiled by Dominic Mitchell and Keith Vinicombe. This list, while up-to-date with its recognition of recent and proposed splits such as Caspian Gull and Siberian Stonechat, takes a more conservative approach with nomenclature. It is hoped that the use of familiar English names instead of their 'global' alternatives, for example Dunnock rather than Hedge Accentor, will make the use of this book more straightforward for readers. Copies of *Birds of Britain: the Complete Checklist* can be ordered from Solo Publishing – call 0208 8810550.

MEASUREMENTS

As distances shown on road signs are in the course of being changed from miles to kilometres, all measurements are given in metric units (see Metric

Conversion Tables at the end of this chapter). The references to maps are all to those of the Ordnance Surveys of the Republic of Ireland and of Northern Ireland (in general to the 1:50,000 series but, where published, to the 1:25,000 series). Grid references are to the 10 km square or squares within which each site is situated.

HABITAT

This section incorporates a brief description of the site or county, emphasising those features that are of particular importance for birds. A brief account is given of other aspects of the fauna and flora and the ownership or reserve status.

SPECIES

This section outlines the most interesting aspects of the birdlife of each site. Breeding, migratory and winter birds are discussed, generally starting with the birds of the season which is best for birdwatching. Common and widespread birds are excluded unless there is a particular feature of interest, and rare vagrants are listed only where they occur with some regularity.

TIMING

This section advises on the best season, time of day, weather conditions, state of tide and so on to see the birds mentioned for each site. Some places, such as the islands where seabirds nest, are better in summer than at any other time: others, such as estuaries, are best in autumn and winter. Early morning tends to be the best time for looking for autumn migrants, while seawatching requires quite precise weather conditions depending on where the site is located.

ACCESS

This is one of the key parts of the book. Nearly all the major sites have an accompanying map showing the roads and paths from which birdwatching can be carried out. The text provides directions to the site, generally commencing from the nearest town or major road, and continuing with detailed instructions to ensure that the site can be located with ease. Most sites are accessible by road or public right of way, and where access is restricted at the time of writing this has been stated. Few of the locations in Ireland are wheelchair-accessible as they are not official reserves or national parks. However, in some cases, where a paved level footpath adjacent to a lakeshore or through a woodland exists, the text will draw attention to this feature and, of course, disabled drivers will be able to make use of their car as a mobile hide, particularly so at some of the seawatch points.

For bird observatories booking information is given and for reserves the name and address of the warden is provided.

The text should be used in conjunction with the outline map accompanying it, and also with the relevant Ordnance Survey maps. References to the 10 km square within which the area is situated have been given for all sites, and the relevant sheets of the Ordnance Survey of Ireland (OSI) and Ordnance Survey of Northern Ireland (OSNI) 1:50,000 maps are referred to at the head of each site account.

CALENDAR

This section is for quick reference to check the most likely species to see at each season. It lists the more interesting species and, where rarities turn up frequently, those most likely to be seen are included as well. At sites good for seawatching, details of species likely to be seen are given here. This section should be used in conjunction with the more detailed Species account.

THE MAPS

The site maps scattered throughout the text are designed to help the visitor to find the best viewing points at the major sites. The location of all sites is shown in general terms on the maps of each province which preface the four main sections of the book.

Intertidal sand and mud is shown in a consistent pale tone on all the maps. Built-up areas are shown in a dark pattern of hatching and are named. Three categories of road are shown, each one thicker than the other. Narrow country roads are the thinnest, main roads the next and motorways the broadest. Road numbers are used more on maps of Northern Ireland sites than in the Republic as the numbers are more widely shown on signposts there. Railways are indicated with a dashed line.

Parking places and hides are indicated with a ringed letter P and H respectively. Particularly good places for viewing birds are given an asterisk.

At times other features are shaded. Where this is done, the map has a key or note to indicate what the feature is.

METRIC CONVERSION TABLES

For readers more familiar with the imperial system, the accompanying tables are designed to facilitate quick conversion to imperial units. Bold figures in the central columns can be read as either metric or imperial: e.g. 1 km = 0.62 miles or 1 mile = 1.61 km.

km		miles	ha		acres
1.61	**1**	0.62	0.40	**1**	2.47
3.22	**2**	1.24	0.81	**2**	4.94
4.83	**3**	1.86	1.21	**3**	7.41
6.44	**4**	2.48	1.62	**4**	9.88
8.05	**5**	3.11	2.02	**5**	12.36
9.65	**6**	3.73	2.43	**6**	14.83
11.26	**7**	4.35	2.83	**7**	17.30
12.87	**8**	4.97	3.24	**8**	19.77
14.48	**9**	5.59	3.64	**9**	22.24

MUNSTER

Waterford
1 Tramore Bay and Brownstown Head
2 Dungarvan Bay and Helvick Head
3 Blackwater Callows
4 River Suir at Coolfin
5 Kilmeaden Ponds
6 Waterford Harbour
7 Dunmore East

Cork
8 Ballymacoda and Knockadoon Head
9 Ballycotton
10 Cork Harbour
11 Old Head of Kinsale and Kinsale Marsh
12 Clonakilty
13 Galley Head and Kilkerran Lake
14 Cape Clear
15 Youghal
16 Courtmacsherry
17 Rosscarbery
18 Lee Reservoirs
19 Kilcolman
20 Lissagriffin and Mizen Head
21 Dursey Island and Allihies

Kerry
22 Castlemalne Harbour
23 Tralee Bay and Barrow Harbour
24 Akeragh Lough and Blackrock Strand

25 Ballinskelligs Bay
26 Lough Gill
27 Dingle Harbour
28 Skelligs
29 Dunquin
30 Blasket Islands
31 Smerwick Harbour
32 Brandon Point
33 Killarney National Park
34 Ballylongford and Tarbert

Limerick
35 South Shore of Shannon Estuary
36 Lough Gur
37 Westfields Marsh
38 Curragh Chase

Clare
39 Shannon Airport Lagoon
40 Fergus Estuary
41 Ballyallia Lake
42 Cliffs of Moher
43 Liscannor Bay
44 Loop Head and Bridges Of Ross
45 Clonderalaw Bay
46 Poulnasherry Bay
47 Mutton Island and Lurga Point
48 Ballyvaughan
49 Lough Atedaun

Tipperary
50 Lough Derg
51 Lough Eorna

MUNSTER

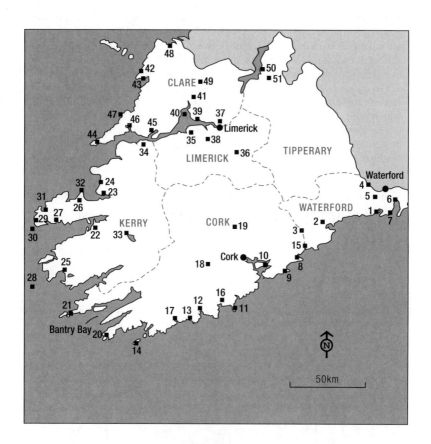

WATERFORD

Waterford comprises a coastal plateau with a row of high mountains behind. The coastline has four estuaries: Waterford Harbour, Dungarvan, Tramore and Youghal (partly in Cork and dealt with under that county). These are interesting for wintering wildfowl and waders. Between the estuaries are long stretches of cliff with colonies of breeding seabirds and Choughs. Some of these lead out to headlands, which provide sites for watching seabird passage.

The major rivers, the Suir and the Blackwater, enter the sea at the eastern and western ends of the county respectively. Both have callows (flood meadows), which hold wildfowl, particularly after heavy rainfall.

The lower slopes of the mountains are afforested but certainly hold interesting breeding birds. In recent years, both European Golden Plover and European Nightjar have been found nesting here.

1 TRAMORE BAY AND BROWNSTOWN HEAD

OSI Discovery map: sheet 76
S60 01; X64 98

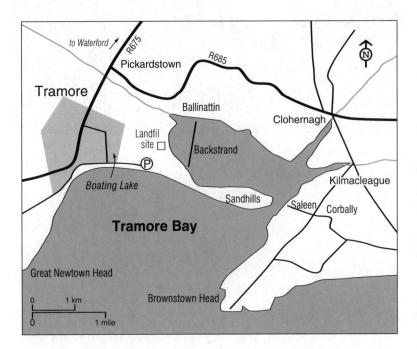

Habitat

Tramore Bay and Backstrand comprise a sandy outer bay and a muddy estuarine system impounded by sand dunes. The town of Tramore is a popular tourist
destination and large numbers of people frequent the strand in summer. The
best bird areas are the Backstrand and the Sandhills.

Birdwatching at the Backstrand is rather difficult at low tide because of the
width of the estuary. There are beds of *Zostera* or eelgrass on the north side providing excellent feeding for wildfowl, especially Brent Geese, and *Spartina* is
well established on the western side. Two embankments crossing the mud to the
east of the old town dump provide high-tide roosts for waders. There is
reclaimed land to the north, behind a sea wall, and at the eastern end there are
low-lying fields which are protected from the tide by raised ditches. At the
south-eastern corner of the bay, Brownstown Head projects well out to sea and
is an excellent seawatching site.

The inner bay is protected from the open sea by an extensive sand dune
system. Privet *Ligustrum vulgare* and Dewberry *Rubus caesius* bushes are found
here. On the seaward side, a sandy beach provides views of the open bay.

Species

The bay is very much a winter birdwatching site. In autumn the most
favoured place for Brent Geese is on the *Zostera*, but in early winter the geese
move to the eastern end of the Backstrand. By mid-winter they are scattered
all across the mud. Several hundred are present each winter, all being usually
of the pale-bellied subspecies, though in recent years single Black Brants, the
Pacific subspecies, have been seen occasionally. Some Shelducks, Mallards,
Wigeons and Teals also feed here, while a few Red-breasted Mergansers can
usually be seen in the channel.

The mudflats hold a diverse wader population. Oystercatchers, Grey Plovers,
Black-tailed and Bar-tailed Godwits, Redshanks, Greenshanks and Dunlins feed
on the mud but can best be seen at their roosts on the embankments or at the
north-eastern corner of the Backstrand. A few Turnstones and Ringed Plovers
can be seen here as well. European Golden Plovers, Northern Lapwings and
Curlews favour the fields at Clohernagh throughout the winter. The Clohernagh
inlet itself is always worth looking at. As well as the increasing Little Egret population, Kingfishers are regular and autumn migrant waders such as Spotted
Redshanks and Green Sandpipers are occasional. The beach and the shingle area
usually hold a small feeding flock of Sanderlings and sometimes a few Ringed
Plovers in winter. In summer Ringed Plovers nest in small numbers.

The town dump is now closed and no longer attracts gulls as it formerly did
but the Boating Pond behind the beach should be checked for roosting and
bathing gulls as Ring-billed Gulls have appeared here regularly. Off the beach,
Gannets can be seen fishing throughout most of the year and both Red-throated
and Great Northern Divers are regular in winter. In autumn, Sandwich Terns
feed off the beach and roost on the sand. Sometimes other tern species occur
with them, and skuas, mostly Arctic, occasionally follow them into the outer bay.
Large numbers of Kittiwakes can be seen at times in winter.

The Sandhills have nesting European Stonechats, Skylarks and Meadow
Pipits and, in winter, Short-eared Owls are not infrequent. Choughs are often
to be seen feeding here and Kestrels are usually present.

Brownstown Head to the south-east is an excellent seawatching and passerine migration watchpoint. Manx Shearwaters, Gannets, Kittiwakes, skuas, Common Guillemots and Razorbills pass in spring, summer and autumn and divers and rarer shearwaters in autumn. Passerine migrants can be found in autumn in gardens and hedges: the large garden at the south end of the road to Brownstown Head has produced many rare migrants in the past, including Yellow Warbler and Northern Parula. The hedges along the narrow lanes and bordering the fields are also productive.

Timing

The Backstrand is best visited between August and the end of March when wildfowl and wader numbers are at their highest. A rising tide bunches the birds and makes viewing easier. The route along one side of the Sandhills and back on the other is a very popular walk.

For seawatching at Brownstown Head, the best conditions are a combination of south-west to south-east winds, mist and rain. Falls of passerine migrants can occur from late March to May and from August to mid-November. South-easterly winds are best for scarcer species.

Access

Tramore town is best approached by the main road from Waterford.

The Backstrand can be viewed from several locations. To see the south-western end drive east from Tramore to the car park at the end of the promenade. Walk out along the embankment, which crosses the mudflats, then follow the Sandhills to the tip. The beach can be viewed from the south side and the mudflats from the north.

The turn off the Tramore-Waterford road at Pickardstown leads after 1 km to Ballinattin. A side road provides space for parking and the Backstrand embankment can be reached by following the lane directly opposite this point. Turn right just before the gate at the end of the lane rather than cross through.

Great Black-backed Gull

Clohernagh inlet can be viewed from Clohernagh on the main road or by turning south-west at Kilmacleague, just before Corbally Church.

Saleen in the south-east has a car park from which the mudflats can be scanned or the eastern side walked.

Brownstown Head is approached from Tramore by turning off the Tramore-Waterford road at Pickardstown, following the narrow road to Corbally Church, then forking right to follow that road to the headland. You can park near ruined farmyard buildings and from there approach the head on foot.

CALENDAR

All year: Shelduck, Cormorant, Shag, Grey Heron, Little Egret, Oystercatcher, Ringed Plover, Rock Pipit.

Spring: divers, Gannet, waders including Whimbrel and Sanderling, Kittiwake, terns, skuas, passerine migrants.

Summer: summer migrants including Sedge Warbler.

Autumn: Brent Goose and other wildfowl, Fulmar, Gannet, occasional Curlew Sandpiper and Spotted Redshank, terns and occasional Little Gull, Arctic Skua. Seawatching and passerine migrants at Brownstown. Possibly rarities at Brownstown.

Winter: Brent Goose, occasional Common and Velvet Scoters, Long-tailed Duck, other wildfowl, divers, waders, gulls including Glaucous and Iceland, occasionally Short-eared Owl and Snow Bunting.

2 DUNGARVAN BAY AND HELVICK HEAD

OSI Discovery map: sheet 82
X27 92; X32 89

Habitat

Dungarvan Bay is a broad, shallow bay fed by three small rivers. The inner part of the bay is impounded by a long, narrow, sandy spit named the Cunnigar. On the seaward side of the Cunnigar is an extensive sandy beach with large tracts of *Zostera* (eelgrass). The inner bay has a wide expanse of mudflats with smaller *Zostera* beds.

Helvick Head to the south projects well out to sea and has high cliffs. The coastline to the north as far as Ballyvoile Head is low-lying.

Species

The inner bay provides good views in winter of Wigeons, Shelducks, Oystercatchers, Curlews, Black-tailed Godwits, Redshanks and Dunlins. From the old swimming baths in the town most wader species can be seen close to the road and small numbers of Great Northern Divers, Great Crested Grebes, Cormorants, Shags, Common Goldeneyes and Red-breasted Mergansers are present in the channel. When the tide is out in spring, Brent Geese feed close to the swimming baths.

The main Dungarvan–Cork road also provides a ready viewing place for Brent Geese, Shelducks and Wigeons as well as Black-tailed Godwits and Redshanks.

Killongford Bridge on the main Cork road crosses the river Brickey. Upstream, Green Sandpipers can be seen frequently by the observer ready to walk along the embankment.

The Cunnigar is perhaps the best place in the estuary for large numbers of birds, especially at high tide. As well as large flocks of Brent Geese, Wigeons, Oystercatchers and Black-tailed Godwits, there are Grey Plovers, Turnstones, Bar-tailed Godwits and Knots. In autumn, Curlew Sandpipers and Little Stints occur here, and there are usually terns, especially Sandwich Terns. The sandy area at the base of the Cunnigar often holds very accessible parties of Ringed Plovers, Dunlins and Sanderlings.

Ballyneety Bridge provides excellent viewing of waders at close range, especially when near to high tide.

On the east side, the road to the Gold Coast provides a number of vantage points for looking out over the bay for grebes and diving ducks. There are good numbers of Great Crested Grebes and usually a few Great Northern Divers and Slavonian Grebes. Red-breasted Mergansers are dotted around the bay. Ballynacourty Pier, at the end of the road, is one of the best places from which to scan the area. North-east of Ballynacourty lies Clonea Strand, which is worth checking for waders and roosting gulls.

Helvick Head is another few kilometres on from the Cunnigar and, as a fishing port, is a good site to look for Glaucous or Iceland Gulls. In autumn, good sea passage of Manx Shearwaters occurs and Great, Cory's and Sooty Shearwaters have all been seen. In the same season the gardens and hedges often hold common migrants and there have been records of rarities, including Radde's Warbler. The headland has breeding Shags, Fulmars, Kittiwakes, Common Guillemots, Razorbills and Black Guillemots as well as Ravens and Choughs.

As with other south-coast headlands, there is always the chance of seeing Harbour Porpoises or dolphins and there are often migrant butterflies and moths in autumn.

Timing

The estuary is best from August to early April. Most areas are best on a rising tide when the birds come closest. The Cunnigar should be walked at or close to high tide.

Helvick Head is worth a look at any time of the year, but the seabird colony is occupied chiefly in summer and migrant seabirds and passerines are most likely in May or from August to October. As elsewhere on this coast, south-westerly or southerly wind and mist provide the best seawatching conditions.

Access

The town of Dungarvan is easily approached by main road from all directions. In the town, cars can be parked at the old swimming baths and the walk around the quays can produce an interesting variety of species.

To the south of the town, the estuary can be watched from the main Cork road. About 4 km on is Killongford Bridge, located just before the left turn for Helvick Head.

The Cunnigar is reached by turning left at the junction for Helvick Head, then taking a left turn after 1.5 km and continuing for about 2 km, where a sharp left turn at a farmhouse leads to the base of the Cunnigar where cars can be parked.

Helvick Head is reached by taking the Dungarvan-Cork road and turning off to the east where signposted about 5 km from the town. The pier is suitable for car parking.

The north side of Dungarvan Bay is readily viewed from the coast road at Abbeyside. Leave the main Dungarvan–Waterford road at the signpost for Clonea and follow the coast road to Kilminnin Bridge.

CALENDAR

All year: Mute Swan, Mallard, Cormorant, Shag, Little Egret, Oystercatcher, Curlew, Redshank, Kingfisher.

Spring: Whimbrel, terns.

Summer: seabirds on Helvick Head.

Autumn: sea passage. Waders including Green and Curlew Sandpipers and, in most years, Little Stint. Passerine migrants.

Winter: Brent Goose, Eurasian Wigeon, Common Teal, Pintail, Shoveler, Common Goldeneye, Red-breasted Merganser, Great Northern Diver, Great Crested and Slavonian Grebes, Ringed, European Golden and Grey Plovers, Northern Lapwing, Knot, Black-tailed and Bar-tailed Godwits, Greenshank, Green Sandpiper, Dunlin, Sanderling. Rarities include regular Dark-bellied Brent Geese and Black Brants.

3 BLACKWATER CALLOWS

OSI Discovery map: sheet 74, 81
W93 99

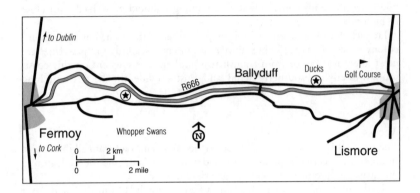

Habitat

The low-lying fields along the river valley of the River Blackwater between Fermoy and Cappoquin are prone to flooding in winter when large shallow pools form. There are deciduous woods on the hilly slopes to the north and south. Lismore Castle, owned by the Duke of Devonshire and available for rent if one tires of hotel life, provides a glorious backdrop at Lismore Bridge.

Species

Several hundred Whooper Swans graze in the fields in winter and large flocks of Eurasian Wigeon and Black-tailed Godwits (often over 1,000) occur on floods at times. Bewick's Swans, Pintail, Shelduck and Common Goldeneye are irregular visitors. Mallard, Common Teal, Shoveler, Tufted Duck, Pochard, Northern Lapwing, Common Snipe and Curlew all winter in small numbers.

The largest numbers of ducks and waders are to be found on the road between Lismore and Ballyduff. The swans are often found between Ballyduff and Fermoy. The southern road is usually the best. At times, there are large numbers of birds between Lismore and Cappoquin so the whole area from Fermoy to Cappoquin deserves investigation.

Large numbers of Redwings and Fieldfares feed on the hedges in winter and the woodlands hold Jays, Woodcocks and Siskins.

Dippers and Grey Wagtails can usually be seen on the fast-flowing river about 100 m to the north-east of Lismore Bridge.

Timing

Whooper Swans are usually present throughout most of the winter, but numbers of Wigeons and Black-tailed Godwits are very dependent on the level of flooding. If there has been little flooding, then bird numbers are low, and when the callows are frozen over most of the waterfowl move to the coast.

Access

Lismore is a good starting point. The river from Lismore to Cappoquin can be seen by taking the northern road to Cappoquin and returning by the southern arm. The north road from Lismore Bridge to Ballyduff provides a number of excellent viewing places commencing at the marshy area just beyond the golf course.

The south road from Ballyduff to Fermoy usually gives better views of swans than the north road, but at times the birds are on the other side. In all cases, they can be seen well from the road and a car acts as an excellent hide.

CALENDAR

All year: Mute Swan, Mallard, Grey Heron, Cormorant, Dipper, Grey Wagtail, Kingfisher, Jay.

Winter: Whooper Swan, Eurasian Wigeon, Common Teal, Shoveler, Tufted Duck, Pochard, Curlew, Black-tailed Godwit, Northern Lapwing.

---

4 RIVER SUIR AT COOLFIN

OSI Discovery map: sheet 75
S48 15

Habitat and Species

Coolfin is a wildfowl sanctuary protected by the National Parks and Wildlife Service. It is an area of grassy fields between the Suir and Clodiagh rivers and the Waterford to Carrick-on-Suir road.

The site holds over 700 Greylag Geese from October to April, one of the largest flocks in Ireland. Whooper Swans also winter here and small numbers of Greenland White-fronted Geese sometimes occur. Ducks, mostly Common Teals and Tufted Ducks, are usually found on the river itself. Northern Lapwings, European Golden Plovers, Common Snipes and Curlews feed in the fields and Green Sandpipers winter regularly.

Kestrels, Peregrines and Sparrowhawks are regular throughout the year.

Access

Coolfin is best approached from the Waterford–Cork road. Take the right turn where sign posted for Portlaw just beyond Kilmeadan, about 11 km from Waterford City. After 5 km a fork is reached: turn right for Carrick-on-Suir, rather than left for Portlaw, and Coolfin is reached on the right-hand side just after the first bridge. The geese can be seen easily from the road, but care should be taken to avoid disturbance.

5 KILMEADEN PONDS   OSI Discovery map: sheet 75
S51 08

Habitat and Species

These ponds are artificially created settling ponds for the nearby creamery, and in recent times have become an important birding spot. The water levels do vary from time to time and the ponds are at their best when there is some mud exposed around the margins.

In recent times these ponds have become a regular wintering site for Water Pipit and can afford decent views of a species which is notoriously flighty and hard to pin down. Green Sandpipers are also regular at this site in autumn and winter, and Water Rails are present and usually visible all year round. Apart from that, the usual freshwater aquatic species are regular while scarcer species such as Garganey and Wood Sandpiper have been recorded.

Access

Kilmeaden Ponds are located quite close to the N25, the main Waterford– Cork road. Going west on the N25, about 10 km from Waterford on the approach to the village of Kilmeaden, turn left just after The Sweep pub and drive about half a kilometre and turn right. Continue for about 1 km until you pass under some power lines; the ponds are accessed from a small road on the right.

6 WATERFORD HARBOUR

OSI Discovery map: sheet 76
S70 10

Habitat and Species

Waterford Harbour has intertidal mudflats on the west side at intervals from Passage East south to Creadan Head. A couple of thousand waders winter here, including Oystercatchers, Ringed Plovers, Curlews, Bar-tailed Godwits, Redshanks and Turnstones, and many Common Gulls roost. Small numbers of Great Crested Grebes, Little Egrets, Brent Geese, Wigeons and Red-breasted Mergansers occur.

Access

Passage East is approached from Waterford by taking the turn for Dunmore East at the Tower Hotel. Turn left at the petrol filling station 3 km south of Ardkeen Regional Hospital. A ferry crosses the harbour at this point and provides convenient access to south Wexford without the necessity to drive north to New Ross. There are some exposed mudflats here.

Follow the road from Passage East south for Woodstown and stop the car just over 3 km from Passage East. Walk down the narrow lane to the left to Geneva Strand where grebes and waders can be seen.

Woodstown is another 2 km south by road and Creadan Strand is farther south again. Take the Dunmore East road from Woodstown, take the next turn left, then the next left again and drive down to the strand. Both these sites afford access to the mudflats.

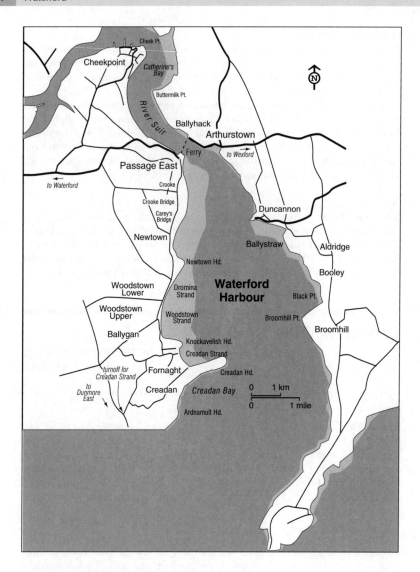

---

7 DUNMORE EAST

OSI Discovery map: sheet 76
S69 00

Habitat and Species

The small town is an attractive fishing port famous for its cliffs, which hold about 560 pairs of nesting Kittiwakes. The birds are present between November and August. Fulmars also breed on the cliffs. A number of Herring Gulls nest on buildings in the town.

Turnstones and Purple Sandpipers feed outside the sea wall in winter. Oystercatchers are present there throughout the year, while large numbers of gulls winter in the harbour with Glaucous and Iceland Gulls both regular.

Access

Dunmore East is 17 km from Waterford city. Take the road to the south at the Tower Hotel and follow the signposts.

CORK

Cork is the largest county in Ireland and it almost certainly has the longest bird list as well. The coast stretches from Youghal in the east, roughly the mid-point of the southern Irish coastline, to Dursey Island in the west and around the corner into Kenmare Bay. The coast is broken by a number of muddy estuaries, most of which hold good numbers of wildfowl and waders, though geese are scarce in the county.

There are several islands and mainland cliffs on which seabirds nest, but the headlands and islands are attractive to the birdwatcher principally because of the opportunities for seeing wind-blown seabirds and passerines. This is the best county for seeing American passerine vagrants. Inland, there are several mountain ridges and a string of lakes in the valley of the River Lee, some of which hold large numbers of ducks.

8 BALLYMACODA AND KNOCKADOON HEAD

OSI Discovery map: sheet 81
X04 73; X09 70

Habitat

The estuary of the Womanagh river at Ballymacoda is a broad area of intertidal mudflats surrounded by low-lying farmland. A ridge of sandstone to the south extends out to Knockadoon Head and Capel Island offshore. As with so many other south coast estuaries, a sand spit impounds the bay. Many of the fields surrounding the bay are marshy and provide feeding for ducks and waders.

Species

The estuary has more waders in winter than any other in Cork apart from Cork Harbour (a far larger area). Diversity, however, is rather disappointing and despite being well watched fewer rare species have been seen than at some of the other Cork sites. Eurasian Wigeons, Common Teals, Mallards, Shelducks, Oystercatchers, Curlews, Black-tailed and Bar-tailed Godwits, Redshanks and Dunlins are all present in good numbers. But the speciality of the estuary is its huge flocks of Northern Lapwings and European Golden Plovers, at times among the largest in Ireland, and its gathering of over 500 Grey Plovers in spring.

Curlew Sandpipers, Ruffs and Green Sandpipers are seen in most years; Little Stints and Wood Sandpipers occur in some autumns. American vagrants have included Killdeer, Spotted and Baird's Sandpipers and Long-billed Dowitcher. A small flock of Brent Geese has wintered in recent years.

In autumn passage migrants can be found in the hedgerows on Knockadoon Head. Goldcrests and Common Chiffchaffs are particularly common in late autumn and Turtle Doves, Pied Flycatchers and Black Redstarts probably occur in most years. Pied Wheatear, Sardinian, Hume's and Pallas' Warblers, Red-eyed Vireo and Woodchat Shrike have been seen. The headland is very much underwatched.

The entire area is good for raptors in winter. Sparrowhawks, Kestrels, Merlins, Peregrines and Hen Harriers are all regular and Short-eared Owls are seen in most winters.

Timing

This is very much a winter estuarine site. It is probably best watched on a rising tide when the waders are pushed in from the extensive mudflats. Knockadoon Head is best in late autumn.

Access

Ballymacoda estuary can be approached from various aspects. The west and north sides can be approached from the road between Ballymacoda and Youghal. This road crosses the estuary at Crompaun Bridge and an energetic visitor can walk south along the bank of the Womanagh river until the estuary opens out. For a more relaxed visit you can drive about 500 m to Clonpriest graveyard and park there. The estuary can be approached on foot by taking a track to the shore about 100 m past the old graveyard. This approach provides access to much of the estuary.

The north-east corner is approached by driving east beyond Clonpriest and turning right for Pilmore strand, where the main road turns sharply left for Youghal, about 2 km beyond Clonpriest. The car can be parked at the beach and the estuary scanned from here.

The south side can be seen by taking the second left turn after passing through the village of Ballymacoda. This narrow road leads down to the edge of the estuary. The third and fourth roads to the left lead down to Ring Strand.

Peregrine

To search for passerines in autumn, take the road out to Knockadoon Head and work backwards, looking at the hedgerows. The area around the caravan park has been productive in the past but the whole area has great and relatively untapped potential.

CALENDAR

All year: Peregrine and Chough at Knockadoon Head.

Knockadoon Head. Small flock of Brent Geese.

Winter: wildfowl, Little Egret, waders, especially large flocks of European Golden Plovers and Northern Lapwings. Divers off

Autumn: passage migrants on the headland. Terns on the beach, especially Sandwich Terns.

9 BALLYCOTTON

OSI Discovery map: sheet 81
W98 65

Habitat

Ballycotton Bay is a shallow, sandy, eastward-facing bay with three shallow lagoons isolated from the sea behind sand bars and a gravel bank. Ballycotton Lake, the largest of these lagoons, was formerly completely open to the sea and

19th-century Ordnance Survey maps show it appearing like an estuary. It became enclosed by a shingle bank as a result of wave action which is also steadily eroding the sand cliffs at the southern end of the bay close to the town. The shingle bank was breached at the request of farmers interested in draining the lake, but the gap in the past was usually closed by south-easterly gales. However, the gap has been open for several years now and the lake has become very saline and very dry around the margins. Reedbeds (*Phragmites australis*) are spreading steadily across the lake, and the area of open water and muddy edge has perceptibly declined in the past 20 years.

Farther north, there are two pools at Shanagarry which remain tidal, although a sand spit separates all except the main channel from the sea. Drainage has taken place at one pool and there is evidence of silting.

The muddy surfaces of these lagoons are extremely attractive to wading birds, both for feeding and roosting. Out on the open beach, the extensive intertidal and rather muddy sands provide feeding for some species, but the combination of brackish lagoon and intertidal flats is what holds such a diversity of wader species in the Ballycotton area.

To the west of the road which crosses the top of Ballycotton Lake from Shanagarry village is a large area of *Phragmites* known as Ballycotton bog. This is an excellent breeding area for ducks but is completely impenetrable.

The town of Ballycotton has many gardens and hedges providing feeding for grounded passerine migrants in spring and autumn. At the end of the town, the pier projects out into the bay and provides a view of two small islands, one of which has a lighthouse.

Species

This is an autumn migration site par excellence. The lagoons and intertidal sands hold a great diversity of waders including parties of Black-tailed and Bar-tailed Godwits, Redshanks, Greenshanks, Ringed Plovers and Sanderlings, but also small numbers of Spotted Redshanks, Ruffs, Curlew Sandpipers, Little Stints and occasional Wood and Green Sandpipers. American waders occur every year. Pectoral Sandpiper is the most regular but most species on the Irish list have been seen including up to three Semipalmated Sandpipers together, near annual White-rumped and Baird's Sandpipers and records of such extreme rarities as Stilt Sandpiper, Killdeer and Greater Yellowlegs. Wintering wader numbers are low and usually much less exciting, but there is always the chance of a surprise wintering vagrant. Long-billed Dowitcher and Lesser Yellowlegs have both wintered in the past. It is not just from America that rare waders wander; this site has also hosted Asian specials such as Red-necked Stint, Long-toed Stint and Sharp-tailed Sandpiper.

The diversity of wildfowl is less marked, but there are usually Whooper and Mute Swans, Wigeons, Teals, Gadwalls, Mallards, Shovelers, Tufted Ducks, Pochards, Red-breasted Mergansers and occasional Pintails and Common Goldeneyes. American Wigeon and Green-winged Teal should both be looked for.

Over the pools, gulls and terns hawk for insects. Look for Mediterranean and Little Gulls at the lagoons: on the beach or at the pier check for Glaucous and Iceland Gulls. Both species are recorded every winter. Many other gull species have been recorded including American Herring Gull, Ring-billed Gull and Ivory Gull.

The bay is always worth checking from the pier. Seabirds drift in at times, especially if fishing boats are arriving, and can include Sabine's Gull, near annual in autumn, as well as three species of skua and both Manx and Sooty Shearwaters. If conditions are good for seawatching, it can be worth taking the road up to the cliff-top car park and watching out to sea. Unfortunately, the cliffs are well in from the two islands and seabirds usually pass rather far out, but good shearwater passage can sometimes be seen.

Interesting passerines can be found throughout the area. Larks and pipits abound in the fields. Northern Wheatears are common on the beach in spring and autumn. The reedbeds hold large numbers of breeding Sedge Warblers (and many more in autumn) and a small population of breeding Reed Warblers. Ballycotton was where Reed Warblers were first proved to be breeding in Ireland in 1981 after a very long absence (the only previous record was in 1935 in Down). Reed Buntings are also common in the reedbeds. The gardens in the village have recorded many passerine rarities, including Booted and Greenish Warblers. Black Redstarts and Pied Flycatchers occur every autumn.

Various birds of prey hunt over the reedbeds. Sparrowhawks and Kestrels can be seen almost every day. Peregrines are regular and Merlins are frequent in winter; Hen Harriers can also be regular in winter in some years and have been known to roost in the bog above Ballycotton Lake. Short-eared Owls are

Sedge Warbler

elusive, but probably winter at the bog. Rare birds of prey recorded here have included Osprey, Goshawk, Red Kite and Marsh Harrier.

In summer, Ringed Plovers struggle to raise their young as the beach is taken over by holidaying humans. Common Terns nested in the recent past and Little Terns before that, but the level of disturbance is now too great. Mute Swan, Shelduck and Mallard nest and Pochard, Shoveler, Common Teal and Gadwall probably breed in most summers.

The cliffs to the west of the town have some breeding Fulmars and several small colonies of cliff-nesting House Martins.

Timing

Ballycotton is best in spring and autumn, but interesting birds can be found at any time of year. Hot summer days, with crowds on the beach and uncontrolled dogs criss-crossing the marshy areas, are probably best avoided. The state of the tide makes very little difference, though waders are usually seen most closely when the tide is high.

Access

The lagoons can be approached by taking the left turn for Ballynamona about 1 km beyond Shanagarry on the road for Ballycotton. This narrow road leads to a car park by the beach. Ballycotton Lake can be seen by walking south along the path at the top of the beach and the Shanagarry lagoons can be watched from the path which runs to the north. All the fields here are private and the landowners do not permit birdwatchers on their land so keep outside the fences.

The western end of Ballycotton Lake can be viewed from the Shanagarry–Ballycotton road. Leave Ballynamona strand and turn left when the Ballycotton–Shanagarry road is reached. At the next junction turn left and park your car about 200 m onwards. The lake can be viewed through gateways from this road.

Drive on to the village and park your car at the end of the pier. Check the bay for seabirds and then, if weather conditions are encouraging, walk back through the village watching for passerine migrants.

To get to the cliffs, turn sharp left after coming up from the pier and drive to the car park at the end of the road.

CALENDAR

All year: Mute Swan, Shelduck, Gadwall, Mallard, Cormorant, Little Egret, Oystercatcher, Ringed Plover, Curlew, Redshank, Reed Bunting.

Autumn: shearwaters, skuas, waders including Curlew Sandpiper, Little Stint, Spotted Redshank, Ruff, rare vagrants from North America. Terns and passerine migrants.

Winter: Whooper Swan, Eurasian Wigeon, Common Teal, Shoveler, Pochard, Tufted Duck, Glaucous and Iceland Gulls.

Spring: waders including Whimbrel, Common Sandpiper and Sanderling. Hirundines, Northern Wheatears, other passerine migrants.

Summer: terns, Sedge Warbler, Reed Warbler.

---

10 CORK HARBOUR
OSI Discovery map: sheet 81, 87
W66 70; W84 63

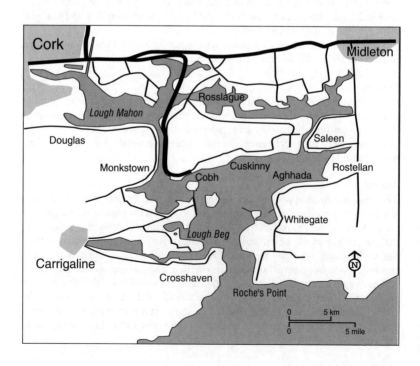

Habitat

With over 5,000 wildfowl and 20,000 waders in winter, Cork Harbour is much the most important estuarine area in Cork county. It is also by far the largest. The area is famous as one of the finest natural harbours in the world and was the departure point for most Irish emigrants to the United States up to the late 1950s. The outer harbour and channels surrounding Great Island are very deep, but there are extensive mudflats around Lough Mahon, the Douglas Estuary and the North Channel on the northern side of the harbour, Lough Beg on the west and around Saleen, Rostellan and Whitegate on the eastern side. These mudflats support sizeable duck and wader populations.

The shallow waters of Lough Mahon, the eastern end of the North Channel and off Rostellan provide feeding for grebes and diving ducks. A lagoon at Lough Beg on the west side has brackish water and a soft edge which attracts migrant waders. There is a small lake at Rostellan and a brackish lagoon at Cuskinny on the south side of Great Island.

There are industrial complexes at Little Island, Ringaskiddy and Whitegate, and there has been much local controversy over the potential for pollution by some of the pharmaceutical factories located here. Because of awareness of the need to collect baseline biological data to support the conservation case, bird numbers have been counted at intervals over the past 20 years so the main concentrations are well known.

Species

The harbour is at its best for birds in winter and the largest numbers are present from October to March. Great Crested Grebes concentrate at Lough Mahon and off Aghada, with over 50 regularly seen in both areas. Little Grebes occur at Douglas Estuary, Rostellan Lake and Cuskinny. Ducks scatter throughout the harbour. Most Shelducks are found in the North Channel and near Carrigaline. Eurasian Wigeons, Common Teals and Mallards are widely scattered but Pintails and Shovelers are scarce. Some diving ducks occur, especially Tufted Duck, Common Goldeneye and Red-breasted Merganser at the Douglas Estuary. The Tufted Ducks tend to assemble around the sewage outfall pipe off the old railway bridge at Rochestown. Red-breasted Mergansers and Common Goldeneyes are also found across Lough Mahon, the North Channel and south-east to Whitegate.

There are concentrations of waders at Douglas, Lough Mahon, Glounthaune and the North Channel. Flocks of up to 5,000 European Golden Plovers, 2,000–5,000 Northern Lapwings, 1,000–2,500 Dunlins and 500–1,500 Black-tailed Godwits can be seen at each of these locations in winter. Smaller numbers of Oystercatchers, Curlews and Redshanks feed throughout the muddy areas of the harbour. Greenshanks can be found feeding in the deep channels or on stonier shores and Grey Plovers are found at Douglas, on the North Channel and east of Carrigaline. Lough Beg, near Ringaskiddy, is particularly well worth a visit in autumn when Wood Sandpiper and Ruff are regular. American waders occur at this lagoon in most autumns. The stony, weed-covered edges of the estuary all support Turnstones.

In autumn, numbers of waders are not so high as in winter but Curlew Sandpipers should be looked for at Lough Mahon and Douglas. In spring, one of the most spectacular sights of the harbour is the return migration of

Whimbrels. Over 2,000 fly north over Cobh each year, usually between mid-April and the first few days of May.

The entire harbour is good for gulls. However, many of the birds which feed in the harbour fly across to The Lough to wash and preen. Iceland and Glaucous Gulls can be seen here each winter and Ring-billed and Mediterranean Gulls are almost always to be found between late October and the end of March. Rarer gulls seen here include Laughing, Kumlien's and American Herring Gulls. As well as the gulls, there is a wildfowl collection to be admired and, amongst the exotic captive birds, parties of wild Shovelers, Teals and Pochards.

Many of the gulls move between The Lough in Cork city, Cobh farther down the harbour and Kinsale to the south-west. The quays at Cobh are excellent for gull watching and have attracted Ross's and Laughing Gulls in the past, as well as Europe's first Thayer's Gull.

In summer Common Terns nest in a small colony on barges near Marino Point. Kingfishers breed near the old railway bridge at the Douglas Estuary, near Passage West, downstream from Carrigaline and close to the Pfizer factory at Ringaskiddy.

Timing

Cork Harbour is at its best for the birdwatcher from September to the end of March when wildfowl, wader and gull numbers are highest. Most sites are best visited within two hours of high tide when the ducks and waders are closest to the observer. At high tide some of the wader roosts in particular can be difficult to study without putting the birds to flight.

Access

All parts of the harbour are worth visiting in winter. Start at Cork and visit The Lough. From the city centre take the road for Douglas and Carrigaline past the City Hall. At the junction beyond City General hospital take the right turn up Summerhill South. At the traffic lights turn left for Turner's Cross. Drive to the next major junction, beyond the modern Church of Christ the King, and turn right. Bear right again at the next major right turn and drive past Musgrave Park rugby ground (on the left) until you see a lake in front of you. This is The Lough. You can park on the perimeter and view the birds from the footpath around the lake.

To see the birds of the north part of the harbour, drive east from Cork for Midleton. At Cobh Cross, about 7 km from Cork, turn right onto Fota Island, following the signposts for Cobh. The first bridge you reach is worth checking for godwits and ducks. After this, drive on to Belvelly Bridge (where a Martello tower faces you). Turn left and left again to drive along the edge of the North Channel where waders and ducks, especially diving ducks, can be seen well. Keep on the road, passing the left turns for East Ferry and the yacht marina, and you will eventually reach the shore at Cuskinny where the lake should be checked for gulls. This is a BirdWatch Ireland reserve. After working the area, travel on westwards to Cobh where the town jetties should be searched for gulls.

Drive back to Belvelly Bridge by taking the western route. A large flock of Shelducks feeds on the open mud just before Belvelly Bridge from December to February.

The north side of the North Channel can be accessed at various points. Turn right on Fota Island, on the way back from Cobh, between the two bridges and take the right hand laneway about 1 km after leaving Fota. There is room to park a car at the entrance to a quarry. A laneway leads down beside the quarry to the estuary and to a large high-tide wader roost. The North Channel can also be viewed at Ballintubbrid and Ahanesk.

The eastern side of the harbour can all be seen from the road from Midleton to Whitegate. Turn right, just over 1 km beyond Ballinacurra on the Whitegate road, for Rathcoursey and East Ferry. The road passes some excellent spots for ducks and, near Saleen, a good viewing spot for checking through the grebes and ducks. The road for Whitegate passes Rostellan, a small lake on the right, and there are several stopping places on the way to Whitegate.

The inner harbour is also very accessible. Lough Mahon can be watched from the road from Blackrock Castle around to the old railway bridge at Rochestown. The Douglas Estuary can be seen well from this bridge.

The best spots on the west side are at Lough Beg, a BirdWatch Ireland reserve, and along the Owenaboy estuary between Carrigaline and Crosshaven. To view Lough Beg, take the left turn for Currabinny at the large church in Carrigaline village. Follow the road for 3 km until a sign is reached at a right turn, sign posted for Currabinny. Follow the road to the SmithKline Pharmaceutical factory and the attractive lagoon in front of it. Cars may be driven across the causeway to the small car park at the hide outside the factory security gates.

CALENDAR

All year: Mute Swan, Mallard, Little Egret, Oystercatcher, Curlew, Kingfisher.

Autumn: waders, including Common Sandpiper, Curlew Sandpiper and Ruff. Terns.

Winter: ducks, Great Crested Grebe, a few Slavonian Grebes and perhaps Black-necked or Red-necked Grebe at Aghada, waders, especially European Golden Plover, Northern Lapwing and Black-tailed Godwit. Gulls, including Glaucous, Iceland and Ring-billed.

Spring: Whimbrel, terns.

Summer: breeding Ringed Plover and Common Tern.

11 OLD HEAD OF KINSALE AND KINSALE MARSH

OSI Discovery map: sheet 87
W63 39; W62 49

Habitat

The strangely named Old Head of Kinsale is the most obviously projecting of the headlands between Hook Head in Wexford and Cape Clear far to the west. It is a sandstone and mudstone promontory with sheer cliffs on the western side. There is a lighthouse at the tip but much of the headland is occupied by a private golf course. Just before the tip of the Old Head are ruins of an old lighthouse and an old coastguard station.

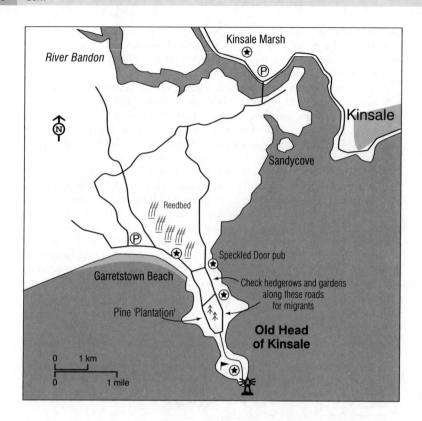

A number of gardens are scattered over the headland between the village of Old Head and the car park. To the west, Garretstown strand is a sandy beach with extensive damp fields behind it and small areas of *Phragmites*. There are large areas of brambles at the western end of the beach which provide more cover for passerines.

Species
A large seabird colony is the principal ornithological feature of the Old Head in summer. On the west side, and visible by walking about 50 m to the cliff edge from the car park, is a colony of several thousand Kittiwakes and Common Guillemots and smaller numbers of Shags, Fulmars and Black Guillemots.

The tip of the Old Head is an excellent seawatching point. In south-westerlies in autumn, Great, Cory's and Sooty Shearwaters appear in numbers surpassed only by Cape Clear. Rarities have included Black-browed Albatross, Fea's Petrel and Wilson's Storm-petrel. Leatherback Turtles have been seen several times and dolphins and small whales are frequent. Manx Shearwaters, Great and Arctic Skuas, Common Guillemots, Razorbills, Kittiwakes and Gannets are to be expected on any autumn day.

There is very little cover on the tip, so it tends not to be good for passerines, though Choughs find the open pasture to their liking. Birdwatchers in autumn tend to spend more time searching the hedges and gardens from the car park back to the Speckled Door bar. These have all proved to be excellent habitat for warblers and flycatchers. Pied Flycatchers, Common Chiffchaffs, Blackcaps and other common migrants are seen here every autumn along with a handful of rarer species including near annual Yellow-browed Warbler. Particular rarities here have included Dusky and Radde's Warblers, Isabelline Shrike, Grey-cheeked Thrush and Siberian Stonechat.

Behind Garretstown beach the fields are excellent habitat for pipits and buntings. The nearby reedbeds are hunted over by Hen Harriers and occasional Marsh Harriers as well as the more frequent Sparrowhawks and, in winter, Merlins. Rarities recorded here include Purple Heron and Red-throated Pipit.

Most visitors to the Old Head check Kinsale Marsh, a brackish pond near the bridge at Kinsale, for waders. This is an excellent place for scarce wader species, especially at high tide. Spotted Redshank, Ruff and Wood Sandpiper are regular and American waders almost annual.

Timing

Seawatching is best in August and September, though it should also be good in May when Pomarine Skuas can be expected. The numbers of seabirds passing are very dependent on weather; in north-westerlies very few are seen, but when south-westerlies are blowing hard and fronts are passing through with mist and rain the Old Head can be one of the most exciting seawatching spots anywhere.

Unfortunately, the best seawatching conditions tend to be among the worst for passerine migrants. A period of south-easterly winds is usually best for eastern migrants, though a spell of calm weather can also be good.

Access

The Old Head of Kinsale is approached from Kinsale by driving west through the town, crossing the modern bridge and following the signposts for the Old Head. About 1.5 km from the bridge, take the sign posted sharp left turn for the Old Head and follow the road straight to the car park near the tip. The entrance to the golf course is located at the end of this road. Access on foot to the tip of the headland is permitted for birders, but please ask permission at the security gate. Kinsale marsh can be seen by keeping straight on for 600 m instead of turning left across the bridge west of the town. The small lagoon is on the right- hand side of the road. Most of the birds can be seen easily from the road, thus minimising disturbance.

CALENDAR

All year: Cormorant, Shag, Peregrine, Rock Dove, Chough, Raven.

Autumn: passage seabirds, passage passerine migrants, possibility of rare seabirds or passerines. Scarce waders and Little Egret at Kinsale marsh.

Winter: Red-throated and Great Northern Divers, Fulmar, Gannet, Kittiwake, Common Guillemot, Hen Harrier.

Spring: terns, breeding and passage seabirds.

Summer: breeding Shag, Fulmar, Kittiwake, Common Guillemot, Razorbill, Black Guillemot. Passage Manx and Sooty Shearwaters, Gannet, Great Skua.

12 CLONAKILTY

OSI Discovery map: sheet 89
W38 38; W41 38

Habitat

The principal bird habitats at Clonakilty Bay comprise two estuaries, a shallow bay and a series of lagoons. At one time there was one estuary with an island in the middle. In the 19th century, Inchydoney Island was connected to the mainland by two embankments and the marshy land in between was drained.

Nowadays there is a rich, muddy zone from Clonakilty town downstream to Ring on the eastern side and to the turn for Inchydoney on the western side. From these points to the sea, the intertidal zone is sandy and of less interest for birds.

At Inchydoney Bay, the south-western estuary, there is similar muddy habitat with sandier strata nearer the sea. Inchydoney Island has sand dunes.

Species

The estuary has about 400 Wigeons and smaller numbers of other duck species in winter, almost all at Inchydoney. A large flock of up to 600 Black-tailed Godwits feeds on the mud at Clonakilty, most of the birds preferring the area close to the town. Up to 100 Bar-tailed Godwits join them in mid-winter and there are good numbers of Oystercatchers, Curlews, Redshanks and Dunlins. Small numbers of Grey and Ringed Plovers, Greenshanks and Knots are also to be found, again mostly at Clonakilty. One or two Spotted Redshanks winter, usually at Inchydoney.

In autumn, scarcer species sometimes occur, usually at the muddy lagoons. Ruffs, Curlew Sandpipers and Little Stints are seen in most years and American waders are almost annual.

Out in the bay in winter, Red-throated and Great Northern Divers feed. They are best seen from Dunmore or from the high ground behind the Inchydoney Hotel. In autumn Arctic Skuas come in close to the beach after terns. No tern species breed in the bay, but Sandwich, Common and Arctic visit frequently in autumn.

There is an enormous nocturnal gull roost in the bay, mostly of Black-headed and Common Gulls. They begin to assemble an hour or so before dusk and scarcer species can sometimes be seen. Ring-billed Gulls have been seen close to the town in most winters, with Iceland and Mediterranean Gulls less frequent.

This estuary is hunted over by several species of birds of prey. The sudden eruption of large clouds of waders is usually a sign of the presence of a Peregrine. Sparrowhawks and Kestrels are common, but rarely have the same effect as a Peregrine. Hen Harriers are sometimes seen over the marshy fields behind the Inchydoney arm of the bay. Short-eared Owls winter here as well, but are rarely seen, unless the area is walked.

Timing

The first Black-tailed Godwits appear in July and are a magnificent sight in their rich red summer plumage. From then until the end of February the estuary has a good variety of waders. Numbers are very low in March, and from then until July only a handful of birds occur. The state of the tide matters little, except that roosts move about and birds can be hard to find at high tide.

Access

This is a most accessible estuary as a road runs around almost the entire shoreline. There is a road on the eastern side from Clonakilty town to Ring and then from Clonakilty around to Inchydoney and Dunmore.

The shallow lagoons should be thoroughly investigated. The nearest pool to Clonakilty is reached by taking the road from Clonakilty town along the west side of the estuary. After 3 km, the road swings right and away from the estuary. At this point, take the narrow road to the left signposted as a 'cul de sac' and drive about 300 m to the small lagoon at the end. To find the other pools, return from the cul de sac, turn left at the junction and drive on to the next arm of the bay at Inchydoney. Turn right when the estuary is reached rather than continuing straight on down the north-east side. There are brackish pools on the right-hand side and migrant waders frequently feed on the muddy edge. At high tide large numbers of waders roost here.

Dunmore at the south-western end of Inchydoney estuary is an excellent vantage point for searching for divers.

CALENDAR

All year: Mute Swan, Shelduck, Mallard, Cormorant, Little Egret, Oystercatcher, Curlew.

Autumn: Eurasian Wigeon, Common Teal, Ringed and European Golden Plovers, Dunlin, Curlew Sandpiper, Ruff, Black-tailed Godwit, Spotted Redshank, Redshank, Greenshank, terns. Possibility of American waders.

Winter: Eurasian Wigeon, Common Teal, Ringed Plover, European Golden and Grey Plovers, Northern Lapwing, Knot, Dunlin, Spotted Redshank, Greenshank, Kingfisher. Occasional Brent Goose.

Spring: Eurasian Wigeon, Common Teal, Dunlin, Redshank, Greenshank.

Summer: occasional terns.

---

13 GALLEY HEAD AND KILKERRAN LAKE
OSI Discovery map: sheet 89
W34 32; W33 34

Habitat

Galley Head projects well out into the Atlantic and has a lighthouse at its tip. As a result, it is the best migration watchpoint (for both seabirds and passerine migrants) between the Old Head of Kinsale and Cape Clear. The tip of the head is private property and clearly indicated as such. It should not be entered without permission.

The principal bird areas are farther back. Sands Cove and Dirk Bay on the eastern side are coastal bays with deciduous trees providing cover for autumn passerine migrants. To the north of Dirk Bay is Red Strand, a sandy beach with a small reedbed and damp fields behind with potential for pipits and buntings. On the road across Galley Head from Dirk Bay to the west are several gardens and an area of hedgerows which also attract migrants. At the western side of the headland is Kilkerran Lake, a shallow, freshwater lake which attracts ducks and waders. Out beyond the lake is the Long Strand, as the name suggests a long stretch of sandy beach, and the surf provides excellent feeding for divers.

Species

Off the Long Strand and Red Strand divers feed in winter. Sometimes sea-ducks are seen: Red-breasted Mergansers are occasional, Common Scoter and Long-tailed Duck rarer. Galley Head is a good watchpoint for shearwaters, skuas and petrels when the conditions are right (invariably south-westerlies, rain or mist).

Sands Cove, Dirk Bay and the gardens at Galley Head all attract a rich mix of passerine migrants in autumn. They may well be productive in spring as well, but they have never been watched at this season. Each autumn they produce Yellow-browed Warblers, Firecrests and at least one major rarity. In the past Hermit Thrush, Philadelphia Vireo, American Redstart, Marsh Warbler and Desert Wheatear have been found (the last at Red Strand). Because of all the cover, passerines can be difficult to find and patience is required.

Kilkerran Lake should be looked at whenever the area is visited. Normally it holds a handful of Little Grebes, Mallards and Tufted Ducks but occasionally rarer birds are seen. Cattle Egret, Black-winged Stilt, Ring-necked Duck and Black-necked Grebe have occurred.

Timing

Most of these sites are best in autumn, but they have been little watched in spring, so they may well repay visits at other seasons.

Access

From Clonakilty take the road along the west side of the estuary and drive on to the causeway at Inchydoney Bay. Keep the estuary on your left until you reach the junction where the road turns left for Dunmore and goes straight on for Ardfield. Take the road for Ardfield and follow the signposts for Red Strand. On the way you will see a signpost to Sands Cove on your left. Follow the narrow road down to a small parking area at the end. There is plenty of cover here to be explored for migrants. Return and turn left at the junction for Red Strand.

After leaving Red Strand, take the next left turn (signposted for Galley Head) about 1 km beyond the beach. The next left, marked as a cul de sac, takes you down to Dirk Bay. There is a small space for parking a car at the end.

Coming up from Dirk Bay, turn left for Galley Head or drive across the junction for an excellent area of gardens and, after about 2 km, Long Strand and Kilkerran Lake are clearly visible on the right. A sharp right turn leads down to the shore of the lake.

CALENDAR

All year: Shag, Gannet, Kittiwake, gulls in the bay, Rock Dove, Chough.

Autumn: Manx and Sooty Shearwaters, Arctic and Great Skuas, occasional Pomarine Skua, warblers, flycatchers, scarce migrants.

Winter: Red-throated and Great Northern Divers, Tufted Duck, Red-breasted Merganser.

Spring: terns in the bay.

Summer: breeding Fulmars.

---

14 CAPE CLEAR

OSI Discovery map: sheet 88
V95 21

Habitat

This is, apart from the Fastnet Rock, the most southerly point of Ireland. Cape Clear is a hilly, sandstone island of about 300 ha, which is almost cut in two by the North Harbour and the South Harbour. It is sharply indented at the south-west end by wave action and has some cliffs on the east and south-west sides. Much of the island is covered by heath with bracken and gorse, but there are large areas of cultivation and some areas of marshland.

About 200 people live on the island and there are a number of small gardens with conifers and shrubs. A Bird Observatory was started in 1959 and has functioned successfully ever since. It is located at the North Harbour and provides accommodation for up to ten people. There is a warden resident from March to early November.

Species

The island is famous for its seabirds and rare passerine migrants. Seawatching from the Irish coastline really started here and systematic recording continues. No two years are quite the same in terms of birds seen, but Manx and Sooty Shearwaters, Fulmars, Gannets, Arctic and Great Skuas, Kittiwakes, Common Guillemots and Razorbills are seen on most days in autumn. Great Shearwaters tend to be seen mostly in August, are almost annual, and can sometimes be seen in large numbers. Cory's Shearwaters are rarer, but can sometimes be seen in hundreds. Persistent seawatchers have a good chance of seeing Wilson's Storm-petrel as this species occurs annually. Other species recorded over the years include Black-browed Albatross, Fea's and Bulwer's Petrels, frigatebirds and Long-tailed Skua.

Although the number and variety of seabird species vary, there are almost always large numbers of passing birds in late July and August. The numbers of Manx Shearwaters alone at this time of year can be up to 30,000 per hour.

The best seawatching spots are at the southern headlands. Blananarragaun, or Blanan' for short, is much the best in poor visibility. Seabirds come very close indeed, close enough for an observer some years ago to notice that Common Guillemots fly with their bills partly open, whereas Razorbills fly with theirs closed. Skuas sometimes come right overhead and shearwaters come within 100 m.

In summer there are nesting Common Guillemots, Black Guillemots, a handful of Puffins, and Great Black-backed, Lesser Black-backed and Herring Gulls. A few pairs of Ravens and Choughs breed and Peregrines also nest. The commonest landbirds are Meadow Pipits.

For autumn passerine migration Cape Clear is famous and the island seems taken over by birdwatchers in October, when vagrants from both North America and Siberia have come to be expected. Rarities such as Yellow-bellied Sapsucker and Indigo Bunting from America have been matched by birds such as Siberian Thrush and Pallas's Grasshopper Warbler from the east. It is not necessary to visit Cape Clear in autumn to see rarities, however; White-throated Needletail and Little Swift were both seen in summer and Scops Owl and Zitting Cisticola in spring.

Passerines should be searched for in all parts of the island, but the best spots tend to be the gardens and hedges in Ballyieragh, Cotter's garden near the North Harbour and the area of bracken and small gardens at the north-west end of the island. Over 300 species have been recorded, a very high percentage of the total of just over 450 species on the Irish list. As well as birds, there are ample opportunities for watching cetaceans and, in August, turtles. Many species of whales have been seen, though Minke Whale is perhaps the most regular.

Timing

Autumn is the best time for seeing seabirds and passerine migrants. The largest numbers of seabirds occur from late July to mid September. The most exciting passerine watching in recent years has been in the month of October. However, the number of birdwatchers is much the greatest in October, and a visitor wanting to enjoy a more relaxed atmosphere might prefer September or indeed May, when Cape Clear can be exceptionally beautiful and tranquil – and the birds can also be exciting.

Access

To stay at the observatory contact to the Booking Secretary, BirdWatch Ireland, P.O. Box 12, Greystones, Co Wicklow. If the observatory is full there is a youth hostel and a number of guest houses on the island.

The ferry leaves Baltimore (south-west of Skibbereen) twice daily. It leaves Cape Clear at 9 am each morning, except Sundays. In the summer months of July and August there are additional sailings. Sailing times can be checked with Cape Clear Co-Operative (telephone 028 39153).

Red-backed Shrike

CALENDAR

All year: Cormorant, Shag, Gannet, Peregrine, Sparrowhawk, Kestrel, Common Guillemot, Razorbill, Black Guillemot, gulls, Rock Dove, European Stonechat, Meadow Pipit, Chough, Raven.

Autumn: seabird passage, passerine migrants, rarities.

Winter: Red-throated and Great Northern Divers, Little Auks at sea, Great Skua, occasional Balearic Shearwater, Redwing, Fieldfare.

Spring: Turtle Dove, other spring migrants, Pomarine Skua.

Summer: breeding seabirds, possibility of rarities.

15 YOUGHAL

OSI Discovery map: sheet 81, 82
X09 80

Habitat and Species

Youghal Bay is the tidal estuary of the Blackwater river. Muddy inlets on the eastern bank, at Kinsalebeg (in Co Waterford), and, on the western bank, between Youghal town and the bridge carrying the main Cork–Waterford road across the bay (in Co Cork), provide wildfowl and wader feeding habitat. The flooded field on the eastern side of the main road, about 1 km on the Youghal side of the bridge, is a particularly good wader roost at high tide.

Shelduck, Mallard, Eurasian Wigeon, Common Teal, Oystercatcher, Redshank, Curlew, Black-tailed Godwit and Dunlin can all be seen well in winter, and migrant waders can be seen in autumn. Great Northern Divers and, sometimes, Red-throated Divers can be seen below the town of Youghal. Little Egrets, Curlew Sandpiper and Lesser Yellowlegs have all been seen from the road at the flooded field to the south of Youghal bridge.

The reedbeds between Youghal and Ballyvergan to the south-west are the largest beds of *Phragmites* on the Cork coast and hold breeding Mallards, Moorhens, Water Rails, Sedge Warblers and about 20 pairs of Reed Warblers. In winter Hen Harriers roost in the marsh and Short-eared Owls are probably annual.

Rarities seen here include Marsh Harrier, Savi's Warbler and Lapland Bunting.

Access

Kinsalebeg at the eastern side of the bay can be approached by turning south off the main Youghal–Waterford road about 3 km from Youghal at a crossroads signposted for Clash more (to the north). At the next junction turn right to Ferry Point pier from where the inlet and mudflats can readily be accessed.

The best place for watching on the western side is at the flooded field on the side of the road about 1 km from the bridge on the road to Youghal. There is space to park a car and, if the tide is out, the mudflats can be searched by walking back towards the bridge and looking out into the bay.

The reedbeds can be seen from the main road from Youghal to Cork about 1 km from the town. More of the marsh can be seen by taking the narrow road towards the beach.

16 COURTMACSHERRY

OSI Discovery map: sheet 87, 8
W50 42

Habitat and Species

Courtmacsherry is another estuary with a sizeable wader population. This is the estuary of the Argideen river and runs from Timoleague to the sea past Courtmacsherry village. There is some *Spartina* on the upper reaches of the estuary, especially on the south side. A large flock of European Golden Plovers is the principal feature, but there are over 100 Black-tailed Godwits and good numbers of Redshanks, Dunlins and other wader species. This is a good site for

Mediterranean Gulls, which are often to be seen on the mudflats below the old Franciscan friary at Timoleague.

Off the town of Courtmacsherry excellent close views may be had of Great Northern Divers in winter.

Access
Drive from Timoleague along the coast road to Courtmacsherry. Stop at intervals to look at waders and gulls. Take the road beyond the hotel to the parking space where the road ends. This is the best spot for divers.

17 ROSSCARBERY
OSI Discovery map: sheet 89
W28 35

Habitat and Species
Rosscarbery Bay is on the main road from Cork to Skibbereen and so is well known to birdwatchers travelling to Cape Clear Bird Observatory. The bay comprises a lagoon north of the causeway, across which the main road runs, and an estuary to the south. The lagoon holds small numbers of Mallards and Red-breasted Mergansers. The estuary has wintering European Golden Plovers, Northern Lapwings, Dunlins, Black-tailed and Bar-tailed Godwits, Redshanks and Greenshanks. Small muddy pools on the side of the roads which run to the sea on both the east and west side of the estuary often hold a Spotted Redshank in autumn and winter. The pier at the end of the road on the western side provides good views of divers in winter.

Access
The estuary is crossed by anyone travelling between Clonakilty and Skibbereen. A road runs around the entire estuary so viewing opportunities are excellent.

18 LEE RESERVOIRS

OSI Discovery map: sheet 79, 80
W32 70; W40 72

Habitat and Species

The Lee Reservoirs were created by the construction of dams at Inniscarra and Carrigadrohid for the generation of electricity. The Gearagh, the section west of Macroom, is much the most interesting botanically. The upper part has woodland cover of oak, birch, willow, ash and hazel which was formerly much more extensive as the blackened stumps of dead trees rising from the water indicate. What remains is of great importance in that it represents an ungrazed natural habitat which is very rare in Ireland. However, it is not of great ornithological significance.

Nowadays, the open water is what attracts the birdwatcher. At the Gearagh, at Carrigadrohid and at other points along the reservoir in winter one can see large numbers of wintering wildfowl including Whooper Swans, up to 4,000 Wigeons, 1,000 Teals and small numbers of Mallard, Shoveler, Tufted Duck, Pochard and Common Goldeneye. Scarcer species such as Goosander, Smew and Ring-necked Duck can occur at times. There are some Greylag Geese in the area, but they are feral.

Access

The reservoirs can be watched from either the northern or southern sides, though the road does not run along the entire shoreline. The northern road from Cork to Coachford provides the best view of the eastern section. Take the road from Cork for Dripsey and follow the reservoir to Macroom, stopping when birds are seen. The section below the town of Macroom is usually good. Instead of driving into Macroom, turn left on the Cork road and take the first right turn (signposted for Bantry) after about 800 m. This road leads directly to the Gearagh which can be viewed from either the south or the north. There are also footpaths leading into the Gearagh which can be used when the water level is low.

The main Macroom-Cork road, about 5 km from Macroom, provides good views of the southern part of the Carrigadrohid reservoir.

19 KILCOLMAN

OSI Discovery map: sheet 73
R58 10

Habitat and Species

Kilcolman Bog is a limestone marsh occupying a glacially-eroded hollow. The marsh floods in winter and, at this time of year, has a small population of Greenland White-fronted Geese and Whooper Swans and a large number of ducks. The most numerous ducks are Eurasian Wigeon, Mallard and Common Teal, but Shoveler, Gadwall, Tufted Duck and Pochard are usually present. Birds of prey include regular Peregrine, Merlin and Hen Harrier in winter.

A castle occupied by the poet Edmund Spenser in the 16th century overlooks the marsh.

A refuge was established here by Richard and Margaret Ridgway in 1969 when they purchased a section of the site. They planted trees, dug out channels, built up islands, constructed hides and an observatory and maintained meticulous records of weather, water-level, bird numbers and bird behaviour. Much of the data they collected has been analysed and is in use for ornithological research.

The refuge is a wonderful place for watching geese, swans and ducks at close quarters. However, because it is private, advance reservation is essential.

Access
To visit Kilcolman, first phone 022 24200 and seek permission. When this is obtained, follow the directions below to get to the site. Mallow is the nearest large town to start from. Leave Mallow on the main Limerick road; at New Twopothouse village, about 3.5 km from Mallow, take the right turn for Doneraile. Drive through Doneraile and keep straight on for about 1.5 km to a crossroads. Turn left following the sign for Rathluirc, and drive on for about 2.5 km until another crossroads is reached. There is a signpost to the right marked Heatherside Hospital. Take the left turn and drive down the narrow road for about 500 m until you reach a gate on the right marked 'Kilcolman Wildfowl Refuge'. This is the entrance to the reserve. Please ensure that you close the gate each time you pass through.

20 LISSAGRIFFIN AND MIZEN HEAD
OSI Discovery map: sheet 88
V76 25

Habitat and Species
Lissagriffin Lake is a shallow, brackish lake impounded by sand hills which have developed behind the strand at Barleycove. It has a sandy edge and some growth of reeds and sedges.

The lake has a small winter population of Whooper Swans, Teals and Wigeons, and Mute Swans and Mallards occur throughout the year. Although wader numbers are small, this is one of the best sites in Ireland for American waders. Pectoral Sandpipers are virtually annual in September, and a long list of other species has been seen. Because the shoreline is so limited in extent, the birds are usually easy to see well.

Choughs feed on the sand dunes and Peregrines are frequent visitors. To the south-west, Mizen Head is a bleak promontory with a lighthouse at the tip which has now been developed as an Interpretive Centre. It is an excellent sea-watching site, probably as good as Cape Clear, which is just across the bay. Sooty and Great Shearwaters and Great and Arctic Skuas are usual in autumn, together with large numbers of Manx Shearwaters, Gannets, Fulmars, Kittiwakes and auks. As is usual with seawatching, optimal weather conditions are essential, This site requires south-westerly winds and mist or rain for its best performance.

There are some small seabird colonies on the cliffs.

Ireland's first Isabelline Wheatear was seen on the cliff-top in autumn 1992, and the gardens at Crookhaven village nearby attract passerine migrants. Rarities recorded here include Buff-bellied Pipit, Red-eyed Vireo and Blyth's Reed Warbler.

Access

From Skibbereen follow the signposts to Schull and thence for Goleen. At Goleen, drive straight on for Barleycove. After about 8 km you will reach a fork where the left turn runs on to Crookhaven village and the right turn to Barleycove past a large caravan park. Follow the road to the right, passing the caravan park, and after about 2 km you will see Lissagriffin Lake below you. The road runs across a causeway through the middle of the lake. A car can be parked here and the lake edge explored on foot.

Mizen Head is reached by turning left after crossing the causeway, then taking the next left turn past the Barleycove Hotel and continuing for about 4 km until the small car park at Mizen Head is reached.

Crookhaven village is reached by forking left after Goleen rather than bearing right for Barleycove. The village has a number of well vegetated gardens and all should be watched from the narrow roadways.

21 DURSEY ISLAND AND ALLIHIES

OSI Discovery map: sheet 88
V48 41; V57 44

Habitat and Species

Dursey Island is a high sandstone island, about 7 km long and 1.5 km wide, located off the tip of the Beara peninsula It has been known as a prime location for rare passerines since the late 1970s when it was first worked regularly. Dr Derek Scott, an English birdwatcher who had come to live locally, found Ireland's second Eastern Olivaceous Warbler on his first visit to the island in 1977. He now resides on the island and his efforts are augmented by a small number of dedicated observers who visit the area every autumn; a number of excellent birdwatching sites have been identified on the island and the adjacent mainland.

The island is long and has rather little cover, so birds can be found almost anywhere. On the mainland there are a few small gardens, some areas of brambles and a glen with steep banks with lots of cover at Firkeel.

Passerine migrants tend to be found on Dursey itself, in Firkeel Glen or in the area around Garinish.

There are rarely large falls of any species in the area, but the diversity of species is remarkable. Common Rosefinch, Lesser Whitethroat and Melodious Warbler are regular in autumn, and major rarities in recent years have included Chimney Swift, Common Nighthawk, Pechora Pipit, Ovenbird and Scarlet Tanager.

Seawatching is quite good from the tip. The species to be seen are similar to those at Cape Clear, but numbers are lower.

Access

Dursey is at the tip of the Beara peninsula. Drive from Glengarriff to Castletownbere, and take the road west. After 15 km of winding road, a junction is reached. The right turn is for Ballydonegan and Allihies; keep straight on for Dursey Sound. Firkeel Glen is reached after another 5 km. A turn to the left runs down to a small slipway and the glen can be seen on the left-hand side. There is a path across the fields into the glen.

Take the road on for another 3 krn and you will reach Dursey Sound.

Access to the island is by cable car. Ask the operator for the times of crossing and, particularly, return. A roadway runs most of the length of the island. Make sure to walk right to the end of the island as the grassy area at the south-west tip can hold waders or pipits.

Garinish is approached by taking the first left turn after leaving Dursey Sound.

KERRY

The Kerry landscape is dominated by the magnificence of the Macgillicuddy Reeks which tower over Killarney, and by the bays which eat into the heart of the county. Kenmare Bay is disappointing for birds as there is little intertidal edge, but both Castlemaine Harbour and Tralee Bay are rich with wildfowl, especially Brent Geese in winter. Off the peninsulas are several groups of rocky islands which provide nest sites for tens of thousands of Gannets, European Storm-petrels, Manx Shearwaters and Puffins, certainly the finest seabird colonies in the country. Passage seabirds are fewer than off the Cork coast, but several headlands present opportunities.

Being situated so far west, Kerry is one of the first landfalls for American waders and ducks. Most have been recorded at Akeragh Lough but there are several other good sites and the potential for autumn passerine migrants exists at the coastal headlands.

The mountains have a thinly distributed avifauna, but breeding birds include Peregrine, Chough and Ring Ouzel and there may well be surprises awaiting the birdwatcher prepared to explore them in summer or winter.

22 CASTLEMAINE HARBOUR

OSI Discovery map: sheet 71, 78
V64 94; Q70 00

Habitat

This wide, sprawling bay is the estuary of Rivers Maine and Laune at the head of Dingle Bay. It comprises a series of interlocking sand spits with broad salt-marshes behind them. There are also extensive intertidal mudflats and poorly drained agricultural land surrounds the estuary, especially at its eastern end. The strata in the outer bay are sandy; the inner bay is much muddier. There are broad sandy beaches on the seaward side of the sand spits on both sides of the mouth of the estuary.

At the north-west corner near Inch there are extensive beds of eelgrass (*Zostera*), *Spartina* is present as well, and there are reedbeds at the eastern end.

The mountains on both sides of the bay make this a magnificently scenic site for birdwatching even if birds are few.

Shooting is prohibited over most of the estuary and there are signs to indicate this around much of the area.

Species

This is one of the major wintering sites of Brent Geese in Ireland and is also an important duck wintering area. Brent Geese arrive in late August, earlier than at most Irish sites, and remain until April. They can be found on both sides of the bay, from Rossbehy around to Inch, but the largest flocks are usually at

Inch. Wigeons arrive early here as well, and the largest numbers are found in autumn. Up to 6,500 have been seen in autumn, but the mid-winter numbers are much reduced. The flock of Wigeons off Inch promontory is one of the great Irish ornithological sights.

Castlemaine Harbour has a flock of up to 100 Pintails. Why this should be, when there are so few elsewhere on the south coast, is a mystery. Nevertheless, they are a magnificent sight as they concentrate behind the sand dunes at Inch. Shelduck, Mallard, Common Teal and Shoveler also occur on the mudflats.

In the upper reaches of the estuary Scaup and Common Goldeneye can be found in flocks of varying size. Sometimes, there can be over 100 Scaups on the southern side.

Great Northern Divers and occasional Long-tailed Ducks frequent the deeper channels. The best place for Long-tailed Ducks is off Dooks Golf Links. There are a few small parties of Red-breasted Mergansers. Off the beaches, on both southern and northern sides, flocks of Common Scoters winter. The flock off Rossbehy numbers up to 2,000 birds.

The numbers of waders are not so spectacular as the flocks of ducks and geese. Oystercatchers, Dunlins, Curlews, Bar-tailed Godwits and Redshanks scatter over the mudflats in small parties. There are some solitary Greenshanks and a few Ringed and Grey Plovers. On the beach at Inch, Sanderlings can be seen. Flocks of European Golden Plovers and Northern Lapwings sometimes occur.

The estuary is regularly hunted over by Peregrines. Being so far west it looks the ideal location for an American vagrant duck or wader, but in fact very few rarities have been recorded. Perhaps more frequent visits by birdwatchers could improve this record.

Timing
This is very much a winter site, at its best from September to the end of March, though the first Brent Geese and Eurasian Wigeon appear in late August. The area is best visited when the tide is rising so that birds can be seen at their closest. The mudflats are very extensive and a telescope is essential.

Access
On the southern side, Rossbehy Creek is approached by driving through Glenbeigh, past the Towers Hotel, and turning right on the turn signposted for Rossbeigh strand. The road leads to a car park and provides views over mud-flats and saltmarsh where geese and Wigeons can be seen.

Drive back towards Glenbeigh, but before reaching the bridge over the River Behy, turn left down a narrow road alongside the fast-flowing river. Dippers can be seen here. Park the car at the end of the tarmac and walk down a short track to the estuary.

For superb views of the scoter flocks, take the narrow road which runs west from the car park at Rossbeigh strand. A lay-by half way up the hill is an ideal vantage point for viewing the ducks.

Returning to Glenbeigh, take the road for Killorglin and turn left 500 m outside the Village. This narrow road leads down to the estuary and provides good views of the outer part of Rossbeigh creek.

Drive back to the main Glenbeigh–Killorglin road again and drive towards Killorglin. Turn left after about 1 km, just after the road crosses the River Caragh where signposts indicate Dooks Golf Links. Follow the road for 4 km to a fork, turn left for Cromane, though bird numbers here are relatively low; or turn right to follow the southern shore of Castlemaine Harbour. Stop after about 1 km and look at the estuary. Scaup and Common Goldeneye can be seen in the channels here in winter and Brent Geese are usual. Also worth checking is Lough Yganavan on the south side of the road from Glenbeigh to Cromane, just before the fork for Cromane. Ring-necked Duck has been regular here in recent years.

To see the northern shore of Castlemaine, drive to Killorglin, then to Castlemaine and, at Castlemaine, take the turn for Dingle. It is about 19 km to Inch strand and there are a couple of left turnings which provide direct access to the inner mudflats. But the mudflats behind Inch strand are the highlight of this bay. Many of the birds can be seen from the main road and the extra height of the road provides a vantage point. However, a walk along the 4 km of sand dune at Inch will present opportunities for magnificent views of great flocks of Brent Geese, Shelducks, Wigeons and Pintails and should be taken.

CALENDAR

All year: Mallard, Oystercatcher, Curlew.

Autumn: Brent Goose, Eurasian Wigeon. Common Teal, Shoveler, Red-breasted Merganser, Great Northern Diver, Northern Lapwing, European Golden and Ringed Plovers, Dunlin, Bar-tailed Godwit, Redshank, terns.

Winter: Brent Goose, Eurasian Wigeon, Common Teal, Shoveler, Common Goldeneye,

Scaup, Long-tailed Duck, Common Scoter, Red-breasted Merganser, Great Northern Diver, Ringed and European Golden Plovers, Northern Lapwing, Dunlin. Sanderling, Bar-tailed Godwit, Redshank, Greenshank.

Spring: Brent Geese and lingering ducks and waders.

Summer: visiting terns.

23 TRALEE BAY AND BARROW HARBOUR

OSI Discovery map: sheet 71
Q81 13; Q74 17

Habitat

Tralee Bay is rather like a small-scale Castlemaine Harbour and shares many of the same bird species. It stretches from Blennerville west to Derrymore Island on the southern side, to Fenit on the northern side, and includes Barrow Harbour to the north. There are extensive intertidal mudflats to the east of Derrymore Island and saltmarsh above the intertidal zone on the southern side. Barrow Harbour also has mudflats, these having built up behind a sand bar. There are beds of eelgrass (*Zostera*) which provide feeding for Brent Geese.

Species

Like Castlemaine Harbour, this bay holds large wintering flocks of Brent Geese, Wigeons and Teals, and smaller numbers of Shelducks, Mallards, Pintails, Shovelers, Scaups and Red-breasted Mergansers. Up to 3,000 Brent Geese have been counted, but there is frequent interchange between this bay and Castlemaine, only 10 km away over the Slieve Mish mountains. In Barrow Harbour, Whooper Swans join the Brent Geese on the *Zostera* in early winter.

Outside the bay there is a wintering flock of Common Scoters and scattered Great Northern and Red-throated Divers.

Wader numbers are lower than at Castlemaine but there appears to be more diversity of species. Oystercatchers, Northern Lapwings, Curlews, Bar-tailed Godwits, Redshanks and Dunlins are all found on the mudflats as in the neighbouring bay, but there appear to be more Grey Plovers, Black-tailed Godwits and autumn migrants such as Spotted Redshank at Tralee Bay. This bay has been much better watched than Castlemaine because it is so much closer to the town of Tralee where several birdwatchers live, but whether the higher coverage is the reason for the apparently greater species diversity is not known.

In autumn Curlew Sandpipers, Little Stints and Ruffs are recorded most years at Blennerville and some American waders have been seen. Spotted Redshanks winter each year. The pier at Fenit has wintering Purple Sandpipers as well as the ubiquitous Turnstones.

The gull roost in Blennerville is a good place for Glaucous, Iceland and Ring-billed Gulls (regular) in winter.

In winter Hen Harriers, Merlins and Peregrines hunt over the salt marshes.

Timing

In autumn look for waders at Blennerville as well as checking the first arrivals among the wildfowl. Winter is good for wildfowl and waders. The tidal channel is at its best for gulls at this time of year as well. In spring numbers of birds are lower, but the area is well worth a visit.

A rising tide is the best for visiting. At high tide the wildfowl and waders are almost inaccessible at their roosts. A telescope is almost essential.

Access

The estuary is difficult to survey thoroughly because the surrounding road runs at some distance from the shoreline for most of its length. The southern side can be watched from the Tralee–Dingle road. The road crosses the river at Blennerville by a large white windmill and the estuary can be scanned from several points. A telescope is essential and it may also be necessary to explore the saltmarsh.

The northern side can be approached at several points by road. From Blennerville, having travelled north across the river take the first left turn and

Redshank

drive to the exit of the disused canal. This provides one vantage point. Another can be reached by driving from Tralee towards Fenit and stopping the car at Spa where there are further views of the bay.

Barrow Harbour can be watched by taking the road on through Fenit until the shoreline is reached, or by turning right just before the village and driving for about 1.5 km until the estuary is reached. There are a number of narrow roads here which give access to different sides of Barrow Harbour.

CALENDAR

All year: Mute Swan, Mallard, Oystercatcher, Curlew.

Autumn: Brent Goose, Eurasian Wigeon, Common Teal, Shoveler, Common Scoter, Red-breasted Merganser, Red-throated and Great Northern Divers, Ringed and European Golden Plovers, Northern Lapwing, Dunlin, occasional Curlew Sandpiper and Little Stint, Ruff, Bar-tailed Godwit, Redshank.

Winter: Whooper Swan, Brent Goose, Eurasian Wigeon, Common Teal, Shoveler, Common Goldeneye, Scaup, Common Scoter, Red-breasted Merganser, Red-throated and Great Northern Divers, Ringed and European Golden Plover, Northern Lapwing, Dunlin, Sanderling, Bar-tailed Godwit, Greenshank, Redshank, occasional Spotted Redshank, Glaucous and Iceland Gulls, Ring-billed Gull.

Spring: Brent Geese and lingering ducks and waders.

---

24 AKERAGH LOUGH AND BLACKROCK STRAND

OSI Discovery map: sheet 71
Q75 26

Habitat

Akeragh Lough is a brackish lagoon behind a line of sand dunes in the northern corner of Ballyheigue Bay north of Tralee. The lagoon has become considerably overgrown and in summer consists of three ponds connected by dykes; in winter the surrounding meadows flood and the area becomes a large shallow lake. Blackrock Strand is on the seaward side of the dunes. In recent years the lake has suffered from varying water levels and Blackrock Strand has tended to attract most waders.

Species

The lough has been famous for over 30 years for the American ducks and waders which occur regularly. The site does not attract as many rarities now as it did in the past, but it is still a premier location for seeking out unusual birds.

Highlights have included flocks of 13 American Wigeons and 14 Pectoral Sandpipers and records of most of the American wader species on the Irish list. The first Irish records of Baird's, Least, Solitary and Stilt Sandpipers were all at this lough. Rare birds come not just from the west: species such as Temminck's Stint and White-winged Black Tern have also been seen here.

As well as being a site with the potential for rarities, Akeragh Lough also has wintering Whooper Swans, Mallards, Wigeons, Teals, Gadwalls, Pintails, Shovelers and small numbers of diving ducks. The numbers of wildfowl vary depending on the water level. Wader species in autumn include Spotted Redshank, Ruff, Little Stint, Curlew Sandpiper, and Green and Wood Sandpipers in most years as well as the more common species. Again, the number of waders depends very much on the condition of the lough. Many of the waders feed on the beach when the lough is unsuitable.

Choughs can be seen in the surrounding fields. Peregrines, Merlins and Hen Harriers hunt over the surrounding area.

Timing
From autumn through winter to spring this is a superb area. In summer it is less likely to be exciting, but is often worth a visit.

Access
Akeragh Lough is best approached from Ballyheigue. Drive south from the centre of the village for 1.5 km along a rough track past caravans. The car should be parked at the open area beside the track and the ponds on the left explored on foot and with care. The new farmhouse at the end of this road is strictly private.

The lough can also be watched from the main road between Ardfert and Ballyheigue, but great care should be taken as the road is busy.

To reach the southernmost pond, take the minor road leading west from the main road about 0.5 km south of the bridge over the stream draining the lough. This minor road degenerates into a track leading to the pond.

Every visitor to Akeragh should take the southerly road which provides access to Black Rock and to the southern side of the lough. Driving from Ballyheigue south for Ardfert, cross the bridge over the river and take the right turn about 1 km south of the Ranch House guest house. This road leads to a sluice. From here, the lough to the north can be explored and the beach offshore can be walked. The small islet, Black Rock, joined to the beach at low tide has waders and gulls.

CALENDAR

All year: Mute Swan, Mallard, Oystercatcher, Ringed Plover, Curlew.

Autumn: Eurasian Wigeon, Common Teal, Shoveler, Red-breasted Merganser, diving ducks, European Golden Plover, Northern Lapwing, Dunlin, Curlew Sandpiper, Little Stint, Ruff, Black-tailed and Bar-tailed Godwits, Redshank, Greenshank, Green and Wood Sandpipers, American waders.

Winter: Whooper Swan, Eurasian Wigeon, Common Teal, Shoveler, Red-breasted Merganser, European Golden Plover, Northern Lapwing, Dunlin, Sanderling, Bar-tailed Godwit, Greenshank, Redshank, Dunlin, Sanderling.

Spring: ducks and late waders.

---

25 BALLINSKELLIGS BAY   OSI Discovery map: sheet 83
V46 66

Habitat and Species
The shallow bay from Hog's Head around to Ballinskelligs is a wintering area for Common Scoters. Velvet and Surf Scoters have been found here in the past and the location of the site, so far west, suggests that it should be worth investigating

regularly for Surf Scoters. Great Northern and Red-throated Divers are also present in winter and Slavonian Grebes turn up regularly.

Access

From Kenmare take the Sneem road. After passing through Sneem, follow the signposts for Waterville. The bay can be seen well from Waterville or the road around to Ballinskelligs. Reenroe Point is the best place for seeing Slavonian Grebes.

26 LOUGH GILL

OSI Discovery map: sheet 83

Q61 14

Habitat and Species

Lough Gill is a shallow lake of 1,800 ha, with rough pasture on its inland side and sand dunes protecting it from the sea. Beds of *Phragmites* surround most of the lake. The outlet from the lake to the sea is a narrow stream at the eastern end and the water level is controlled by a sluice. The entire area is subject to a no-shooting order.

This is a wonderfully productive lake with great numbers of wintering wildfowl. The lake has varying numbers of swans and ducks throughout the winter. At times there are large flocks of Whooper Swans (up to 200 with the occasional Bewick's) and large numbers of Mallards, Teals, Wigeons and Scaups. Smaller numbers of Gadwalls, Shovelers, Tufted Ducks, Pochards and Coots can also be seen.

The lake is quite large and many ducks spend their time in the reedbeds, making them difficult to see.

As well as being a good bird area, this is also the centre of the Irish population of Natterjack Toads.

Access

Drive from Tralee to Castlegregory. At Castlegregory bear left rather than taking either of the two right turns in the village, and drive straight on for about 200 m. Take the right turn marked Lough Gill and drive to a small parking area where a pier projects into the lake. Much of the lake, especially the eastern end, can be surveyed from here.

To see the eastern end, drive back onto the road out of Castlegregory and turn right (rather than returning to the village). Drive on for about 800 m and you will have a good view across fields of the western end of the lake. Many ducks can be seen best from here.

27 DINGLE HARBOUR   OSI Discovery map: sheet 83
Q44 01

Habitat and Species

The Dingle Peninsula is a well-known tourist resort in Kerry and the main town of Dingle is also a fishing port. In winter, it attracts a variety of gulls in the harbour area and loafing on offshore rocks and vessels. As such should be scanned for Glaucous and Iceland Gulls, particularly in late winter and spring. In late summer, it is often used as a departure point for pelagic birding trips which have a high success rate for Wilson's Storm-petrel.

About three kilometres west of Dingle Harbour on the coast road is Burnham Lagoon which is one of the few areas of exposed mudflat on the south shore of the Dingle Peninsula and is worth a look to check the small number of waders, as well as Little Egret there, while at high tide, the open water is particularly sheltered from the prevailing south-westerly winds and is good for divers, grebes and diving ducks.

Access

The town of Dingle is located on the south side of the Dingle Peninsula and can be reached by the N86 from Tralee or the R561 from Castlemaine

28 SKELLIGS

OSI Discovery map: sheet 83
V27 61

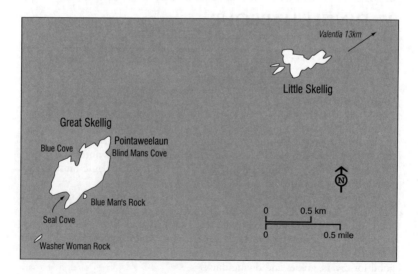

Habitat and Species

The Skelligs are two towering rocks projecting out of the Atlantic about 13 km off Valentia Island. The islands are red sandstone and slate. Skellig Michael, much the larger of the two islands at 48 ha, has a lighthouse which was manned from 1826 up to the very recent past. The Little Skellig is smaller, only 7 ha in extent, with sheer cliffs and no room for human habitation. It holds almost 30,000 pairs of nesting Gannets.

The Great Skellig has no Gannets but holds several thousand nesting pairs of Puffins, European Storm-petrels and Manx Shearwaters, and smaller numbers of Fulmars, Kittiwakes, Razorbills and Common Guillemots. It is a unique experience to stand in front of the beehive huts on the Great Skellig, built by monks over 1,000 years ago, and to hear Manx Shearwaters groaning on their nest scrapes in crevices in the walls.

The Little Skellig is a BirdWatch Ireland reserve.

Access

Boats travel to the Great Skellig in summer from Valentia, Caherciveen, Portmagee and Derrynane. Timetables are available in local hotels and guest-houses. If possible, negotiate a trip which will take you close to the Little Skellig for a good view of the Gannet colony. Landing on the Little Skellig is prohibited.

---

29 DUNQUIN

OSI Discovery map: sheet 70
Q32 00

Habitat and Species

Dunquin is at the western tip of the Dingle peninsula, a spectacularly beautiful part of west Kerry. The village of Dunquin, with plenty of cover, and the fields and valleys around it have been shown in recent years to attract rare migrants in autumn. Red-eyed Vireo has been seen, and Yellow-browed Warbler, Western Bonelli's Warbler, Icterine Warbler and Red-throated Pipit have also been recorded. The area has obvious potential for American passerine vagrants.

Seawatching can be carried out from Clogher Head, to the north of Dunquin, and in west or north-west winds good numbers of Sooty Shearwaters have been seen and smaller numbers of Great Shearwaters, Great, Arctic and Pomarine Skuas and Grey Phalaropes. Rarer seabirds seen include Long-tailed Skua and Sabine's Gull.

Access

Dunquin is reached by driving from Dingle to Ventry and then following the road around Slea Head until the village is reached. There is a Youth Hostel in the village and numerous guest houses in the vicinity.

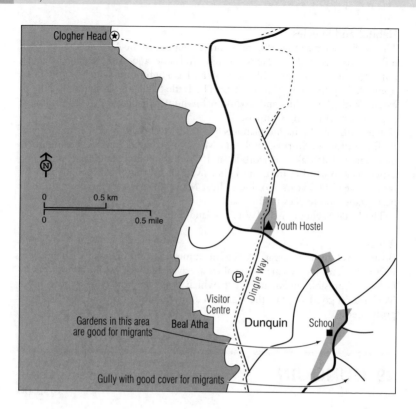

30 BLASKET ISLANDS   OSI Discovery map: sheet 70
V27 97

Habitat and Species

The Blasket Islands are a group of islands off the Dingle peninsula with substan-tial colonies of breeding seabirds. Some thousands of pairs of Manx Shearwater and Puffins and several tens of thousands of pairs of European Storm-petrels nest on the small islands of Inishtearaght, Inishvickillane, Inishnabro and Inishtooskert, together with small numbers of Fulmars, Common Guillemots, Razorbills and gulls. Leach's Storm-petrels have been seen in the surrounding waters during summer and several have been caught at night on the islands, so a small number possibly breed. The neighbouring islands of Beginish and Young's Island have important tern colonies.

Cover on the islands is almost non-existent, but nevertheless a few passer-ine migrants have been recorded, most notably Yellow-rumped Warbler and Rose-breasted Grosbeak. There are old records of migrants striking the light-house on Great Blasket, so a visit to that island at least might be productive in autumn.

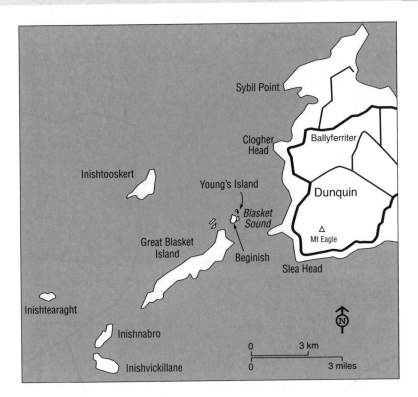

Access

Unfortunately, the islands are uninhabited and access is only possible by nego-
tiating with local fishermen and bringing camping equipment. Permission is
required to land on Inishvickillane. There is a Blasket Islands Interpretive
Centre (Ionad an Bhlascaoid) situated in Dunquin.

While the Great Blasket is visited regularly in summer by organised boat
trips from Dunquin Pier (details in Kruger's pub in Dunquin), there are very
few trips in autumn when the potential for seeing migrants should be
highest.

31 SMERWICK HARBOUR

OSI Discovery map: sheet 70
Q37 05

Habitat and Species

From an ornithological perspective, Smerwick is a comparatively recently discovered coastal inlet which has yielded an impressive number of American

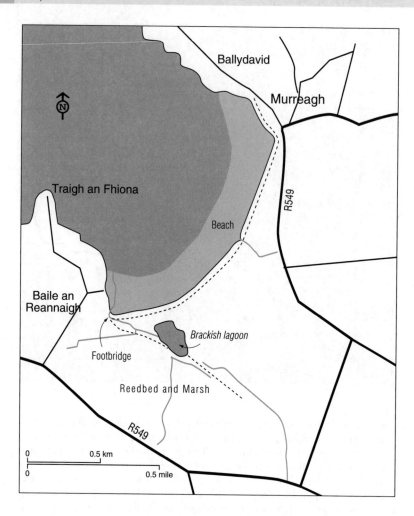

waders and other rarities. In a comparatively small area it comprises brackish lagoon, sandy shore and reedbed, all of which are worth checking, particularly in autumn.

Access

The best access to the beach and lagoon is from Baile an Reannaigh which is 2 km north of Ballyferriter on the R559. Small flocks of waders feed on the beach and should be thoroughly searched for Nearctic vagrants. There is a footbridge over the river channel which bisects the beach and a path inland towards the lagoon which provides some limited access to the reedbed and views over the lagoon.

32 BRANDON POINT

OSI Discovery map: sheet 70,
OSI Mount Brandon Map 1:25000
Q52 17

Habitat and Species

Brandon Point is a classic seawatching point in north-west winds. It is located at the western end of a north facing bay and seabirds which are funnelled into the bay by strong gales exit almost below the feet of the observer at Brandon.

As well as Manx Shearwaters, Gannets, Fulmars, auks and skuas, large numbers of Great and Sooty Shearwaters have been seen, though not usually in such numbers as at Cape Clear. This site gets a somewhat different mix of species, reflecting its much more westerly location. The west coast of Ireland appears to have many more Sabine's Gulls, Leach's Storm-petrels and phalaropes offshore than the south coast, and this has been reflected on days when small flocks of all three species have been seen.

Access
Follow the road from Tralee to Castlegregory and, at the fork for Dingle some 10 km beyond Castlegregory, turn right for Cloghane and drive out to the end of the road at Brandon Point. Remember, however, that this site requires northwest winds. If short of time, stop at Fermoyle, signposted just after the turn for Cloghane, and check the beach. Skuas and Sabine's Gulls can be seen assembling off here when the winds are suitable.

33 KILLARNEY NATIONAL PARK

OSI Discovery map: sheet 78,
OSI Killarney NP Map 1:25000
V95 88

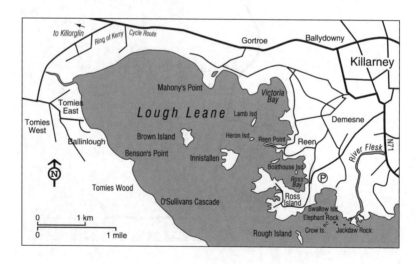

Habitat and Species
The Killarney National Park covers 10,000 ha of lake, mountain and woodland, principally of sessile oak, but with extensive coniferous wood, wet alder

Goldcrest

swamp and a fine yew wood. The old woodland holds a rich diversity of breeding species. The commonest birds are Chaffinches, Robins. Goldcrests, Blue Tits, Coal Tits and Wrens, but there are also Jays, Long-eared Owls, Blackcaps, probably a few Common Redstarts and perhaps a few Wood Warblers. Garden Warblers are also regular breeders. The park is now the focus of a re-introduction program for White-tailed Eagle and more than a dozen birds have been released in the area.

The lakes attract occasional rarities including Ring-necked Duck, Garganey and Osprey. The best area is on Lough Leane from Ross Castle around to Killarney Golf Club.

Access

There are several large tracts of deciduous woodland in the Killarney vicinity. Ross Island has woodland close to the town. Follow the signposts for Ross Bay and park your car in the car park.

Tomies Wood is on the far side of Lough Leane from Killarney town. Drive out on the Killorglin road and turn left after 5 km; turn left after a further 2 km and the road leads down to the lake shore. A path leads along the lake shore to the wood.

There is more woodland on the southern shore of the upper lake.

Take the road for Kenmare and explore the various tracts of woodland within 15 km of Killarney. Even if birds are few, the views are justly famous.

34 BALLYLONGFORD AND TARBERT

OSI Discovery map: sheet 63, 64
Q99 47; R07 47

Habitat and Species

The mudflats on the Shannon Estuary at Ballylongford and Tarbert are two
small sections of an enormous complex which holds large numbers of wildfowl
and waders. These two bays each hold up to 1,500 ducks (and Tarbert has had
3,000) and 3,000 waders. The main duck species are Eurasian Wigeon,
Common Teal and Mallard, with some Shelducks, Pintails and Shovelers and a
few Red-breasted Mergansers off the mudflats. There are usually some wintering Scaups in both bays. Waders include Oystercatcher, Northern Lapwing,
European Golden Plover, Grey Plover, Curlew, Bar-tailed Godwit, Redshank,
Greenshank and Dunlin.

Access

Ballylongford Bay is easily watched by taking the road from Ballylongford west
towards Ballybunion. Turn right 1 km after leaving Ballylongford and follow
the narrow road down to Carrig Island.

The Tarbert mudflats can be viewed from the road leading from Tarbert village to the pier and ferry terminal. The road runs right alongside the estuary.
Cars can be parked at the ferry terminal. The best time is when slightly more
than half the mud has been covered by a rising tide.

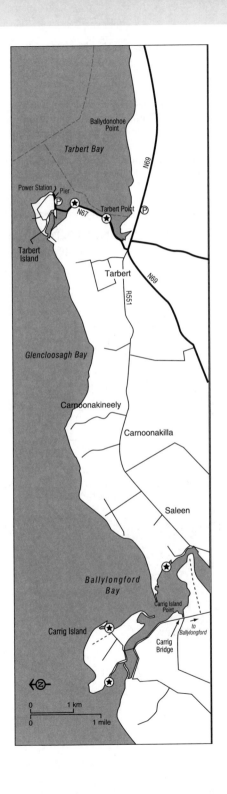

LIMERICK

Limerick is a rich and rather low-lying agricultural county, with its only coastline the south shore of the Shannon estuary. As a result, there are no seabird colonies to see, and the chances of finding unusual passerine migrants are slim.

The Shannon estuary runs from the city of Limerick to the border with Kerry and beyond and, while difficult to access, has a great deal of variety in its winter bird species. It has certainly been very much underwatched.

35 SOUTH SHORE OF SHANNON ESTUARY

OSI Discovery map: sheet 64
R26 52; R46 56

Habitat

The Shannon Estuary is approximately 80 km from Limerick to the open sea, and has numerous bays, many of which hold flocks of wintering wildfowl and waders. On the southern side, the stretch from the Maigue Estuary to Aughinish Island is unquestionably the most productive for birds. There are a number of inlets and the coastline around Greenish Island is particularly indented. The tide recedes for nearly 2 km in places. Behind the intertidal zone is an extensive area of saltmarsh and poor agricultural land with a number of drains. The road does not run alongside the mudflats and access is therefore difficult.

This is a wild and attractive estuary, but one for the enthusiast. The visual impact of the enormous alumina extraction factory at Aughinish Island detracts somewhat from the experience of birdwatching on the saltmarsh, but the relative inaccessibility of the best birdwatching sites means that the visitor is highly unlikely to come across another birder. This also means that if you simply want to see the species which occur here, you can probably get closer and better views at a number of other sites.

Species

The wintering wildfowl and waders of the Shannon estuary were not thoroughly surveyed until the 1970s when regular aerial surveys were carried out. These ceased when the aircraft ditched into the Shannon estuary close to the islands north of this shoreline. Fortunately, both pilot and ornithologist were able to scramble to safety. The counts, however, showed that between 3,500 and 6,000 wildfowl and between 5,000 and 11,000 waders used this area in winter.

Some wader ringing was also carried out near Greenish Island in the 1970s, but little birdwatching has been carried on here since.

The principal wildfowl species are Shelduck, Eurasian Wigeon, Common Teal, Mallard and Scaup. Small numbers of Shovelers and Red-breasted Mergansers also occur. There are small populations of both Greylag Geese and Greenland White-fronted Geese in the area, but the birds are very mobile and difficult to find. The Greylag Geese usually frequent the Maigue Estuary and the Greenland White-fronts are further downstream between Beagh Castle and Aughinish. The best section for ducks is to the east of Aughinish Island and around Greenish Island.

Most of the waders are further east, from Beagh Castle to the mouth of the River Maigue. The principal species are Northern Lapwing, European Golden Plover, Curlew, Black-tailed Godwit, Redshank, Greenshank and Dunlin. Some Grey and Ringed Plovers and Knots occur. Robertstown Creek is a haunt of Spotted Redshanks in autumn, winter and spring.

Timing

The estuary is very quiet from spring to early autumn, so the best time for visiting is between early September and the middle of March. Numbers of some wader species are higher in autumn, but duck numbers are certainly highest from November to February. The area is shot over in winter.

Access

Access is difficult and requires serious commitment. From Limerick take the road for Mungret and Askeaton. This is well signposted.

After passing Mungret keep on the main road for about 12 km until you reach a right turn for Pallaskenry. Take the road to Pallaskenry and drive straight through the village. At a junction about 400 m past the village bear left; drive for nearly 2 km to another junction; then turn right and immediately afterwards turn left and drive down to Ringmoylan Quay. There are good views of the mudflats here.

Drive back to Pallaskenry and turn right. Drive straight for 5 km and then take the right turn for Beagh Castle. This road leads right onto the edge of the mudflats again.

Return from Beagh Castle and turn right. Follow this road into Askeaton. There are several stopping places where the saltmarsh and estuary can be approached on your right, but remember that the land here is all privately owned. The only access by road is on the narrow road to the right at Ballysteen.

To see Robertstown Creek drive on through Askeaton and turn right at Robertstown church. This road provides access to the western arm of the creek; the eastern arm can best be seen from the main road.

CALENDAR

All year: Mute Swan, Greylag Goose, Mallard, Cormorant, Grey Heron, Curlew.

Autumn: Greylag and Greenland White-fronted Geese, Shelduck, Eurasian Wigeon, Common Teal, Shoveler, Red-breasted Merganser, Oystercatcher, Northern Lapwing, European Golden and Ringed Plovers, Black-tailed Godwit, Redshank, Greenshank, Spotted Redshank, Dunlin.

Winter: Greenland White-fronted Goose, Shelduck, Eurasian Wigeon, Common Teal, Shoveler, Scaup, Red-breasted Merganser, Great Crested Grebe, Oystercatcher, Ringed, European Golden and Grey Plovers, Northern Lapwing, Knot, Dunlin, Black-tailed Godwit, Redshank, Greenshank.

Spring: lingering geese, ducks and waders.

36 LOUGH GUR

OSI Discovery map: sheet 65
R64 41

Habitat and Species

This shallow lake is better known for its archaeological remains than its birds. There is an ancient lake dwelling or crannog in the lake which when excavated produced many artefacts, which can be seen in the National Museum in Dublin. The lake holds between 1,000 and 2,000 ducks in winter. Eurasian Wigeon and Tufted Duck are most numerous, but up to 200 Shovelers and smaller numbers of Mallards, Gadwalls and Common Teals also occur.

At night up to 50 Whooper Swans roost on the lake, having travelled from their daytime feeding site on pasture fields at Rathcannon, Bruff and near Herbertstown.

Several rare duck species have been recorded, including Ring-necked and Ferruginous Ducks. There is very little standing water in the vicinity so it is not altogether surprising that this lake has attracted rarities.

Access

Lough Gur is close to Kilmallock. Driving from Cork to Limerick on the main road between these two cities, turn off at Charleville for Kilmallock. Drive through Kilmallock on the road for Bruff and Holycross. Turn right at Holycross and view from the layby beyond the cemetery or from the main car park at the northern end of the lake. There is a pathway running along a portion of the lakeshore which is wheelchair accessible.

To get to Rathcannon, where the Whooper Swans feed, drive from Lough Gur to Bruff. Turn right just beyond the main bridge. The swans can be seen from November to April on fields to the right about 1.5 km from Bruff.

---

37 WESTFIELDS MARSH   OSI Discovery map: sheet 65
R55 57

Habitat and Species

This is a small freshwater marsh on the north shore of the River Shannon in Limerick City. It is not particularly interesting, but its location makes it extremely convenient for anyone visiting Limerick City and who has limited time available. The marsh supports small numbers of ducks and other waterbirds including Water Rail and, in winter, Common Snipe.

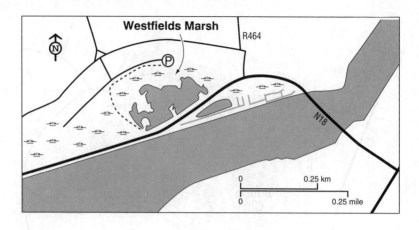

Access

The entrance to the marsh is located on North Circular Road, just 10 mins walk from the City Centre. Take the N18 bridge to cross the river from south to north and take the first turn right on the north side to North Circular Road roundabout. Turn left onto North Circular Road, the entrance is on the left-hand side.

38 CURRAGH CHASE   OSI Discovery map: sheet 65
R41 49

Habitat and Species

The mixed woodlands at Curragh Chase offer some of the best woodland birding in Co Limerick, with all of the usual Irish woodland species to be found, but with the possibility of something rarer. In the late 1980s this woodland supported the largest flock of Hawfinches recorded in Ireland and there have been sporadic sightings there since. Among the variety of deciduous trees planted are a number of stands of mature hornbeam *Carpinus* sp. which attracted the Hawfinches. There is also an ornamental lake which is big enough to attract some wintering wildfowl and extensive parkland.

Access

The park entrance is located on the N69 Limerick to Askeaton Road, approximately 4.5km west of the crossroads at Kildimo. Many of the forest paths are wheelchair-accessible including those by the lakeshore.

CLARE

Clare is bordered on the east and south sides by the River Shannon and its estuary. To the west lies the Atlantic and to the north is Galway Bay and a stretch of limestone between the sea and the Slieve Aughty hills. The limestone pavement of the Burren dominates north Clare and the visitor in spring or summer should certainly explore this habitat for its flowers and butterflies.

The county has large numbers of wintering wildfowl on the Shannon estuary and the many lakes scattered across the county. Waders are most numerous on the Shannon estuary.

To the west there are breeding seabird colonies on the Cliffs of Moher and a good seabird and passerine migration watchpoint at Loop Head in the extreme south-west of the county.

39 SHANNON AIRPORT LAGOON

OSI Discovery map: sheet 58
R37 60

Habitat

The area described as the lagoon at Shannon Airport comprises three habitats. The lagoon proper is a shallow brackish lake, created when two embankments were built between Dernish Island and the mainland. A sluice gate controls the water level. Sometimes the water level drops and a muddy shoreline is exposed.

Coots

There are reedbeds alongside the lagoon and these have been heavily mist-netted as part of a study of Sedge Warblers. The principal species is *Phragmites*. Around the reedbed is an area of marsh with stands of rushes and some invading willows (*Salix*).

Outside the lake, the estuarine mudflat stretches into the distance beyond Rineanna in the west. However, the mudflat close to where the causeway around the eastern rim of the lagoon partially encloses the intertidal mud is one of the last areas to flood when the tide rises and is a particularly attractive area for large numbers of waders. Unfortunately, *Spartina* is spreading in the area.

Species

Mute Swans and sometimes Whooper Swans assemble on the lagoon proper, as do wintering flocks of up to 300 Mallards, 500 Eurasian Wigeons, 600 Common Teals, 200 Shovelers, 20 Pintails, 40 Gadwalls, 150 Pochards and 400 Coots. Flocks of Mallards, Eurasian Wigeons and Shovelers also occur on the estuary, as do Shelducks and, in the channels, parties of Scaups.

Numbers of waders vary greatly, but have reached 20,000 at the mudflats off the lagoon. Up to 5,000 Dunlins, 1,000 European Golden Plovers, 1,000 Redshanks, 1,500 Black-tailed Godwits, 200 Bar-tailed Godwits, 300 Knots, and smaller numbers of Grey and Ringed Plovers, Turnstones, Greenshanks and Spotted Redshanks winter here. In autumn, Ruffs, Curlew Sandpipers and Little Stints all occur. Rarities recorded in recent years include Broad-billed and Least Sandpipers, Wilson's Phalarope and Laughing Gull.

The lagoon holds breeding Water Rails, large numbers of Sedge Warblers and a few pairs of Grasshopper Warblers. In autumn, a few Reed Warblers have been caught among the migrant Sedge Warblers and rarer species trapped include Savi's Warbler and Bluethroat.

Timing

The area is worth visiting at any time of the year, but visits should ideally be made when the tide is rising and the mudflats are partially inundated. When the tide is fully out waders are difficult to see owing to the extent of the mudflats.

Access (see Map 35 Shannon Estuary)

The lagoon proper is owned by the Shannon Airport Authority, and is subject to patrols by security staff sympathetic to birdwatching. Park in the Airport Hotel car park (just before the Airport on the left-hand side) and walk out onto the lagoon causeway which commences just beyond the rear of the hotel. A disused hide, on the western side of the lagoon can be reached by driving past the main terminal building and taking the first left turn for the golf club-house. Walk through the gate at the far end of the clubhouse car park and follow the track to the wooden hide. The mudflats can easily be watched from the public road. Follow the signposts to Shannon Airport. Drive right to the airport itself, park your car in one of the public car parks and walk over to the edge of the estuary.

CALENDAR

All year: Mute Swan, Shelduck, Mallard, Little Grebe, Coot, Moorhen, Water Rail, Curlew, Black-tailed Godwit, Reed Bunting.

Autumn: Eurasian Wigeon, Common Teal, Shoveler, Pintail, Pochard, Oystercatcher, Ringed and European Golden Plovers, Turnstone, Northern Lapwing, Knot, Dunlin, Curlew Sandpiper, Little Stint, Ruff, Bar-tailed Godwit, Spotted Redshank, Redshank, Greenshank, Swallow and Starling roosts, Sedge and Reed Warblers, Northern Wheatear, White Wagtail.

Winter: Whooper Swan, Eurasian Wigeon, Common Teal, Shoveler, Pintail, Pochard, Scaup, Oystercatcher, Ringed Plover, European Golden Plover, Grey Plover, Northern Lapwing, Knot, Dunlin, Bar-tailed Godwit, Spotted Redshank, Redshank, Greenshank, Turnstone, Merlin.

Spring: late ducks and waders, Sedge and Willow Warblers, Common Whitethroat, Swallow, Northern Wheatear, White Wagtail.

Summer: Sedge Warbler, Grasshopper Warbler.

40 FERGUS ESTUARY

OSI Discovery map: sheet 58
R32 68; R36 64

Habitat
The Fergus is an enormous and daunting estuary, shaped rather like an inverted 'V' with its apex at Clarecastle and broadening out to Shannon in the east and Killadysert in the west. Both sides have extensive saltmarshes and, while access is possible at intervals on both sides, no road providing an opportunity for continuous views runs around the edge of the estuary. The mudflats, which cover many square kilometres, stretch right to the Shannon and birds interchange freely between this estuary, the Limerick shore of the Shannon, and the area around the Airport (see map on page 94).

Species
This is an exceptionally important wildfowl and wader wintering area, but a very frustrating place to watch birds because of the distances involved. The entire estuary holds several thousand wintering Eurasian Wigeons and smaller numbers of Whooper Swans, Shelducks, Mallards, Common Teals, Shovelers and Scaups.

Wader numbers are also enormous, with similar species to Shannon Airport Lagoon. This area, however, is renowned as a spring staging point for Black-tailed Godwits returning to Iceland. Several thousand, sometimes over 6,000, have been seen here in March and April. They are a magnificent sight, as most are in full summer plumage. Islandavanna, Ing and Clenagh are the best places for them.

This estuary also holds flocks of Grey Plovers in spring.

Timing
The best time for the Fergus Estuary is between September and early April. It is essential to visit it on a rising tide if reasonable views of the birds are to be had.

Access (see Map 35 Shannon Estuary)

Ing on the eastern side has a small hillock from which good views can be had over the estuary with a telescope. Drive from Limerick on the Ennis road and pass through Newmarket-on-Fergus. About 1 km on the Ennis side of the village, take the next left turn and turn right at the junction reached after 2 km. Take the next left turn after 1.5 km and drive to the estuary at Ing.

Further south on the eastern side is Clenagh, which is approached from the same left turn just beyond Newmarket-on-Fergus. At the junction reached after 2 km turn left (instead of right for Ing) and follow the road to the estuary, by keeping to the right.

The western side is best watched from lslandmagrath and Islandavanna. To get to Islandmagrath, keep straight on after crossing the River Fergus at Clarecastle rather than going into the town proper. After less than 1 km take the left fork and drive on to Islandmagrath. The saltmarsh and estuary can be explored from here.

Islandavanna is reached by taking the Killadysert road out of Clarecastle and driving for 6 km. A narrow road on the left leads to Islandavanna.

CALENDAR

All year: Shelduck, Mallard, Black-tailed Godwit, Curlew, Reed Bunting.

Autumn: Eurasian Wigeon, Common Teal, Shoveler, Pintail, Oystercatcher, Ringed Plover, European Golden Plover, Turnstone, Northern Lapwing, Knot, Dunlin, Bar-tailed Godwit, Redshank, Greenshank.

Winter: Whooper Swan, Greenland White-fronted Goose, Eurasian Wigeon, Common Teal, Shoveler, Pintail, Scaup, Oystercatcher, Ringed, European Golden and Grey Plovers, Northern Lapwing, Knot, Dunlin, Bar-tailed Godwit, Redshank, Greenshank, Turnstone.

Spring: late ducks and waders. Large flocks of migrating Black-tailed Godwits.

41 BALLYALLIA LAKE

OSI Discovery map: sheet 58
R34 81

Habitat

Ballyallia is a small lake on the River Fergus situated in a limestone depression in undulating countryside. It is surrounded by cattle pasture and there are woodlands around Ballyallia House to the north. Shooting is prohibited and there is a small public car park at the eastern side.

This is a particularly attractive place to see large numbers of wildfowl because they can be approached more readily than on the Shannon estuary or at the other nearby lakes.

Species

Both Mute and Whooper Swans can be found on the lake, usually concentrating at its western arm. Large flocks of Eurasian Wigeons and Common Teals can be seen, often up to 1,500 of the former. Smaller numbers of Pintails,

Gadwalls, Tufted Ducks and Pochards occur, but the lake is chiefly famous for its large numbers of Shovelers. Up to 500 or so have been recorded, making this one of the most important sites for the species in the country. There is also a large Coot population.

Waders occur on the pasture around the water's edge. Curlews, Northern Lapwings, Black-tailed Godwits, Dunlins and occasional Ruffs are the principal species.

Rarities recorded here include American Wigeon, Blue-winged Teal and Ring-necked Duck.

Timing
Ballyallia is best between October and March.

Access
The car park is the first place from which to look at the lake. Driving north from Ennis on the Galway road, take the first left turn, about 1.5 km outside the town. Drive straight for a couple of hundred metres until the lake and car park appear. Wildfowl are usually easily seen from here.

To see the rest of the lake, turn the car and take the narrow road to the right just before the main road. The road crosses a small stream and runs within sight of the lake for about 1 km. The lake is briefly lost to view and then reappears as a long, narrow channel. This part is usually good for swans.

CALENDAR

All year: Mute Swan, Coot, Mallard, Tufted Duck

Autumn: Eurasian Wigeon, Gadwall, Common Teal, Shoveler, Pintail, Pochard, Northern

Lapwing, Dunlin, Ruff, Black-tailed Godwit, Curlew.

Winter: Whooper Swan, ducks and waders.

Spring: late wildfowl and waders.

---

42 CLIFFS OF MOHER   OSI Discovery map: sheet 51
R04 92

Habitat
The Cliffs of Moher comprise 10 km of cliffs stretching from Fisherstreet to Cancregga Point. The cliffs rise sheer from the sea to just over 200 m and are one of the most popular tourist destinations in County Clare. The cliffs have several rock strata: beds of black shale at sea level alternate with layers of sandstone and flagstones. This layering of rock has led to the development of narrow horizontal ledges which provide excellent nest sites for seabirds.

Species
The most numerous seabirds breeding on the cliffs are Fulmars, Kittiwakes, Common Guillemots, Razorbills and Puffins. This is probably the most accessible breeding site of Puffins in the country and over 1,000 pairs nest here. They can be seen easily from the Visitor Centre at O'Brien's Tower as they wheel in to land on the grassy slopes of Goat Island. Over 3,000 pairs of Fulmars nest on the cliffs and they can be seen on ledges to the south of the Visitor Centre. Below them are scattered Razorbills, crouched in nooks and crannies in the rock; further down the cliff are rows of Common Guillemots and Kittiwakes on ledges. There are in the region of 7,000 nesting Razorbills, 7,000 Kittiwake nests and almost 20,000 Common Guillemots occupying ledges. Small numbers of Shags, Great Black-backed Gulls and Herring Gulls also breed here.

Ravens and Choughs usually attract attention with their characteristic calls, and Peregrines should be seen on a summer visit. Jackdaws and Rock Doves are also common on the cliffs. Above the cliffs Northern Wheatears are easily seen, but the handful of pairs of breeding Twites are more difficult to find and may now be extinct.

Timing
The best time to see seabirds at the Cliffs of Moher is at the height of the breeding season, from early May to the end of July. Some species are on the

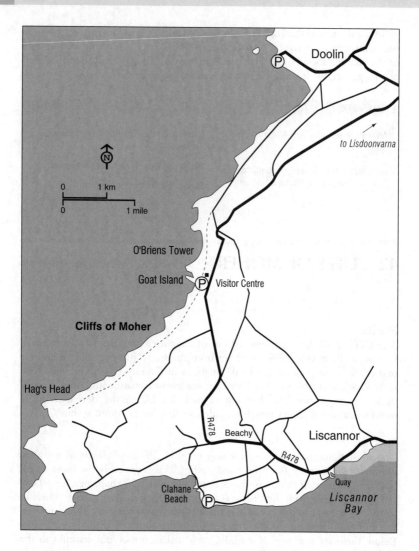

cliffs throughout much of the year, but they cannot be depended upon in autumn and winter.

Access

The Cliffs of Moher are well signposted from the surrounding villages of west Clare. From Lisdoonvarna or Ennistimon follow the signposts west and park in the public car park. This is a very popular tourist centre so do not be surprised by large numbers of buses.

There are walks along the clifftop north to Fisherstreet and south to Cancregga.

Puffins

43 LISCANNOR BAY

OSI Discovery map: sheet 51
R06 88

Habitat and Species

Liscannor Bay is a broad and rather exposed bay but when viewing conditions are calm, it is well worth a look. Divers, grebes, scoters and gulls all gather in the bay in autumn and winter and should be scanned from the pier in the village of Liscannor.

On the north shore of the bay is Clahane Beach, where accumulations of kelp and other rotting seaweed are picked over by pipits and wagtails.

Access

Liscannor is located on the R478, about 6 km south of the Cliffs of Moher. The best vantage points are on the north shore of the Bay, particularly the pier at Liscannor. Clahane Beach can be reached by taking the R478 west from Liscannor Pier and take the third turn on the left. Drive 1 km to the seashore. At full tide, the scoter flock can also be viewed (with a telescope) from the promenade at Lahinch, about 3 km further south.

44 LOOP HEAD AND BRIDGES OF ROSS

OSI Discovery map: sheet 63
Q68 47; Q73 50

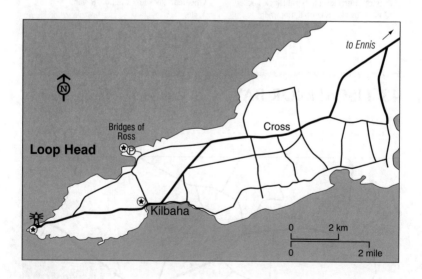

Habitat

Loop Head is at the western extremity of Clare. To the north of the peninsula is a seawatching site, the Bridges of Ross, and to the south are some patches of cover on the road from Kilbaha village to the lighthouse. The clifftop around the lighthouse is very exposed. The cliffs on the northern side are quite steep and provide nesting sites for seabirds.

Species

The area has nesting Fulmars, Shags, Herring and Great Black-backed Gulls, Kittiwakes, Razorbills and Common Guillemots, breeding mainly on the northern side, but the Loop is chiefly known for the marvellous seawatching from the Bridges of Ross. In west and north-west gales in autumn, Sabine's Gulls, Leach's Storm-petrels and Grey Phalaropes are regular. As many as 460 Sabine's Gulls have been seen in a season. Wilson's Storm-petrel and Fea's Petrel has been recorded annually in recent years. Manx Shearwaters are numerous as one would expect and Sooty Shearwaters are common in some years, but Great and Cory's Shearwaters are not as frequent as on the south coast. Long-tailed Skuas are seen in most autumns, while the three regular skua species are common.

The variety of passerines recorded here in recent years has been quite remarkable for a site so far west, although its potential was apparent as long ago as 1905 when Ireland's first Dark-eyed Junco was shot here. They include Red-eyed Vireo and Yellow-rumped, Yellow and Canada Warblers from the west, while from the east Pied Wheatear, Rustic and Black-headed Buntings, Rock and Siberian Thrushes and Arctic Warbler have occurred as well as regular Yellow-browed Warbler. Migrant numbers are generally low, but the unexpected frequently turns up. The road from Kilbaha to the west and the area around the lighthouse are the best places.

The area has been seriously watched only in autumn. Spring visits might be very worthwhile.

Winter seawatching, which has only been carried out on a handful of occasions, has shown that large numbers of Little Auks occur in westerly or north-westerly gales.

Timing

Breeding seabirds can be seen in summer, but this is a long way to travel to see species which are much more accessible on the Cliffs of Moher to the north-east. Autumn is the time to visit this site.

Good seawatching can be had from early August to the middle of October and sometimes later. Make sure, however, that the wind is from the north-west or west. Passerines are unlikely in these conditions, so look for them in south-easterlies or calm conditions. Early morning is much the best for passerines, as they move inland rapidly after dawn.

Access

To get to Loop Head from Limerick, drive north-west for Ennis, then south-west for Kilrush and then Kilkee. At Kilkee, follow the signposts for Loop Head. The Bridges of Ross are on the north side about 5 km before the lighthouse. There is a small car park. If the birds are passing close inshore, it would be possible to seawatch from the carpark, but the best views will be obtained by walking out to the rocky promontory.

The lighthouse is at the end of the headland. Kilbaha village is on the southern side of the head, about 5 km back.

45 CLONDERALAW BAY   OSI Discovery map: sheet 64
R11 54

Habitat and Species

This deep inlet faces the south-west so is heavily exposed to the prevailing winds. It holds a winter duck population of 1,000–1,500 birds, of which the Pintail flock is the most noteworthy. There are 2,000–3,000 waders as well. The area has been very little watched.

Access

Roads lead down to several points on each side of the estuary. On the south-east side, the road south-west of Labasheeda which runs to Kilkerin Point, has two right turns off it, both of which lead down to the estuary. The road from Labasheeda to Kilrush runs around the northern side of the bay. To see the north-west side, take the road for Killimer and follow either of the two left turns down to the estuary (1 km apart), about 3 km after you cross the bridge over the Clon river at the head of the bay.

46 POULNASHERRY BAY OSI Discovery map: sheet 63
Q92 58; Q95 55

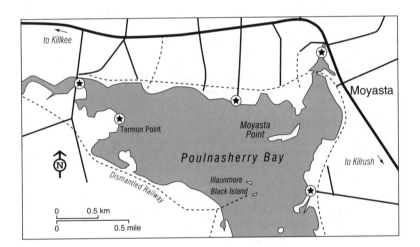

Habitat and Species

This is a relatively isolated bay on the north-west side of the Shannon estuary and it has been very little watched. It is much more sheltered than Clonderalaw and holds a flock of 200 or so Brent Geese, about 1,000 Eurasian Wigeons and smaller numbers of Shelducks, Mallards, Common Teals and Scaups. There are 2,000–3,500 waders in winter.

Access

Several roads run to the shore of this estuary. Driving from Kilrush for Moyasta, take the second left turn (about 3 km from Kilrush). Beyond Moyasta, several left turns lead to different sections of the estuary.

47 MUTTON ISLAND AND LURGA POINT

OSI Discovery map: sheet 57
Q99 74

Habitat and Species

Mutton Island is a 75-ha island lying off the west coast. The island is windswept and rocky with a cover of maritime grass. It has one of the largest wintering flocks of Barnacle Geese in the country, the total sometimes reaching over 400, though more usually there are fewer than 200.

Opposite the island on the mainland, at Seafield, Lurga Point, large counts of Purple Sandpipers have been recorded – some of the largest ever in Ireland. Up to 350 have been counted in February. Turnstones and Sanderlings also winter in the area.

Access

Lurga Point is reached from Quilty, which is south of Spanish Point. Take the road along the coast south-west from Quilty. Mutton Island can be viewed from the mainland by telescope.

48 BALLYVAUGHAN

OSI Discovery map: sheet 51
M27 13

Habitat and Species

Ballyvaughan Bay is on the southern side of Galway Bay. Its shoreline is stony as befits the northern rim of the Burren. Off the beaches there are concentra-

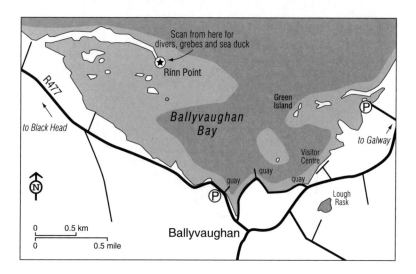

Scan from here for
divers, grebes and sea duck

Rinn Point

R477

Green
Island

to Black Head

Ballyvaughan
Bay

to Galway

Visitor
Centre

quay

N

quay

quay

Lough
Rask

0   0.5 km

0   0.5 mile

Ballyvaughan

tions of divers in winter. Great Northern Divers are particularly numerous but Red-throated also occur. More importantly, this is the best place in Ireland for seeing Black-throated Divers. There are usually a few throughout the winter and up to 100 have been seen. Up to 150 Brent Geese are sometimes found on the shore. Snow Buntings have been seen in winter at Rine Point.

Access
Ballyvaughan is well signposted from Kinvarra to the east or Lisdoonvarna to the south-west. If travelling in the area in spring or summer, extend your trip to see Black Head to the west and do some 'botanising'.

49 LOUGH ATEDAUN   OSI Discovery map: sheet 57
R29 88

Habitat and Species
Lough Atedaun is a small, shallow lake east of Corofin which holds large numbers of wildfowl when it is not being shot over. It is a good site for Mute, Whooper and occasional Bewick's Swans. Large numbers of Eurasian Wigeons and Common Teals also winter here and smaller numbers of Tufted Ducks, Pintails, Shovelers and Pochards can also be seen. Significant numbers of Dunlins and Black-tailed Godwits have been recorded.

Access
From Corofin the lake can be viewed at several points. Drive on the Gort road and turn right at the fork after 1.5 km. This road gives views of the northern

side. The western side can be easily viewed by taking the first right turn off the Gort road for Corofin, following the signpost for Lough Atedaun. The road leads to a slipway at the edge of the lake. The south-western side can be seen from the road south for Ennis. Take the first left turn (after about 1.5 km) to get access to the southern side.

TIPPERARY

Tipperary is a large county bordered on the north-west side by Lough Derg and the River Shannon, on the north by the Little Brosna and on the south by the Galtee Mountains. To the east, stretch fertile agricultural lands.

Because the county has no large centres of population and no coastline it was underwatched until the mid-1980s. Since about 1983 a Tipperary Ringing Group has been very active: this formed the nucleus of a branch of BirdWatch Ireland which has discovered a number of worthwhile bird sites in the county, two of which are described below.

One of the best sites in the county is the Little Brosna, but this site is more easily approached from the Offaly side so it is dealt with under that county.

50 LOUGH DERG   OSI Discovery map: sheet 53, 59

M85 03; R76 83

Habitat and Species

Lough Derg is the largest lake on the River Shannon and most of its eastern shore lies in Co Tipperary. It is not particularly interesting for birds but the islands in the lake have important inland breeding colonies of gulls and terns and such a large water body is sure to attract the unusual from time to time. The best access points in Co Tipperary are at Youghal Bay at the south-east end and Slevoir Bay at the north-east end; both are good for winter concentrations of wildfowl.

Access

To access Youghal Bay, take the R494 west from Nenagh to Portroe and turn right in the village of Portroe, the lakeshore is about 3 km from Portroe. Slevoir Bay can be viewed from the N52 approximately 4 km east of Portumna. Portumna Castle and Estate is located just across the county border in Galway and offers access to the flooded fields of the north-western shore of the lake which often holds large numbers of dabbling ducks.

For spring and summer birding, Goat Island on the eastern shore holds an important inland colony of Common Terns. The island can be viewed from the shore near Coolbaun. Take the R493 north from Nenagh and pass through the village of Coolbaun which is about 15kms north of Nenagh, turn left 2 km past Coolbaun. This brings you to a dead end and requires you to cross a field in order to access the lakeshore.

51 LOUGH EORNA   OSI Discovery map: sheet 59
R87 86

Habitat and Species

There are several small lakes near the town of Borrisokane in the north-west of Tipperary, of which Lough Eorna has perhaps the best track record for scarcer species. There is a large colony of Black-headed Gulls in summer and the lake attracts a good variety of ducks in winter. The lake is situated in the grounds of Ashley Park guesthouse but birders are welcome to visit the lake and there is some nice beech woodland habitat in the grounds of the house.

Access

Lough Eorna is located on the west side of the N52 between Borrisokane and Nenagh, about 9 km south of Borrisokane and 5 km north of Nenagh. Look for the turn in to Ashley Park.

CONNACHT

Galway
52 Galway Bay
53 Lough Corrib
54 Rahasane Turlough
55 River Suck
56 Inishbofin
57 Coole Park Lake
58 Rossaveal

Mayo
59 The Mullet
60 Killala Bay
61 Kilcummin Head
62 Lough Cullin
63 Clare Island
64 Rostaff Lake

Sligo
65 Sligo Bay
65A Lissadell
65B Ballysadare
66 Bunduff Lake

Leitrim

Roscommon
67 River Shannon, Athlone to
    Shannonbridge
68 Cloonlaughnan
69 Lough Croan
70 Lough Funshinagh
71 Lough Ree

CONNACHT

GALWAY

Galway is a large county with an extremely indented coastline to the west and south-west, the rolling Slieve Aughty mountains to the south, the Rivers Shannon and Suck to the east and a mixture of lowland and hilly blanket bog to the north. Lough Corrib separates the western mountains and blanket bogs from the eastern lowlands.

Apart from Galway Bay itself, which is an important site, there is relatively little mudflat or saltmarsh to provide wildfowl or wader feeding on the coast, and there are few mainland cliffs to provide breeding sites for seabirds. Some of the offshore islands have breeding seabird colonies but they have been little studied.

The western blanket bog is difficult to traverse, as there are few roads crossing it, but it holds small populations of Merlins, European Golden Plovers and Red Grouse in summer, scattered flocks of Greenland White-fronted Geese in winter and a large population of Grey Herons which nest on lake islands and feed on the coast. The mountains are little known and would repay visiting at any time of year.

Inland the most obvious physical features of the county are Ireland's second largest lake, Lough Corrib, and to the west the peaks of the Twelve Bens.

The most significant wetlands for birds are Lough Corrib, Rahasane Turlough and the Shannon and Suck system which border the eastern side of the county.

52 GALWAY BAY   OSI Discovery map: sheet 45, 46, 51, 52
M23 23; M30 19

Habitat

Galway Bay is a broad bay, about 10 km wide, bordered on the southern side by the limestone hills of the Burren in Clare, on the northern side by the west Galway hills and at its eastern end by low-lying agricultural land.

There is a boulder shore on the southern side from Black Head (in Clare) to Kinvarra and on the northern side from Barna westwards, neither of which is particularly productive for birds. The best bird sites are all in the inner bay, which is divided into two sections by Tawin Island. The south-eastern part from Kinvarra to Clarinbridge has rather little intertidal sand or mud, but the section from Clarinbridge to Oranmore, and including Tawin Island, has a number of areas of mud and sand, several areas of saltmarsh and some shallow inlets and lagoons.

From Oranmore to Barna are stretches of mud at Oranmore Bay, stretches of sand and mud close to Galway city, a brackish inlet at Laugh Atalia and a sandy bay at Loc Ruisin near Barna.

The birds of the inner bay have been counted regularly by the local BWI branch since 1976 so they are well known.

Species

The outer reaches of the bay hold wintering populations of divers. Great Northern is the most frequent, with many counts of over 20 in the bay, but Red-throated and Black-throated also occur, mainly south and west of Tawin. Great Crested Grebes in contrast tend to winter to the north of Tawin, though numbers are variable with up to 70 having been counted in the bay in the recent past. These are probably birds which breed on the nearby Lough Corrib. At the Claddagh, right in Galway city, over 300 Mute Swans assemble in spring and early summer and up to 600 moult on Lough Corrib in August.

Brent Geese arrive in the bay in late October and build up to reach a peak in the period from January to March. As elsewhere in the country, numbers have been increasing and now reach almost 600 in the bay. The bays on the south side of Tawin hold the largest numbers but, as the population has increased, so they have spread around the northern side of Galway Bay as well. Up to 1,500 Eurasian Wigeons have been counted in the bay in winter, widely dispersed around the shoreline, but numbers of Shelducks, Mallards, Common Teals and Shovelers are much lower.

Some diving ducks winter. A small flock of Scaups usually spends the early winter on Lough Atalia and some also occur on the south side of Tawin. Very small parties of Long-tailed Ducks (up to 14) occur in late winter or early spring in the southern part of the bay. Common Scoter sometimes occurs on open water in the bay but does not winter regularly. Red-breasted Mergansers are widely distributed, with large numbers on Lough Atalia at times.

Galway Bay has the typical wintering waders of much of the Irish coastline. Up to 600 Oystercatchers winter, while Ringed Plovers are numerous, probably reflecting the extent of sand in the bay, and have exceeded 900. European Golden Plovers and Northern Lapwings can be found in winter on many parts of the bay. Grey Plovers are most easily met with near Tawin. Dunlins, Bar-tailed Godwits, Curlews, Redshanks and Turnstones are all quite numerous. Small numbers of Greenshanks winter, and slightly more occur in autumn and spring; Loc Ruisin is usually the best place for them. Knots are scarce and Black-tailed Godwits curiously rare.

The bay is an excellent place for gull watching. Nimmo's Pier provides a vantage point for seeing large gulls which feed on the shore and smaller gulls which may be farther out in the bay. Great Black-backed, Herring and Common Gulls are common; Black-headed Gulls are numerous. Glaucous and Iceland Gulls should be sought for at Nimmo's Pier, although you should not expect a repeat sight of the 80 Glaucous Gulls seen here in February 1981 at the time of an exceptional sprat fishery. Waterside is an alternative place to seek out gulls; the weir and open stretches of water are good for bathing and roosting gulls. Little Gulls should be looked for at Nimmo's Pier, especially between January and March, when quite large influxes can occur (once over 150 birds). Ring-billed and Mediterranean Gulls are both nearly annual and Ross's Gull has been seen here several times.

Timing
The bay is at its best from October to the end of March. Goose and most duck numbers are highest after December. Scarcer gulls are most frequently recorded from January to March, though Glaucous and Iceland can be found in early winter as well. Birdwatching is much easier at low tide at all locations mentioned above.

Access
All the sites referred to are easily accessible by road. On the southern side there are a number of turns to the left off the main road from Kinvarra to Clarinbridge which lead down to the edge of the bay To the west of Kinvarra, driving west towards Black Head, there is a right turn, about 2 km from Kinvarra, which leads to Aughinish causeway and provides a number of viewing points for the outer reaches of the bay.

Tawin Island, in reality a peninsula, is an essential area to visit. Turn left at Clarinbridge off the main Limerick-Galway road. After 4 km take the right-

Black-throated Diver

hand turn at a T-junction and turn left after a further 1.5 km. Follow the road out to Tawin and stop wherever birds are seen. Excellent views can be had of geese here.

Drive back to the main Limerick-Galway road and follow the signposts for Galway. Lough Atalia comes into view on the left-hand side of the main road.

In Galway City follow the coast road beside Lough Atalia and around the docks to the Claddagh. The River Corrib flows south into Galway Bay at this point and Nimmo's Pier is on the western side of the little harbour. You can park here and explore the area on foot. Nimmo's Pier is wheelchair accessible. The entire Galway docks area should be checked for gulls. Finally follow the course of the river upstream about 2 km from Nimmo's Pier to Waterside on the east bank; check the gulls loafing around the weir.

Drive west through Galway, pass Salthill and 5 km later Loc Ruisin can be seen on your left. Take the left turn just after the bay, follow the signposts for Silver Strand and park your car at the beach.

CALENDAR

All year: Mallard, Cormorant, Shag, Great Black-backed and Herring Gulls.

Autumn: early wildfowl and waders, Black-headed and Common Gulls.

Winter: Brent Goose, Shelduck, Eurasian Wigeon, Common Teal, Mallard, Shoveler, Scaup, Long-tailed Duck, Red-breasted Merganser, divers, Great Crested Grebe, Oystercatcher, Ringed, European Golden and Grey Plovers, Northern Lapwing, Dunlin, Common Snipe, Bar-tailed Godwit, Curlew, Redshank, Greenshank, Turnstone, Black-headed, Common, Glaucous and Iceland Gulls, possibly Little and Ring-billed Gulls.

Spring: late wildfowl and waders. Possible influxes of Little Gulls, Glaucous and Iceland Gulls, probably Ring-billed Gull.

53 LOUGH CORRIB

OSI Discovery map: sheet 45
M25 42; M29 30

Habitat

Lough Corrib, with an area of 17,000 ha, is the second largest lake in Ireland. It can be divided conveniently into two sections. The narrow, south-eastern arm is very shallow, with a maximum depth of about 6 m, and lies on limestone. The much larger and broader northern part is considerably deeper and lies mainly on granite, schist, shales and sandstones. A depth of up to 45 m has been recorded in this part.

Much of the lake is surrounded by bare limestone or a thin covering of bog over the limestone. At the southern end is an extensive area of fen. The lake is one of Ireland's finest brown trout fisheries.

The shallower southern end, Lower Lough Corrib, is far and away the best for winter wildfowl.

Species

This is an excellent wildfowl lake in winter with large flocks of Pochards and Coots the highlight, although numbers have declined since the mid 1970s when over 20,000 Pochards and 16,000 Coots were counted. Nowadays, the peak counts are in the region of 10,000 Pochard and 10,000 Coots. Smaller numbers of Tufted Ducks occur among the Pochards, together with some Common Goldeneyes, and, on the shoreline, there are small parties of Eurasian Wigeons, Common Teals, Mallards and Shovelers.

Pochards probably breed in small numbers, but the large flocks result from immigration commencing in late July and building to a peak in October or November, before declining again. Presumably these are birds moulting on Lough Corrib.

Coot numbers appear to be very volatile. Large numbers have been seen in September, October and December, but in some years there are very few in mid-winter. There is a substantial breeding population.

In summer Great Crested and Little Grebes nest and as one would expect there is a good scattering of breeding Mute Swans and Mallards. Gadwall and Shoveler probably nest at the Mount Ross inlet and Tufted Ducks and Red-breasted

Mergansers breed on many of the islands. In recent years a small breeding population of Common Scoters has become established as well.

The islands on the lake hold sizeable colonies of breeding Black-headed and Common Gulls. There are about 400 pairs of Black-headed and nearly 200 pairs of Common. A few pairs of Lesser Black-backed Gulls also nest, but Herring Gulls, which once bred in numbers up to 300 pairs, no longer breed here. The decrease, which mirrors similar declines all over Ireland, has been attributed to death of adult birds from botulism. A few Great Black-backed Gulls also nest. Terns can be found on the small islands as well: Common and Arctic Terns both breed in small numbers. The colonies are scattered on islands around the lake.

There were records in February and March 1990 of several thousand Common and Black-headed Gulls in the upper lough, presumably on passage to breeding grounds in Scotland. This was not repeated in subsequent years so appears not be a regular phenomenon.

Timing
Winter wildfowl are best seen from August to February. As the lake is large, and flocks of diving ducks can be well offshore, a calm and bright day is recommended. Gulls and terns, as well as nesting ducks, should be watched for from April to July.

Access
This is an enormous lake and, unfortunately, the road does not always run around the water's edge providing vantage points for viewing. At the southern end, the best place for getting good views is Angliham Marble Quarries where diving ducks, often including Common Goldeneye, can be seen and, in the narrows, the Mount Ross inlet holds wintering Gadwalls and breeding Shovelers and Gadwalls.

Angliham is reached by taking the road for Headford out of Galway. After about 5 km, at the village of Ballindooly, take the left turn and follow it down to the lake shore.

Mount Ross is reached by taking the same road from Galway, but driving almost as far as Headford. Turn left at Clooneen about 3 km before Headford and follow the road to the lake shore.

CALENDAR

All year: Mallard, Tufted Duck, occasionally Red-breasted Merganser, Cormorant, Little Grebe, Coot, Black-headed Gull, Herring Gull, Great Black-backed Gull.

Autumn: Gadwall, a few Shovelers at the southern margin, Pochard, Great Crested Grebe, large numbers of Coots, other wildfowl.

Winter: Eurasian Wigeon, Common Teal, Shoveler, Pochard, Great Crested Grebe, Northern Lapwing, Common Snipe, Curlew.

Spring: Whimbrel, early terns, return of breeding gulls, passage of migrant gulls.

Summer: breeding wildfowl, gulls and terns. Breeding Common Scoter, Ringed Plover, Redshank and Curlew, migrant Whimbrel.

Pochard

54 RAHASANE TURLOUGH

OSI Discovery map: sheet 52
M45 18

Habitat
Rahasane is one of the few remaining turloughs in Ireland and is certainly the best for wildfowl of those which survive. There are a number of different kinds of turlough, and some have argued that Rahasane is not really one (turloughs are lakes which fill with water at times and then drain off through underground channels). Two aquatic mosses are found at most turloughs: *Cinclidotus fontinaloides*, a blackish moss, and *Fontinalis antipyretica*, a dark green one. Both can be seen at Rahasane.

The doubt about Rahasane's authenticity as a turlough arises because of arguments whether the water fills the lake through swallow-holes or rises purely due to the flooding of the Dunkellin River.

Whatever the case, this is an area of rich, green, alluvial pasture in summer with a narrow river running through it. When the winter rain comes, the water level rises and a shallow lake about 3 km long and 1 km wide appears within hours. The blackthorn around the lake is the habitat of one of Ireland's scarcest butterflies, the Brown Hairstreak.

In late autumn 1992, drainage works lowered the water level significantly. However since then water levels have continued to fluctuate and can be quite high at times.

Species
This is a wonderful wildfowl haunt in winter and, at times, a good place for wader watching. Up to 4,000 Eurasian Wigeons occur in winter, together with smaller numbers of Mallards, Common Teals, Pintails, Shovelers, Tufted Ducks and Pochards. Whooper Swans can be seen throughout the winter and a flock of about 100 Greenland White-fronted Geese is frequently present. Pintail is now a scarce duck in Galway and numbers at Rahasane are generally low.

Flocks of up to several thousand Northern Lapwings and European Golden Plovers and small numbers of Curlews, Black-tailed Godwits, Redshanks and Dunlins are regular. Larger flocks of godwits occur in spring on passage north to Iceland.

In winter the fields and hedgerows hold large numbers of Redwings and Fieldfares.

Water levels fluctuate and there can be a lot of disturbance at times, so bird numbers are unpredictable. Galway Bay is not far and birds move in and out of Rahasane frequently.

Timing
The best time to visit Rahasane is when the turlough is flooded to a level where there are grassy islets still visible. When the water level is very high some ducks have difficulty grazing and leave the area.

It could repay autumn visits as the habitat looks ideal for migrant waders; Ruffs are regularly recorded in small numbers while a number of American waders have occurred.

Access
Rahasane is approached by turning right off the main Limerick–Galway road at Kilcolgan, where the signpost indicates Craughwell. Follow the narrow road for about 5 km until you see the turlough to the south on your right-hand side.

Park the car and scan the water from the roadside or, if the water level permits, walk across the pasture to the edge of the water and watch from there.

CALENDAR

All year: Mallard, Grey Heron, Meadow Pipit, Skylark, Reed Bunting.

Autumn: Common Teal, Shoveler, Eurasian Wigeon, Pintail, Pochard, Tufted Duck, European Golden Plover, Northern Lapwing, Dunlin, Ruff, Curlew, Black-tailed Godwit, Redshank.

Winter: Whooper Swan, Greenland White-fronted Goose, Common Teal, Shoveler, Eurasian Wigeon, Pintail, Pochard, Tufted Duck, European Golden Plover, Northern Lapwing, Dunlin, Black-tailed Godwit, Curlew, Redshank.

Spring: late wildfowl and waders.

---

55 RIVER SUCK

OSI Discovery map: sheet 47
M80 50; M82 42

Habitat

The River Suck rises north of Lough O'Flynn in Roscommon and meanders in a generally south-south-east direction to join the Shannon at Shannonbridge. From close to Athleague it forms the border between the counties of Galway and Roscommon until it reaches the Shannon.

It is a narrow, slow-flowing river surrounded by extensive bogs and poorly drained agricultural land. The flood plain is low-lying and floods frequently in late autumn and winter. The flooded callows, or water meadows, which occur at Muckanagh to the south of Ballygar, between Ballyforan and Ballinasloe, and between Ballinasloe and the Shannon, provide feeding for large numbers of wildfowl.

In patches there are areas fringed with reeds and behind them rushy pastures where Northern Lapwings and European Golden Plovers feed.

Species

The species found are those typical of the Shannon system. Whooper Swans are widespread; there is a flock of several hundred Greenland White-fronted Geese at Muckanagh; thousands of Eurasian Wigeon and Common Teals can be seen and smaller numbers of Mallards and Shovelers. Some Tufted Ducks and Pochards and good numbers of Coots occur.

The callows and the rough pasture are frequented by thousands of Northern Lapwings and European Golden Plovers and smaller numbers of Curlews and Common Snipe. Some Redshanks occur and Black-tailed Godwits can sometimes be found.

Timing

This is very much a winter wetland. Visits are best when the river has flooded.

Access

Because this is a meandering river with no road running along its bank, access is often difficult. However, there are two particularly good spots.

Muckanagh, to the south of Ballygar, is a marvellously wild place for watching geese and swans in winter. Drive from Mount Talbot to Ballygar and turn left in the village on the Ballyforan road. After just over a kilometre turn left down a narrow road and follow the lane for 2 km to a fork; take the right turn and follow the road to the callows where you should have excellent views of wildfowl.

Derrycahill, to the south of Ballyforan, gives access to the next stretch of the river to the south. Take the road from Ballyforan for Athlone and, after about 1 km turn right and follow the road for about 5 km to a right turning. Take this turn to Derrycahill and access to the river.

Access to the stretch between Ballinasloe and Shannon bridge is difficult but several narrow roads lead close to the river and may produce views of wildfowl.

CALENDAR

All year: Mallard, Grey Heron, Meadow Pipit, Skylark, Reed Bunting.

Autumn: Eurasian Wigeon, Common Teal, Pintail, Pochard, Tufted Duck, European Golden Plover, Northern Lapwing, Curlew, Redshank.

Winter: Whooper Swan, Greenland White-fronted Goose, Common Teal, Shoveler, Eurasian Wigeon, Pintail, Pochard, Tufted Duck, European Golden Plover, Northern Lapwing, Dunlin, Black-tailed Godwit, Curlew, Redshank.

Spring: late wildfowl and waders.

56 INISHBOFIN

OSI Discovery map: sheet 37
L49 65; L55 66

Habitat and Species

Inishbofin is the larger of two neighbouring islands off the Connemara coast and is inhabited by about 250 people; the smaller of the two, Inishshark has long been deserted. The southern part of Inishbofin is cultivated and the remainder is rough moorland and bog. There are some hedges and shrubs, and several gardens near the harbour, which provide cover for passerines. Inishshark is much bleaker and has no cover at all.

Inishbofin is notable for its surviving population of Corncrakes – which are now very scarce in Ireland. While they have declined on Inishbofin, they can be easily found in the cultivated quarter. Corncrakes were once so numerous that they were quite impossible to count at night. Nowadays there are a few pairs left, mostly at the east end of the island. Inishbofin was also one of the last remaining haunts of the Corn Bunting, which became extinct in Ireland in the 1990s.

Inishshark has good numbers of nesting Fulmars and small numbers of other breeding seabirds. Peregrines nest on the island.

Access

The ferry for Inishbofin leaves from Cleggan near Clifden. Kings Ferries (tel: 095 44649) or MV Dun Aengus (tel: 095 45903) operate several sailings per day between April and September but this reduces to just a few per week in the winter months. There are two small hotels on the island and some self-catering accommodation. Inishshark can only be reached by making special arrangements with local boatmen.

57 COOLE PARK LAKE

OSI Discovery map: sheet 52
M44 05

Habitat and Species

There are a number of small lakes and turloughs set in wooded parkland in this area of South Galway and while not a rarity hotspot, by any means, the area does support a good variety of birdlife. Coole Park, which is associated with W.B.Yeats, is maintained by the National Parks and Wildlife Service which makes access very easy as there is a network of trails and other facilities available.

The lakes are important wintering areas for Whooper Swan and other wild-fowl, while the deciduous woodland is quite extensive and provides a habitat which is quite scarce in the West of Ireland.

Access

The entrance to Coole Park is located about 2 km north of Gort on the N18. Some of the woodland paths are wheelchair accessible.

58 ROSSAVEAL

OSI Discovery map: sheet 47
L96 25

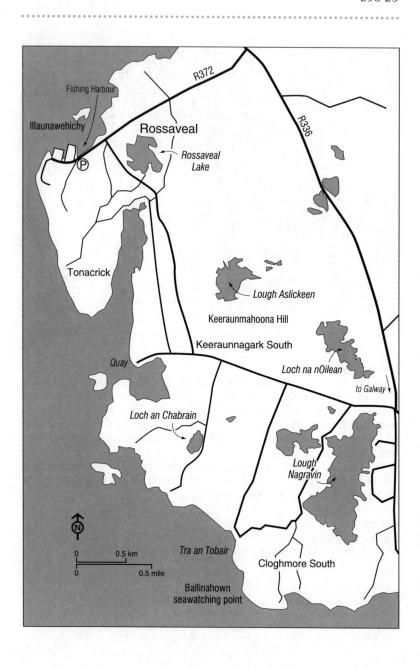

R372

Fishing Harbour

R336

Illaunawehichy

Rossaveal

Ⓟ

*Rossaveal
Lake*

Tonacrick

Lough Aslickeen

Keeraunmahoona Hill

Keeraunnagark South

Quay

Loch na nOilean

to Galway

Loch an Chabrain

*Lough
Nagravin*

N

0   0.5 km

0   0.5 mile

Tra an Tobair

Cloghmore South

Ballinahown
seawatching point

Habitat and Species

For those with an interest in gulls, Rossaveal is a fishing port and depending on the comings and goings of the trawlers can be very good for the numbers and varieties of large gulls. The harbour is located within a sheltered inlet and in stormy conditions should also be checked for divers, gulls and Little Auk. During the summer, it is also a departure point for the ferry to the Aran Islands, itself an opportunity for some pelagic birding.

Seawatching can also be conducted from Ballinahown (Baile na hAbhann) which is about 4 km south of Rossaveal on the north shore of Galway Bay. The north shore of Galway Bay is rarely as good as the south shore for divers and grebes, but in autumn, in westerly or south-westerly winds, this can be a good seawatch point for petrels and skuas.

Access

Rossaveal is located about 40 km west of Galway and is signposted off the R336. To reach Ballinahown, go south from Rossaveal on the coast road and, after about 2 km, the road veers east at a sharp bend. Continue for one more kilometre and turn right (this is the third right after the bend), following this road down to the seashore.

MAYO

Mayo is another large county, but the landscape is very different from that of Galway, with much more extensive areas of blanket bog and, particularly in the north-east, large tracts where there are no roads. The human population density is low, and birdwatchers are very few. The visitor, therefore, has a good chance of finding something new, especially on the coast or one of the lakes.

The western coastline has a variety of habitats. From Killary Harbour north to Roonagh Quay the shoreline is low-lying, despite Mweelrea Mountain dominating the skyline. The shore is sandy, with Sanderling and Ringed Plover the principal wader species, but there are a number of small lakes behind the sand dunes which attract a number of other species and look as though they should attract migrant waders. Clew Bay has numerous islands and is difficult to watch because of the relative inaccessibility of so much of the habitat.

The Mullet peninsula forms the north-western corner of the county and has a number of good bird sites. Off the Mullet are the Inishkea Islands, long deserted by humans, but now providing a refuge for wintering Barnacle Geese and breeding terns and waders. Several smaller islands have large seabird colonies: Inishglora, in particular, has a large European Storm-petrel colony and Illaunmaistir off the north Mayo coast has substantial numbers of Puffins.

The north coast has steep cliffs with breeding Fulmars, Kittiwakes and auks as well as good numbers of Choughs and Peregrines. However, access is chiefly on foot as there are few roads.

Killala Bay, the estuary of the river Moy, forms the eastern boundary of the county on the northern coast and has a history as a good bird site. Richard Warren, one of the authors of *Birds of Ireland*, published in 1900, spent much of his life here and made many interesting observations of seabirds, wildfowl and waders.

There are several large lakes in the centre of the county. Lough Mask is famous for fishing but is generally too deep for birds. Lough Carra, to its north, is shallower and well worth a visit. Farther north, Loughs Conn and Cullin have not been very well watched, but appear to have potential, especially Lough Cullin.

59 THE MULLET

OSI Discovery map: sheet 22
F62 34; F65 27

Habitat

The Mullet is a long peninsula, really almost an island as the inlets of Broadhaven to the north and Blacksod Bay to the south virtually meet at the town of Belmullet. The western side of the peninsula mainly comprises sandy beaches with dune systems behind them and areas of wet machair. To the west are the long and low Inishkea Islands and several smaller islands including Inishglora, famous for the European Storm-petrels which nest in its boulder beach. The entire area is wild and windswept.

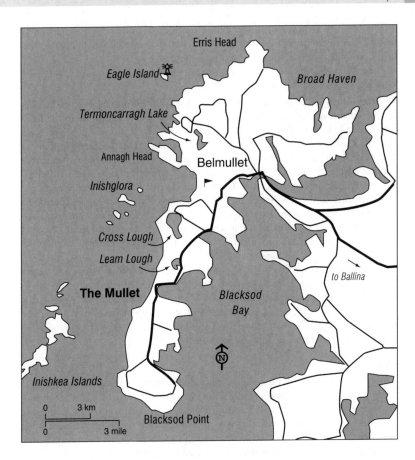

There are several headlands on The Mullet, and both Erris Head to the north and Annagh Head to the west are good seawatching promontories. These promontories have very little cover but look attractive for buntings and pipits, and support small numbers of breeding Twites. Along the main road, which runs along the Mullet, are some small gardens which can hold migrant passerines.

Three lakes on The Mullet are well worth visiting: Termoncarragh Lake to the north, Cross Lough in the centre and Leam Lough towards the south all have the potential to attract interesting wildfowl and waders. The eastern end of Termoncarragh Lake is owned by BirdWatch Ireland.

Termoncarragh is a relatively shallow lake surrounded by stands of clubrush. A number of streams flow into the lake and, where they enter the lake, there are marshy areas. There is damp grassland surrounding the lake, classic damp machair, providing habitat for nesting waders.

Annagh Marsh, to the west of Termoncarragh Lake, is a marshy area which provides excellent breeding wader habitat. This marsh was purchased in the 1950s by the Irish Society for the Protection of Birds as a sanctuary for the now extinct colony of Red-necked Phalaropes there. When the ISPB merged with other organisations in 1968 to form the Irish Wildbird Conservancy, ownership passed into the hands of the new body (now BirdWatch Ireland).

The town of Belmullet has a small winter flock of gulls, which is principally famous because it was here that Ireland's first Ring-billed Gulls were seen. Glaucous and Iceland Gulls are regular.

Species

Termoncarragh has a flock of up to 40 Greenland White-fronted Geese in October and wintering Whooper Swans and ducks. Barnacle Geese commute to the fields around the Lake from the Inishkea Islands offshore. The principal duck species are Mallard, Common Teal, Eurasian Wigeon and Tufted Duck. Large numbers of Northern Lapwings, European Golden Plovers and Curlews pass through in autumn and many also winter. Ruffs occur on passage and rarities such as Green-winged Teal, American Wigeon and American Golden Plover are quite regular.

This is one of the few remaining places where Corncrakes can be found; the margins of Termoncarragh are a good place to search for them. Water Rail also nests here as well as Northern Lapwing, Common Snipe and Dunlin. Scarcer waders can also occur, and Wilson's Phalarope and Buff-breasted Sandpiper have both been seen in the area.

Seabird passage has been shown to be excellent at times. Great and Sooty Shearwaters and Great, Pomarine and Arctic Skuas are all regular and the site is so far west that Long-tailed Skuas, which are known to migrate well off the west coast of Ireland, could be expected in strong westerlies. They have been seen in spring in the past from the Inishkeas so some should be seen from Annagh or Erris Head in May or in autumn.

Timing

The Mullet is a place which can be visited at almost any time. In summer the nesting waders, Corncrakes and Twites are the main attractions. Common Rosefinch has been recorded singing in the area in recent years. In spring and autumn, there is the possibility of good seawatching. The presence of a BirdWatch Ireland warden at Termoncarragh in recent years has resulted in a significant number of rare and scarce migrants being recorded.

The area is so far west that it gets American waders and passerines most years. Red-eyed Vireo has been seen and some waders but, rather surprisingly, quite a number of Continental European rarities are seen. Collared Pratincole, Short-toed Lark and Booted Warbler have all been seen in recent years. In winter there can be a good variety of wildfowl and again the chance of some exotic vagrant. In recent years, it has become a regular site for Snowy Owl, recalling its pre-eminence for this species in the 19th century.

Access

The Mullet is a long drive from Dublin, Belfast or Cork. It is hardly a place for a day trip, but an excellent place for a full weekend or a few days.

Termoncarragh Lake can be viewed from the public road which runs north-west from Belmullet to Scotch Port.

Cross Lough and Leam Lough are both accessible from the road south along the peninsula.

Annagh marsh is at the southern end of Termoncarragh and can be visited by turning left off the road for Scotch Port, about 3 km beyond Belmullet and following the narrow road down to the inlet. The marsh is a bird reserve, with a local warden, and visitors should not walk in places where waders may be breeding.

Northern Lapwing chick

CALENDAR

Autumn: divers, Fulmar, Manx Shearwater, Sooty Shearwater, Gannet, Oystercatcher, Ringed Plover, European Golden Plover, Northern Lapwing, Dunlin, Sanderling, Ruff, Curlew, Redshank, Greenshank, skuas. Migrant passerines, particularly Greenland Redpoll, Snow and Lapland Buntings. Possibility of vagrant waders and passerines.

Winter: Greenland White-fronted Goose, Eurasian Wigeon, Common Teal, Mallard, Tufted and Long-tailed Ducks, Red-breasted Merganser, divers, Oystercatcher, Ringed and European Golden Plovers, Northern Lapwing, Dunlin, Bar-tailed Godwit, Curlew, Redshank, Greenshank, Turnstone, Glaucous and Iceland Gulls, possible Ring-billed Gull.

Spring: late wildfowl and waders. Sea passage, including Pomarine Skua and possibility of Long-tailed Skua.

Summer: breeding seabirds, Northern Lapwing, Common Snipe, Dunlin, Corncrake, Water Rail, Twite.

60 KILLALA BAY

OSI Discovery map: sheet 24
G20 30; G26 29

Habitat

Killala Bay comprises the estuary of the Moy river, from Ballina northwards to the sand dunes of Bartragh Island, and the outer bay which is reasonably sheltered from westerly winds. The inner estuary is muddy but the strata are sandier close to Bartragh Island.

Any visitor seeking a historical account of this estuary should dip into Ussher and Warren's great *Birds in Ireland*, published in 1900. Richard Warren, one of the authors, lived in this area for much of his life and the book contains many observations of birds around Bartragh Island and in the bay generally.

Species

In winter, there is a flock of about 200 Brent Geese, several hundred Common Teals and smaller numbers of Eurasian Wigeons and Mallards in the estuary. This section of the bay is one of the better places to see waders on the west coast and Curlews, Oystercatchers, European Golden Plovers, Northern Lapwings, Redshanks, Dunlins and a few Knots and Grey Plovers can all be seen. In autumn Black-tailed Godwits, Spotted Redshanks, Curlew Sandpipers and Little Stints have been seen but not every year.

The outer bay holds Great Northern and Red-throated Divers, Red-breasted Mergansers and a handful of Long-tailed Ducks in winter.

In autumn seawatching can be excellent if north-westerlies funnel birds into the bay. Large numbers of skuas of each of the three commonest species have been seen in these conditions.

The sand dunes have Snow Buntings in late autumn and winter.

Timing
The estuary is at its best between August and May.

Access
The inner bay is difficult to cover adequately, but it can be reached by walking west along the sand dunes from Inishcrone.

The western side of the bay, and in particular the outer bay, is easier to see. Drive from Ballina towards Killala and, just before the town, park your car and walk east along the edge of the bay.

Killala Pier and the car park at Ross beach, just before Ross Point, are both excellent vantage points.

CALENDAR

All year: Shelduck, Mallard, Oystercatcher, Curlew, gulls.

Autumn: wildfowl, seabirds including Gannet, Fulmar, Manx Shearwater, Arctic Skua, Pomarine Skua, Great Skua and terns. Migrant waders including Curlew Sandpiper and Little Stint in most years.

Winter: Brent Goose, Eurasian Wigeon, Common Teal, Red-breasted Merganser, Long-tailed Duck, Red-throated and Great Northern Divers, wintering waders including European Golden and Grey Plovers, Northern Lapwing, Knot, Dunlin, Redshank, Greenshank.

Spring: late wildfowl and waders.

Summer: a few terns.

---

61 KILCUMMIN HEAD OSI Discovery map: sheet 24
G20 38

Habitat
In recent years, Kilcummin Head has emerged as one of the top seawatching sites in Ireland, and unlike the exposed wind-blown sites in the south-west, you can seawatch here from your car, simply pull up and roll down the window! Kilcummin Head is at its best in north-westerly winds as this forces the birds into Killala Bay and to regain the open sea they must fly past the Head.

Species
The variety of birds tends to reflect the passage of north Atlantic species migrating to their winter grounds (skuas, Leach's Storm-petrels, Sabine's Gulls and Grey Phalaropes) rather than southern ocean migrants (large shearwaters and Wilson's Storm-petrels) which can be more typical of the south-western headlands but nevertheless, anything can turn up here and it has established a very impressive list of rarities in the comparatively short period of time for which it has been watched.

Access

Take the R314 from Killala to Belmullet and after 4 km take a right turn and continue for another 4 km to a crossroads. Take the right-hand turn at the crossroads to Ballinlena Pier and continue past this Pier and take the first right which brings to a car park at the end of this narrow road. You can seawatch from the car park or else walk out to the cliff edge (taking due care).

CALENDAR

Autumn: seawatching, Sooty Shearwater, European Storm-petrel, skuas; good chance of Sabine's Gull, Leach's Storm-petrel, Grey Phalarope.

Winter: Little Auks on seawatches in suitable conditions.

Spring: possibly good seawatching and passerine migration.

---

62 LOUGH CULLIN   OSI Discovery map: sheet 31
G21 05

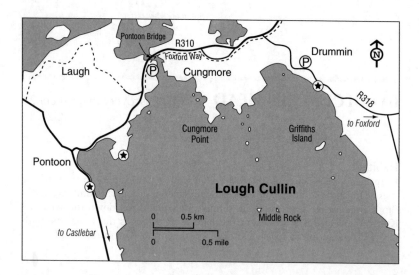

Habitat and Species

Lough Cullin is a moderate-sized lake, about 1,100 ha in extent, which lies to the south of the much larger Lough Conn. The village of Pontoon divides the two lakes. Conn is much deeper than Cullin, so its wildfowl populations are much smaller. Most of Lough Cullin is no more than 4 m deep, though there are substantial fluctuations in water level between summer and winter, and the shallow waters provide feeding for large numbers of diving ducks.

A small and declining population of Common Scoters breed on Loughs Conn and Cullin, but the best time for birdwatching is from July onwards. A moulting flock of up to 600 Tufted Ducks, which is present from July, is joined by up to 400 Pochards and 150 Coots in October. Rarer species are sometimes among them; Scaup, Goosander, Smew and Ring-necked and Ferruginous Ducks have all been recorded.

The lake was well watched in the late 1980s, and the value of regular observations was shown by the list of rare ducks and, in addition, the recording of Mediterranean and Bonaparte's Gulls among the Black-headed Gulls.

Access
Cullin is best viewed from the peninsula which projects south into the lake about 1 km west of Pontoon Bridge and from the bridge itself. There are also several places where a car can be parked on the north-east shore on the road from Pontoon to Foxford.

63 CLARE ISLAND

OSI Discovery map: sheet 30
L71 85

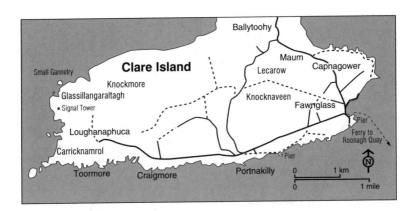

Habitat and Species
Clare Island lies off the west Mayo coast, just outside the mouth of Clew Bay. It is a particularly hilly island with a summit of approximately 400 m. The island is famous in the scientific literature because of the study of its natural history carried out in 1909–1911 under the auspices of the Royal Irish Academy. In 1990 research into the island's natural history recommenced and an updated Clare Island Survey was produced. As the island has a hotel and guest houses, birdwatching can be carried out in some comfort.

The island has spectacular cliffs on the north side which hold breeding Fulmars, Kittiwakes, Razorbills and Common Guillemots. A small number of Puffins and Black Guillemots also nest, and Lesser Black-backed, Herring,

Great Black-backed and Common Gulls all breed in scattered little colonies. In 1978, Gannets were first found breeding on the island, the single pair choosing a low stack north-east of the old tower. Breeding continues, albeit in small numbers.

Choughs are numerous, up to 25 pairs nesting, and Peregrines and Sparrowhawks are present in summer, perhaps breeding. Skylarks, Swallows, Wrens, Blackbirds, Northern Wheatears, Meadow and Rock Pipits and Linnets are among the commoner landbirds.

Access

The ferry for Clare Island leaves from Roonagh Quay. From Westport, drive west to Louisburgh. In Louisburgh, follow the signposts for Roonagh Quay.

There are numerous ferry sailings per day furing the summer, but this reduces to just two ferries per day in winter. Contact O'Grady's Ferries (tel: 086 8515003) or O'Malley's Ferries (tel: 098 25045).

64 ROSTAFF LAKE

OSI Discovery map: sheet 45
M24 48

Habitat and Species

Rostaff is a shallow lake close to Lough Corrib overlooked by a hide built by the local branch of BirdWatch Ireland in conjunction with the Black River Gun Club and the National Parks and Wildlife Service.

A flock of between 100 and 200 Greenland White-fronted Geese, small parties of Whooper Swans, occasional Bewick's Swans, several hundred Eurasian Wigeons, up to 150 Common Teals and up to 70 Shovelers are regularly present in winter. Peregrines are frequent visitors.

Access

The lake is close to the road from Headford to Ballinrobe. It is on the left-hand side of the road, about 3 km from Headford. The hide is reached by going north from Headford on the R334 and turning left after about 3km. Continue for about 500 m and take the first left. The hide is located about 1 km along this road on the left-hand side. This area holds most birds in autumn and winter when the lake floods.

SLIGO

Sligo has a varied coastline backed by impressive mountains. From Killala Bay in the west, the coast is rocky to Ballysadare Bay, but then the inner reaches of the shallow, sandy and muddy Sligo Bay are met. There are three separate bays here – Ballysadare Bay, Cummeen Strand and Drumcliff Bay – before the coast swings around north-eastwards from Raghly to Mullaghmore.

Inland, the Ox Mountains dominate the south-west of the county and the Curlew Mountains the south-east. There are several fine lakes, including Lough Gill, which was made famous by the poet William Butler Yeats. The scenery is very different from any other part of Ireland, and the spectacular Ben Bulbin dominates the view from Sligo town northwards.

65 SLIGO BAY

OSI Discovery map: sheet 16, 25
G63 39; G68 37

Habitat

The large, shallow bay between Sligo town and the sea is shaped rather like a bottle with Coney Island, at the mouth, forming a loosely fitting cork. The sea has a narrow exit to both north and south of Coney Island and most of the bay drains dry at low tide, giving access to Coney Island by a narrow road. The sand flats are most extensive at the southern side of the bay, known as Cummeen Strand.

Species

Cummeen Strand is a place of arrival in autumn for large numbers of Brent Geese and Eurasian Wigeons. In October and November there are brief periods when over 400 Brent Geese and about the same number of Eurasian Wigeons occur; numbers decline later. Shelducks and Mallards also winter.

Some hundreds of waders spend the autumn and winter. Oystercatchers, Ringed Plovers, Northern Lapwing, Dunlin and Curlew all occur, and the location of the bay, at the western side of the country, is such that occasional American vagrants should occur; the Brent Goose flock has included at least one Black Brant in recent years.

Over 2,000 gulls frequent the harbour and inner estuary. Glaucous and Iceland Gulls are seen every winter and rarer species have also been recorded.

Timing

Late autumn is much the best for this site, as wildfowl peak at this time. Since the tide runs out for 3 km, the best time for a visit is within two hours of high tide.

Access

The upper part of the strand can be watched from the Rosses Point road north-west of the town and along the edge of the inner bay. The strand itself is best watched from the end of the narrow road which turns right off the Sligo-Strandhill road and crosses the strand to Coney Island. Take the road west for Strand Hill out of Sligo and turn right after 4 km. The narrow road reaches Cummeen Strand after about a kilometre.

CALENDAR

Autumn–winter–spring: Brent Goose, Shelduck, Eurasian Wigeon, Common Teal, Mallard, Red-breasted Merganser, Oystercatcher, Ringed Plover, Northern Lapwing, Dunlin, Curlew, Redshank, Greenshank, gulls including Glaucous and Iceland, and possibility of Ring-billed and Mediterranean.

65A LISSADELL

OSI Discovery map: sheet 16
G64 43

Habitat

A large field between Lissadell and the north shore of Drumcliff Bay is the finest site on the Irish mainland for Barnacle Geese. The site is managed by the

National Parks and Wildlife Service for the geese and the field has been fertilised specifically to improve the grass for them. A hide provides excellent viewing.

Species

This site is one where Barnacle Geese are the highlight. Some ducks and waders do winter on the mudflats of Drumclilf Bay, but the numbers are lower than at Cummeen Strand or Ballysadare. Lissadell has over 1,000 Barnacle Geese at times nowadays, having increased from only 300 or so in the mid-1970s. This increase has been due to good management, as it far exceeds the rate of increase in the wintering population generally, but the birds move about the general area on the north side of Drumclilf Bay and spend much of their time at Ballintemple.

Timing

The geese are present from October to April.

Access

Take the road from Sligo to Drumcliff. Just beyond Drumcliff, turn left for Lissadell and drive for about 5 km, forking left at Carney village. The geese can be seen easily from the road to Lissadell. To see them from the hide which overlooks the field traditionally used by the birds, enter the driveway to Lissadell House and walk back in an easterly direction through the trees along the shoreline, taking care not to disturb the geese.

Ballintemple is farther out along the road towards Raghly and should also be explored.

CALENDAR

Autumn–winter–spring: Barnacle Goose.

65B BALLYSADARE

OSI Discovery map: sheet 25
G65 29

Habitat and Species

Ballysadare is the most southerly of the three inlets of Sligo Bay. It is the estuary of the Ballysadare river and is a long inlet. The upper reaches of the estuary are muddy and hold wintering Shelducks, Mallards, Common Teals, Eurasian Wigeons, Red-breasted Mergansers and Common Goldeneyes. Oystercatchers, Curlews, Bar-tailed Godwits, Redshanks, Greenshanks and Dunlins are also found here. Some Brent Geese also winter: they can be found in most parts of the bay, but tend to prefer the Streamstown inlet.

In autumn, the sandbank at the mouth of the bay attracts feeding terns. It should be a good place for interesting gulls.

Access

The head of the bay is best viewed from the shoreline by Ballysadare Quarry. The inlet by Streamstown, to the west of Ballysadare and accessible by taking the first right turn about 1.5 km outside Ballysadare on the Ballina road, is good for seeing Brent Geese. The mouth of the estuary can be reached most easily by taking the road from Ballysadare to Strandhill and stopping on the road as it passes alongside the bay.

66 BUNDUFF LAKE   OSI Discovery map: sheet 16
G71 55

Habitat and Species

North of Sligo, close to Mullaghmore, lies Bunduff Lake, a small lake surrounded by marshy fields, which holds up to 180 Whooper Swans in October and about 50 in winter. Small numbers of Common Teals, Mallards, Tufted Ducks and Pochards also winter here, together with occasional Scaups.

Located as it is, so close to a coastal headland, it looks an ideal site for a vagrant.

Access

Take the road from Sligo to Bundoran and take the left turn for Mullaghmore, just after passing through the village of Cliffony. Bunduff Lake is on the right-hand side of the road, about a kilometre after the junction. Bunduff Lake can be well viewed from the road which leads to the right immediately after passing the south-west end of the lake.

LEITRIM

Leitrim is undoubtedly the least birdwatched county in Ireland. It suffers from having only a very short coastline, but has numerous small lakes. There are no sites known to be of particular importance for birdwatching but Fermanagh, which adjoins this county, has been better watched and found to have a very rich mix of breeding birds.

Lough Allen, the large lake in the centre of the county, is deep and holds relatively few birds. Loughs Boderg and Bofin on the Shannon, at the south-eastern end of the county, hold Whooper Swans and good numbers of ducks. These lakes are difficult to access, other than from a boat on the river.

In summer, Great Crested Grebes nest on many of the Leitrim lakes and Garden Warblers nest on the shorelines of some.

Overall, this is a county about which little is known of its birds but which might well repay more intensive study.

ROSCOMMON
● ●

Introduction

Roscommon is a large county bordered to the east by the River Shannon, to the south-west by the Suck, a tributary of the Shannon, to the north-west by the Curlew Mountains and stretching out in the west to the landscape of small fields mixed with areas of bogland which dominates east Galway and Mayo.

The Suck and the Shannon are surrounded by bogs and, to the west of these rivers, there are a number of shallow lakes and turloughs which hold quite large numbers of passage and wintering wildfowl and waders.

The Suck, which divides Roscommon from Galway, is dealt with under that county.

67 RIVER SHANNON, ATHLONE TO SHANNONBRIDGE

OSI Discovery map: sheet 47
N04 40; M96 25

● ●

Habitat

The River Shannon between Athlone and Shannonbridge is surrounded by extensive bogs and poorly drained agricultural land. In winter it floods and the surrounding callows hold large numbers of birds. The river is difficult to access because the only road crossings between Lough Ree and Lough Derg are at Athlone, Shannonbridge and Banagher where eskers, which formed under the glacial ice sheet, provide firm ground on both banks. The roads run along the eskers at right angles to the river, rather than following the line of the Shannon.

The pasture land on either side of the river provides excellent feeding for wildfowl when the river floods.

Species

The principal species to be seen in winter are those typical of the Shannon system generally: parties of Whooper Swans, Greenland White-fronted Geese, huge flocks of Eurasian Wigeons and smaller flocks of Common Teals and Mallards. Mute Swans are common. In winter the fields hold great clouds of Northern Lapwings and European Golden Plovers, and smaller numbers of Curlews. The drains are full of Common Snipes and small flocks of Black-tailed Godwits can often be found.

In summer the wildfowl mostly return to the north to breed and only some Little Grebes, Moorhens, Mute Swans and Mallards nest. However, this is one of the last refuges of the Corncrake. As the water drains from the fields which have flooded in winter, a glorious growth of meadow emerges and this provides cover for Corncrakes. They can be heard at night, and sometimes by day, along much of this stretch of river.

Some wader species also nest here. Common Snipes, Redshanks, Curlews and Northern Lapwings all breed in small numbers, especially in the vicinity of Clonmacnoise, and Black-tailed Godwits have nested in the past.

Timing

To see the breeding birds and hear the Corncrakes, the best time to come is in June or early July.

For wildfowl the best time is from October to the end of March. Weekends should be avoided if possible as the river is very heavily shot over.

Access

Much the best way to see birds on the Shannon is from a boat. Cruisers can be hired at Portumna, Banagher and Athlone and provide a great summer holiday. In winter they are not available, so the wildfowl enthusiast must take the various roads which cross the river or, alternatively, come close to the Shannon. There are a number of points where access has been provided to the river for coarse fishing.

Common Snipe

The road crosses the river at Shannonbridge and at Athlone and comes close to the river at Clonmacnoise and a number of points on both banks south of Athlone.

CALENDAR

All year: Mute Swan, Mallard, Little Grebe, Heron, Cormorant, Moorhen, Curlew, Common Snipe, Kingfisher, Reed Bunting. Wigeon, Common Teal, European Golden Plover, Northern Lapwing, Black-tailed Godwit.

Autumn–winter–spring: Whooper Swan, Greenland White-fronted Goose, Eurasian **Summer:** Redshank, Corncrake, Swallow, Sand Martin, Sedge Warbler.

---

68 CLOONLAUGHNAN   OSI Discovery map: sheet 40
M84 52

Habitat

Cloonlaughnan is a turlough close to Mount Talbot which has the great advantage of being much easier to watch than the rather inaccessible callows on the Shannon and the Suck. This shallow lake lies in a large field partially hidden from the road by high hedgerows. The area is very open so geese and ducks can see danger from a considerable distance, yet the hedges provide cover for the birdwatcher.

Species

When Cloonlaughnan is flooded a flock of up to 100 Greenland White-fronted Geese, parties of Whooper and occasionally Bewick's Swans, hundreds of

Eurasian Wigeons, Common Teals and Mallards and smaller numbers of Shovelers and Pintails can be seen well. At times, indeed, there are well over 1,000 Eurasian Wigeons here.

Large numbers of Northern Lapwings and European Golden Plovers occur, as is usual on wet land in the Shannon valley, and Curlews and Black-tailed Godwits as well. Less common in the Shannon are the wintering Dunlins which can also be found.

Timing
This is a site to be visited only in winter. It is best between October and March.

Access
Cloonlaughnan is not marked on the Discovery Series Ordnance Survey map; the townland of Cloonlaughnan is marked about 0.5 km to the south. It is best located by taking the road from Athlone for Mount Talbot (R362 leading on to R357). Turn right (north) at Four Roads, a junction about 5 km before Mount Talbot. The turlough at Cloonlaughnan is on the left-hand side of the road just after the crossroads.

CALENDAR

Autumn–winter–spring: Whooper and Mute Swans, Greenland White-fronted Goose, Eurasian Wigeon, Common Teal, Mallard, Shoveler, Pintail, European Golden Plover, Northern Lapwing, Dunlin, Black-tailed Godwit, Curlew.

69 LOUGH CROAN
OSI Discovery map: sheet 47
M88 48

Habitat and Species
Croan is a small permanent lake which holds a reasonable wildfowl population in winter and is an excellent breeding site for ducks in summer. The lake has

up to 900 Eurasian Wigeons and smaller numbers of Common Teals, Mallards, Shovelers and Pintails in winter. Northern Lapwings, European Golden Plovers and Curlews utilise the surrounding pastures.

In summer Great Crested and Little Grebes nest and Black-necked Grebe has been proved to breed in the past. A number of duck species breed including Mallard, Common Teal and Shoveler.

The lake dries out considerably in summer and the breeding ducks are vulnerable to disturbance so the area should not be walked over.

Access

Lough Croan is close to the road from Athlone to Mount Talbot. Take the left turn about 2 km before Four Roads and then take the narrow road to the left which is found after about 2 km. This road runs along the edge of the lake and provides good views.

70 LOUGH FUNSHINAGH

OSI Discovery map: sheet 40, 47
M93 52

Habitat and Species

Funshinagh, like Croan, is a famous wildfowl breeding lake. In the past this lake was the stronghold of the Irish Black-necked Grebe breeding colony that

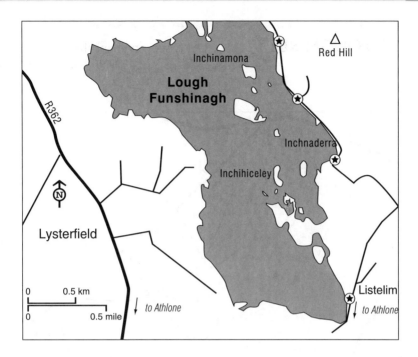

was plundered by egg-collectors year after year. As well as the rare Black-necked, both Great Crested and Little Grebes bred. Mallard, Common Teal, Gadwall, Pintail, Shoveler, Tufted Duck, Pochard, Red-breasted Merganser, Mute Swan, Coot, Moorhen, Northern Lapwing, Ringed Plover, Common Snipe, Common Sandpiper, Redshank and Dunlin have all been known to nest.

The lake has a naturally fluctuating water level and extensive stands of clubrush and reeds, which make observation of both wintering and breeding birds very difficult.

Following several decades of rather poor numbers of wildfowl, this lake appears to have become much more attractive. Undoubtedly, the area would repay further investigation as it is very much underwatched since egg-collecting has fallen out of favour (as well as being illegal).

Access

The best way to approach Funshinagh is by turning right off the road from Athlone to Mount Talbot. Take the first right turn after passing through Milltown Pass, about 2 km after the village. Follow the road straight through the crossroads which is reached after 1.5 km. The road soon runs past the south-east corner of the lake. A narrow road runs along the southern side.

71 LOUGH REE

OSI Discovery map: sheet 40, 47
M96 60; N07 46

Habitat and Species

Lough Ree is the second largest lake on the Shannon system but has rather low numbers of wintering ducks when compared with the great flocks which occur on the callows. At times in winter, when the water level is low, the east side in particular can hold good numbers of ducks. The north-east holds over

1,000 Tufted Ducks and the south-east several hundred Eurasian Wigeons, Mallards and Common Teals.

There are a number of islands and these provide nest sites for Tufted Ducks, Red-breasted Mergansers, Mallards and, in recent years, a small but growing population of Common Scoters. Common Goldeneyes have been recorded in summer and are also suspected of breeding.

Some Common Terns and Black-headed Gulls also nest on the lough.

Access

In summer, access is best by boat, but the lake is very broad and can be dangerous when winds get up.

In winter, the wildfowl can be best seen by driving down to the shoreline at the many points where access is available. The shoreline is very indented and there are quite extensive reedbeds in parts so birdwatching is frequently rather unsatisfactory. One gets the feeling that only a small proportion of the birds are being seen.

LEINSTER

Louth
72 Dundalk Bay
73 Clogher Head
74 Boyne Estuary
75 Carlingford Lough
76 Braganstown

Meath

Dublin
77 Rogerstown Estuary
78 Malahide Estuary
79 North Bull
80 South Dublin Bay
81 Skerries
82 Howth Head
83 Ireland's Eye
84 Baldoyle Estuary
85 Knock Lake

Wicklow
86 Kilcoole
87 Blackditch BWI Reserve
88 Broad Lough
89 Bray Head
90 Wicklow Head
91 Blessington Reservoir
92 Glendalough
93 Glenmalure
94 Roundwood Reservoirs

Wexford
95 North Slob

96 Curracloe
97 Rosslare Back Strand
98 Lady's Island Lake
98A Nethertown
98B Carnsore Point
99 Tacumshin Lake
100 The Cull
101 Saltee Islands
102 Hook Head
103 Bannow Bay
104 Cahore Marshes

Kilkenny

Carlow

Laois

Kildare
105 Pollardstown Fen

Offaly
106 Little Brosna
107 Bullock Island
108 Lough Boora Parklands

Westmeath
109 Lough Derravaragh
110 Lough Owel
111 Lough Iron
112 Lough Ennell

Longford
113 Lough Kinale and Derragh Lough

LEINSTER

LOUTH

Louth is the most northerly county in Leinster, pressing up against the mountainous south-east corner of Down. The coastline is largely low-lying and there are extensive mudflats on the shore of Carlingford Lough and, especially, around the sweep of Dundalk Bay which resembles an enormous bite taken out of the county. South of Dundalk Bay the headlands of Dunany Point and Clogher Head project out into the Irish Sea. Sandy beaches run from Dunany Point southwards to Baltray and the Boyne Estuary where the county boundary with Meath follows the line of the river to the sea.

Inland, the Cooley Peninsula, dividing Carlingford Lough from Dundalk Bay, incorporates a wild stretch of hill country with few roads. Most of the remainder of the county is low-lying, flat agricultural land.

A number of rivers flow from west to east, entering the sea in Dundalk Bay or farther south. The Fane, for example, runs into Dundalk Bay at Lurgangreen, and the Dee at Annagassan. The Boyne, which enters the Irish Sea at Baltray, runs through Meath for much of its length rather than Louth.

72 DUNDALK BAY

OSI Discovery map: sheet 36
J06 08; O09 94

Habitat

Dundalk Bay is an enormous sandy bay with extensive intertidal flats where wildfowl and waders feed securely at low tide. Behind these flats are a number of areas of saltmarsh where large roosts form.

Ballymascanlan in the north is a small muddy inlet which has rich feeding for Redshanks and Black-tailed Godwits. To the immediate south, Dundalk Harbour at low tide is also quite muddy. However, these two inlets represent only a tiny part of the wader feeding area. The tide exposes an area of sand and mud which stretches for up to 3 km between the high tide mark and the water's edge. This expanse stretches from Giles' Quay on the Cooley peninsula in the north to Annagassan in the south and covers 4,500 ha.

The land behind the bay is all very low-lying but at the South Marsh and Lurgangreen there are extensive saltmarshes. The South Marsh lies to the east of the town of Dundalk and is a large area of mixed pasture and saltmarsh, divided in places by muddy channels, many of which are impassable, especially at high tide. Lurgangreen lies to the south of Blackrock, just south of where the Fane river meets the bay. It too is an area of saltmarsh, divided by channels, and behind it are fields protected from the sea by embankments.

Farther south again, near Annagassan are shingle banks where waders frequently roost at high tide.

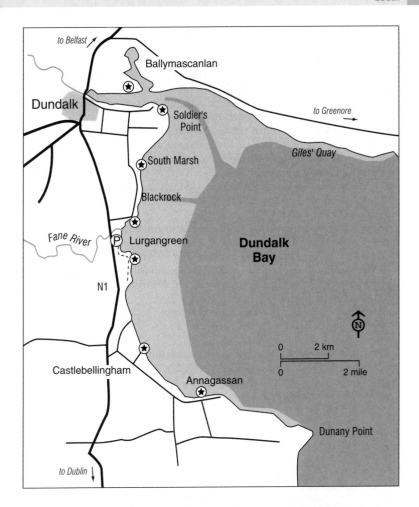

Species

The outer bay holds small numbers of divers and grebes. Both Red-throated and Great Northern Divers can be seen from Giles' Quay and some Great Crested Grebes also occur. Slavonian Grebe has been recorded and might well be found more frequently if the area was more thoroughly covered by bird-watchers. Common Scoters and Red-breasted Mergansers also winter off Giles' Quay.

Wildfowl numbers are not particularly high when one considers how large the area is, but there is great diversity. Mute Swans congregate at Dundalk docks; Whooper Swans are occasional visitors to Lurgangreen; Greylag and Greenland White-fronted Geese come and go at both Dundalk Bay and Lurgangreen; Brent Geese are regular in autumn and spring; Shelduck, Eurasian Wigeon, Common Teal, Mallard, Pintail, Shoveler and Common Goldeneye all winter in varying numbers. Eurasian Wigeons and Common

Teals gather principally at the South Marsh and Lurgangreen, Mallards at Ballymascanlan and off Annagassan. Shoveler is probably the scarcest of the regularly occurring ducks.

The bay is best known among birdwatchers, however, for its enormous wader numbers. In Ireland as a whole, only the Shannon estuary and Strangford Lough have had more waders recorded. On the Atlantic coast of Europe and north Africa it ranks among the top twenty estuaries.

About 10,000 Oystercatchers winter, and many more occur in autumn. Winter numbers of Northern Lapwing and European Golden Plover are among the highest on the east coast, with flocks of several thousand of each. Bar-tailed Godwits, Curlews, Redshanks, Dunlins and Knots all winter in numbers surpassing 1,000. Winter flocks of Black-tailed Godwits at both Ballymascanlon and Dundalk Harbour have been building steadily over many years and now number several hundred at each site.

Many other wader species also occur, but in small numbers. Grey Plover, Ringed Plover and Greenshank all winter in small numbers. Ruff and Spotted Redshank occur in autumn and sometimes in winter. Curlew Sandpipers are seen in autumn most years and Little Stints occasionally. Common Sandpipers teeter about the estuary at Ballymascanlan and Dundalk Harbour in late July. Gulls roost in the bay and terns feed in late summer.

The South Marsh is probably the best site on the Leinster coast for wintering Twites. Over 50 have been seen in the area from Soldier's Point southwards.

Overall, this bay has potential which has hardly been touched. Regular watching should turn up many more species, but, even for a brief day visit, the sight of huge wader flocks Swirling over the saltmarsh at the South Marsh or Lurgangreen is well worth a detour.

Curlew

Access

Begin a visit from the north at Giles' Quay. Take the Belfast road north from Dundalk and turn right after 3 km on the road to Carlingford. Follow the road past Ballymascanlan and on for 7 km to a right turn for Giles' Quay. Turn down the narrow road to the quay. The open bay can be scanned from here and from several points on the road back towards Ballymascanlan.

The top of Ballymascanlan Bay can be seen from the road west of Ballymascanlan village. The outer part of the bay is accessible on the west side from a narrow road which runs to the east from the main Belfast road about 600 m north of Dundalk.

Dundalk Harbour is readily worked by following the road to the east along the edge of the harbour out to Soldier's Point. Park the car here and explore the north part of the South Marsh. Much of the marsh is not directly accessible because of the drains which cross it, but most of the birds can be seen with the use of a telescope. The south part of the marsh can be seen from the road from Dundalk to Blackrock, just where it joins the coast.

At low tide, or on a dropping tide, the estuary can be seen well from the road to Blackrock. Just west of Blackrock, the road joins the main Dundalk–Dublin road. A couple of hundred metres to the south, the road south crosses a bridge over the River Fane. Park on the south side of the bridge and follow the lane down to the edge of the saltmarsh. There is a path south to the sea wall and, from there on to the south, the embankment provides cover for viewing the roosting flocks of birds.

The south part of Dundalk Bay can be seen by driving south to Castlebellingham and then turning left for Annagassan. The road runs along the side of the bay for a couple of kilometres and good views are available at the old mill at Annagassan.

Timing

The bay is best from August to March, but passage waders in April and May could be interesting. Observations are much easier if the tide is within two hours of high water. At low tide most of the birds are too far distant, even with a good telescope, but they can be well seen as they are pushed up by a rising tide to the roosts. At full tide, many of the waders are hidden among the long grass on the saltmarsh but they become visible again as the tide ebbs. The best conditions of all are about one hour after high tide in the afternoon, with the sun behind the observer.

CALENDAR

Autumn–winter–spring: Mute and Whooper Swans, Greylag, Greenland White-fronted and Brent Geese, Shelduck, Eurasian Wigeon, Common Teal, Mallard, Pintail, Shoveler, Common Goldeneye, possibility of Long-tailed Duck, Red-throated and Great Northern Divers, Great Crested Grebe, Oystercatcher, Ringed, European Golden and Grey Plovers, Northern Lapwing, Knot, Dunlin, Black-tailed and Bar-tailed Godwits, Curlew, Redshank, Greenshank, Turnstone.

Autumn: Curlew Sandpiper, possibility of Little Stint, Ruff, Spotted Redshank, Common Sandpiper

73 CLOGHER HEAD

OSI Discovery map: sheet 36
O17 84

Habitat

Clogher Head protrudes well out into the Irish Sea and is well situated for sea-watching and searching for passerine migrants. Its potential was first thoroughly explored by a small group of Dublin birdwatchers in the early 1970s. They were anxious to see if the variety of migrants which could be seen at Saltee in Wexford and Cape Clear in Cork might be found on the east coast, and they visited Clogher Head regularly at weekends throughout the year for a period, but eventually the lure of rarities in Wexford and Cork drew them away. Clogher Head is now very much underwatched.

The head itself has a scattering of cover in gardens above the harbour of Port Oriel. The harbour is busy and attracts gulls, especially where the water outflows from the fish processing plant to the west of the harbour. There is rocky shore each side of the harbour, and a sandy beach from a few hundred metres west of Port Oriel which stretches north to Dunany Point.

Species

Systematic seawatching in spring and autumn showed that quite substantial passage could be seen from the head. In the autumn of 1974 all four species of skua were recorded as were Cory's and Sooty Shearwaters, Sabine's and Little Gulls and Black Terns. Subsequent observations have been far less regular but have shown that Arctic and Great Skua are both regular and Pomarine Skua occasional. The Irish Sea, in the right conditions, obviously has considerable numbers and diversity of seabirds and Clogher Head is an ideal headland for seawatching.

Large numbers of gulls appear off the harbour, especially in winter, and Glaucous and Iceland are regular. Mediterranean Gulls often occur among the Black-headed Gulls which roost on Cruisetown beach to the north of the head. Both Laughing Gull and Franklin's Gull have been recorded there.

Passerine migration is good in both spring and autumn. Clogher Head's rarest bird, Ireland's first Rock Thrush, was found in May 1974. Willow Warblers, Common Chiffchaffs, Northern Wheatears, Whinchats, Common Whitethroats, Grasshopper Warblers, Sedge Warblers and Spotted Flycatchers all pass through in April and May. Other species recorded in spring include Turtle Dove, Serin and Red-breasted Flycatcher.

In autumn, Blackcap and Garden Warbler are probably annual. Rarities seen in autumn have included Barred Warbler, Yellow-browed Warbler and Lesser Whitethroat.

Northern Wheatear

Late in autumn Clogher Head has good numbers of finches, including occasional Twites.

Timing
Visits are worthwhile in spring from March to early June and in autumn from August to the end of October if seawatching or passerine watching is planned. The best conditions for skuas are after periods of strong westerly and south-westerly gales accompanying the passage of areas of low pressure.

Passerines are best in both spring and autumn in quite different conditions, when the winds are south-easterly or during periods of calm weather accompanying high pressure systems.

Access
Clogher Head is easily found. Drive from Drogheda for Termonfeckin and follow on through the village to Clogher Head. Park the car at the harbour and explore on foot.

CALENDAR

All year: Red-breasted Merganser, Fulmar, Oystercatcher, Curlew, Turnstone, Black-headed, Herring, Lesser Black-backed and Great Black-backed Gulls, Kittiwake, Common Guillemot, Razorbill, Linnet, Tree Sparrow.

Autumn: Red-throated and Great Northern Divers, Manx Shearwater, Gannet, Arctic, Pomarine and Great Skuas, passerine migrants.

Winter: Common Scoter, divers, European Golden Plover, Northern Lapwing, Purple Sandpiper, Iceland and Glaucous Gulls, finch and thrush flocks.

Spring: divers, seabird passage with likelihood of Arctic Skua, passerine migrants including Grasshopper Warbler, Sedge Warbler, Whinchat

---

74 BOYNE ESTUARY
OSI Discovery map: sheet 43
O14 78; O16 76

Habitat
The Boyne estuary divides the eastern margin of the counties of Louth and Meath. The land is low-lying on both sides and the estuary is muddy with some saltmarsh. Various efforts have been made over the years to reclaim parts of the estuary and there are a number of sea walls.

The estuary is narrow from the town of Drogheda downstream as far as Mornington where it broadens out to about 1.5 km in width. This is the widest part of the estuary; shortly afterwards the estuary narrows again to reach the sea through an exit between the sand dunes of Baltray to the north and Queensborough to the south.

Species

This is a rather good site for seeing wildfowl and waders, but it has been over-shadowed by the impressive sites of Dundalk Bay to the north and the North Bull to the south. The site has been surveyed regularly and duck numbers appear to have been reasonably stable over the past 20 years. Up to 200 Shelducks, 800 Eurasian Wigeons, 300 Common Teals and 250 Mallards can be expected and, in recent years, as their Irish wintering population has increased, a small flock of Brent Geese occurs. The geese are most regular in spring.

The wader species are typical of those of the east coast, but the Boyne has the largest numbers of Black-tailed Godwits (up to 450) of any estuary north of Wexford. Passage waders also occur and Spotted Redshank, Little Stint and Ruff are annual. Rarities recorded include Little Egret, Avocet and Pectoral Sandpiper.

The dunes at Baltray hold a small colony of Little Terns in summer and a handful of Ringed Plovers. Carrion Crows are more often reported from the Baltray area than any other part of Leinster.

Timing

The best time for visiting the estuary is within two hours of high tide. However, timing is not so critical as at Dundalk Bay, as the estuary is relatively narrow and easily watched.

Access

Both sides of the Boyne can be watched by driving east from Drogheda. To see the northern side take the road for Baltray and stop where birds are seen. The southern side, which is not usually so good, can be watched by taking the road for Mornington. To cover the area thoroughly, both sides must be watched.

CALENDAR

Autumn–winter–spring: Brent Goose, Shelduck, Eurasian Wigeon, Common Teal, Mallard, Oystercatcher, European Golden and Grey Plovers, Northern Lapwing, Knot, Dunlin, Black-tailed Godwit, Curlew, Redshank, Greenshank.

Autumn: Spotted Redshank, Ruff, Curlew Sandpiper, Little Stint, Whimbrel.

Summer: terns, especially Little Tern.

75 CARLINGFORD LOUGH

OSI Discovery map: sheet 36
J14 16; J22 11

Habitat and Species

Carlingford Lough is divided in two by the border between Northern Ireland and the Republic. This section, therefore, deals only with the south-west shore. The north-east side is dealt with under the accounts for County Down.

The lough is a deep fjord-like sea lough surrounded by mountains. The Mourne Mountains loom over the Down side and the Carlingford Mountains dominate the Cooley peninsula on the Louth side. The mouth of the lough is shallower than much of the lough itself, a characteristic of fjords, and the bay is surrounded by moraines.

The lough holds an impressive population of seaducks. Over 500 Scaups and up to 100 Common Goldeneyes, 50 Red-breasted Mergansers and, in some years, over 20 Long-tailed Ducks winter here. Great Crested Grebes are common, but divers are very thinly distributed. Some Brent Geese, Shelducks, Common Teals, Mallards and Eurasian Wigeons winter here, along with small numbers of Grey and European Golden Plovers, Northern Lapwings, Oystercatchers, Dunlins, Bar-tailed Godwits, Redshanks and Greenshanks. The muddy area between Greenore and Carlingford is the best part of the bay for waders.

Access

Access could hardly be easier. From Dundalk, take the main road for Greenore. Park at Greenore and scan the bay. Work back along the road to Carlingford and then back to Omeath. The border crossing is just beyond Omeath.

76 BRAGANSTOWN

OSI Discovery map: sheet 36
O02 94

Habitat and Species

Braganstown, just to the north of Stabannon, has become an important swan and goose wintering site since the early 1980s. In the maps of Louth, which form part of the centrepiece of the Irish East Coast Bird Report, it did not appear until 1984. The site is an area of farmland on the southern edge of the River Glyde between Ardee and Castlebellingham, which attracts large numbers of Greylag Geese and smaller numbers of wild swans and other geese. The farm was formerly marshland but was drained and is now farmed intensively for grass, cereals and root crops.

Up to 1,000 Greylag Geese are regular, though numbers do fluctuate considerably. A few Pink-footed and Greenland White-fronted Geese are usually among the Greylags and Barnacle Goose has been recorded. Up to 50 Whooper Swans could be expected, and very occasionally a few Bewick's. As well as wildfowl, there are flocks of European Golden Plovers, Northern

Lapwings and Curlews, as well as good numbers of wintering thrushes and finches. This is a good spot for seeing Bramblings and it is a regular site for Common Buzzard.

The best time for a visit is between late October and March.

Access

The birds can be watched by taking the road north from Ardee towards Dundalk and turning right for Castlebellingham about 1 km beyond Ardee. The road runs along the north side of the River Dee. Drive for about 5 km to Stabannon. At Stabannon, turn left at the junction and Braganstown is reached on the left side of the road after about 1.5 km. The estate is strictly private, but most of the birds can be viewed from the road.

MEATH

Meath is a large county with rich agricultural land. The coastline is small and limited to a stretch of shelving beach between the Boyne estuary (see under Louth above) and the Dublin border, although because it is regularly watched it has proved to be rather productive. Inland the county is relatively flat and has very few areas of standing water. For a county so close to Dublin, there have been surprisingly few unusual species found.

Bird records are included in the annual Irish East Coast Bird Report. Coastal birdwatching at Laytown and Gormanston is good in winter.

Red-throated and Great Northern Divers occur in small numbers. Large flocks of Common Scoters winter in some years, though numbers fluctuate from year to year, and small numbers of Velvet Scoters and an occasional Surf Scoter can be found among them. A small flock of Scaups sometimes winters on this coast as well. The mixed gull and tern flock on this beach is a good spot to look for Roseate Tern in late summer and autumn and both Elegant Tern and Franklin's Gull have been recorded. Waders, some Eurasian Wigeons and Common Teals and a small flock of about 50 Brent Geese winter on the estuary just to the south of Laytown. A few Purple Sandpipers can be seen on the rocky coast north of Laytown.

The lakes in the west and north of the county have breeding Great Crested Grebes and Blackcaps.

DUBLIN

Dublin is dominated by the city which sprawls both inland and along the coast to north and south from Dublin Bay. Over a million people live in the capital and its suburbs, and inevitably they put pressure on the best places for birds. Yet the county has a magnificent series of estuaries, large seabird colonies on sea cliffs and fine mountains.

The coast from the Meath border south to Rogerstown estuary is low-lying with a shelving beach off which scoters and Red-breasted Mergansers feed. Then there is a series of estuaries: Rogerstown, Malahide, Baldoyle and Dublin Bay. On the north side of Dublin Bay the promontory of Howth Head projects far enough out to be a useful seawatching site and its cliffs support large numbers of seabirds. South of Dublin Bay, the coast swings around the arc of Killiney Bay and then, just across the border with Wicklow, the shallow coast terminates at Bray Head.

Offshore, there are several islands. Rockabill, a tiny rock marked with a lighthouse, lies off Skerries, but visiting is prohibited. The island has the largest colony of Roseate Terns in north-west Europe and a team of wardens protect them from disturbance. The birds can be seen in summer from the adjacent coast. Farther south, Lambay Island has wintering geese and large numbers of breeding seabirds but is privately owned so not accessible. Ireland's Eye, a smaller island off Howth, can be reached by boat from Howth Harbour and also holds a seabird colony.

Inland, there are attractive habitats for riverine birds along the River Liffey and the banks of the Royal and Grand Canals. The Phoenix Park, on the western side of Dublin city and within easy reach of the centre city by public transport, has a long list of the commoner breeding and wintering landbirds.

The birds of the county are probably the best watched in the country as there is a greater concentration of birdwatchers here than anywhere else. BirdWatch Ireland has three branches within County Dublin.

Perhaps the finest aspect of birdwatching in Dublin is that most of the sites can be reached easily by public transport.

77 ROGERSTOWN ESTUARY

OSI Discovery map: sheet 43
O22 52

Habitat

Rogerstown is the most northerly of the Dublin estuaries and is situated in the heart of the rich vegetable-growing belt of north County Dublin. The estuary is broad and muddy, but is divided in two by the causeway which was built in 1844 to carry the railway line between Dublin and Belfast.

Above the causeway, the estuary is very muddy and is edged with saltmarsh at the inner end. The mud is quite treacherous and slopes down to the meandering river channel at low tide. There are clumps of *Spartina anglica* and a large expanse of *Salicornia europaea*. On the northern side is a large and expanding tiphead, operated by Fingal County Council since the early 1970s. The tip has reduced the area of mud by about 50 ha and has covered what used to be one of the main wildfowl feeding areas.

The outer section of the estuary has coarser sediments and is scarred with mussel beds. There are extensive beds of green algae *Enteromorpha* and *Ulva lactuca* which provide feeding for Brent Geese. Large areas of *Ruppia maritima* are grazed by Eurasian Wigeons. The estuary is partly impounded by terminal sand dune systems to both north and south and narrows sharply before meeting the sea.

The outer portion of the estuary is a National Nature Reserve and a Ramsar site, while the north shore of the inner section is a BirdWatch Ireland Reserve.

Species

Rogerstown is very much an estuarine site with its best birdwatching between late August and March. The principal wildfowl species here are Brent Goose (up to 1000), Greylag Goose (200), Shelduck (over 800), Eurasian Wigeon (fluctuating from 300–1,000), Common Teal (up to 900), Mallard (peaking at about 500 in August when local breeding birds assemble), Pintail (20–30) and

Shoveler (30–60). In addition, occasional Gadwalls are seen and, in among the Brent Geese, one or two Black Brants and one or two Dark-bellied Brents have been seen in most recent years among the Pale-bellied birds.

Numbers of ducks have decreased somewhat in the past 20 years. Wader numbers are quite high with the principal species being Oystercatcher (up to 1500), Ringed Plover (up to 180 in autumn), European Golden Plover and Northern Lapwing (occasional large flocks in winter, especially after cold weather), Grey Plover (up to 300), Knot (fluctuating between 100 and 2,000), Dunlin (2,000–2,500), Black-tailed Godwit (500–1,000), Curlew (up to 1,000), Redshank (up to 1,600 in autumn), Bar-tailed Godwit, Greenshank, Spotted Redshank and Green Sandpiper (a few of each).

The estuary is far and away the best place on the east coast to see Green Sandpipers and is also one of the most likely places to come upon an American vagrant in autumn. Ten species of American wader have been recorded here, with Pectoral Sandpiper the most frequent.

Green Sandpipers can be found in late summer and autumn along the river between Newhaggard Bridge and the saltmarsh, but the land here is privately owned and warning notices have been erected.

Other scarce migrant waders, such as Curlew Sandpipers, Little Stints and Ruffs, have also been seen here in autumn with some regularity.

This is an excellent site for winter birds of prey; Common Buzzard, Peregrine and Merlin are regular; Hen Harriers are seen some winters, while Osprey and Marsh Harrier have been seen in recent years as passage migrants. The rough pastures provide suitable habitat for Short-eared Owls which can sometimes be seen in winter.

The fields around the estuary hold large flocks of thrushes and finches in winter and are among the best sites in the country for flocks of Tree Sparrows.

Timing

The estuary is best visited between August and March. Green Sandpipers can be found from July, sometimes June, so an earlier visit could be worthwhile. Most of the Brent Geese arrive at this site in November.

Access

Take the bus or drive along the M1 Dublin–Belfast road to the Skerries exit about 2 km north of Swords. Take the exit for Skerries, going north on the R132 where a large warehouse can be seen on the right-hand side and signposts for Skerries and Lusk. Turn right here (R127) if you have a car and turn right again at the fork about 1 km on, following the signs to Balleally tiphead. If you have travelled by bus, you will have to get off at the main road and continue on foot. Approximately 1 km along this road is a gateway on the right-hand side with the entrance to the BirdWatch Ireland Reserve. If driving, go slowly as it is easy to miss the entrance. Follow this track to the bird hide.

You can then return to the road and continue east past the tiphead, where a track under the railway bridge continues to the north shore of the outer estuary. However the visitor with a car will prefer to take the road inland towards Rush (R128). After crossing over the railway bridge take the first turn right (Spout Road, which is well-signposted) towards Rush Pier at the mouth of the estuary.

To access the south side, return to the R132, go south for half a kilometre and then turn east on the R126 towards Donabate. Continue for about 1 km before coming to a sign indicating the BirdWatch Ireland hide. Turn left at this sign and drive through an open gate along an unsurfaced road through the fields and then take a right-hand turn past the allotments to the hide. This hide is accessible to key holders only, but it is still possible to scan the mudflats from beside the hide. Be advised that the gate at the main road closes before dusk, so be sure to return before this time. The best access to the south shore of the outer estuary is by the road which runs directly north from Donabate Village to the edge of the estuary.

Grey Heron

CALENDAR

All year: Mute Swan, Shelduck, Mallard, Grey Heron, Little Egret, Common Buzzard, Sparrowhawk, Kestrel, Oystercatcher, Curlew, Herring and Great Black-backed Gulls, Skylark, Meadow Pipit, European Stonechat.

Autumn: arriving wintering wildfowl and passage waders including Green Sandpiper. Common Sandpiper, Ruff, Curlew Sandpiper; possibility of American waders, terns at the mouth of the estuary.

Winter: Brent and Greylag Geese, duck and wader species, Tree Sparrow.

Spring: late wildfowl and waders, Whimbrel, Common Sandpiper, terns.

78 MALAHIDE ESTUARY   OSI Discovery map: sheet 50
O20 47

Habitat

This estuary, the next one south after Rogerstown (see map on page 173), is similar in that it is also divided in two by a causeway built to carry the railway northwards from Dublin. The habitat, however, is rather different because the area impounded behind the causeway is here an expanse of open water with only a slight tidal rhythm.

This estuary can be considered to have three principal habitats for birds. East of the railway causeway are open mudflats exposed at low tide and with some mussel beds and extensive swards of *Zostera angustifolia* and the scarcer *Z. noltii*.

Immediately west of the causeway is an area of water known as Broad Meadows (after the River Broad Meadow which empties into it) which is deep and only drops a few centimetres on the ebb tide. This is a popular sailing and windsurfing area.

At the head of this part of the estuary, just below the M1 Motorway Bridge, is a small area of grassy islands and muddy creeks.

The whole area has changed dramatically in the past 20 years as housing estates have extended around both Malahide and Swords and boating has become more popular on the open water.

Arctic Tern

Species

On the open mudflats, a large flock of Brent Geese and smaller numbers of ducks winter. Numbers have increased in recent years. Up to 400 Shelducks, 150 Eurasian Wigeons, 250 Common Teals, 200 Mallards and a handful of

Pintails occur. Among them are 1,200 or more Oystercatchers, occasional large flocks of European Golden Plovers and Northern Lapwings, up to 1,500 Dunlins and smaller numbers of Bar-tailed Godwits, Black-tailed Godwits, Curlews and Redshanks.

The deeper waters at Broad Meadows hold up to 100 Great Crested Grebes, 100 Pochards (as many as 400 have been seen), 200 Common Goldeneyes, a handful of Scaups, one or two Long-tailed Ducks and the possibility of something unusual such as a Smew or a Slavonian Grebe, both of which are recorded here periodically.

The head of the estuary, traditionally known as Swords estuary, holds a large flock of Mute Swans which have been studied for many years as part of a research programme on the swans of Co Dublin. Many of them have white numbered rings on their legs. Indeed, Mute Swans ringed in Dublin as part of this programme have been seen as far east as Wales, as far south as Wexford and as far west as Cork.

The muddy creeks among the small islands at the head of the estuary provide perfect habitat for migrant waders in autumn. They hold Spotted Redshank, Curlew Sandpiper, Little Stint and Ruff almost every autumn, and many rarities have occurred here including both American and Pacific Golden Plovers and Short-billed Dowitcher. Gulls roost here and Mediterranean Gull should be looked for at any time of the year.

In summer and early autumn, terns feed in the estuary. Common, Arctic, Sandwich and Black Terns all occur regularly and Roseates from the Rockabill breeding colony occasionally.

Timing

The estuary is best from August through the winter to April. Wildfowl and wader numbers are highest and there is always the possibility of a rarity in autumn. Coverage is best within two hours either side of high tide.

Access

The main wader roost on the outer estuary can be viewed well from the southern shore, about 200m east of Malahide village. The road along the southern shore of Broad Meadows has several points where a car can be parked and the area scanned in comfort.

A road runs around the entire head of the estuary, providing excellent viewing at a number of points.

CALENDAR

All year: Mute Swan, Shelduck, Mallard, Grey Heron, Little Egret, Oystercatcher, Curlew, Herring and Great Black-backed Gulls.

Autumn: early wildfowl, passage waders and terns; Ruff, Curlew Sandpiper, possibility of American waders.

Winter: Brent Goose, duck and wader species.

Spring: late wildfowl and waders, terns.

79 NORTH BULL

OSI Discovery map: sheet 50
O23 37

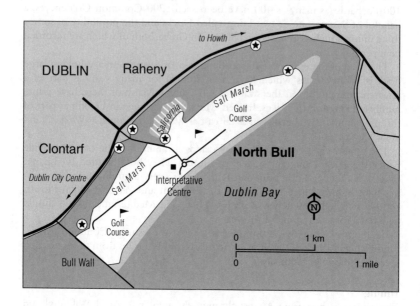

Habitat

The North Bull is a dune-covered sandy spit which runs parallel to the coast between Clontarf and Sutton on the northern side of Dublin Bay for a distance of 4.85 km. The island is bordered to the south by the Bull Wall which was completed in 1825 with the objective of improving the approaches to Dublin Harbour. The word 'bull' may derive from 'ball', which means a sandbank. Certainly, there was a sandbank here in the late 18th century, which emerged following extensive dredging activities and the construction of new walls on the south side of the port. A map drawn by Captain Bligh (of *Bounty* fame) in 1800 shows a tiny area of permanent dry sand.

After the Bull Wall was built, the island extended rapidly. Sand was deposited on the seaward side of the bank and what was described by the Directors-General of Inland Navigation in Ireland as soft ooze from the sewers of the city was swept down from the river and deposited on the strand opposite the growing island.

In 1964, a causeway was completed to carry traffic across the middle of the muddy lagoon to the centre of the island.

There are two golf courses on the Bull and the beach on the seaward side is a very popular recreational area.

There are several habitats of special interest to the birdwatcher, and the intertidal flats and saltmarsh are the principal ones. The inner side of the Bull, from Clontarf out to Sutton, is an extensive intertidal zone where thousands of wildfowl and waders feed at low tide. The area of flats to the north of the causeway comprises a mixture of bare mud and *Salicornia*-covered mudflat. Farther to the north, and to the south of the causeway, most of the remaining intertidal flats are comprised of sandier sediments.

Above the intertidal zone, an extensive saltmarsh runs almost the entire length of the island between the dune complex and the high water mark of neap tides. When there are high spring tides, the entire saltmarsh is inundated at high water. The saltmarsh has numerous drainage channels and shallow, muddy pans.

Towards the tip of the island, known as the Point, about 1 km from the end, is the Alder Marsh, an area of low-lying ground with a stand of alder trees and a terrestrial marsh vegetation. This habitat, quite different from others on the Bull, attracts occasional passerine migrants.

The Bull has been much studied and written about. A very attractive little book, *An Irish Sanctuary – Birds of the North Bull*, was published in 1953 by Rev P.G. Kennedy S.J. but is long out of print. More recently, the Royal Dublin Society sponsored the publication of a major volume on the natural history of the island (see references) and a slim paperback, entitled *A Students' Guide to North Bull Island,* subsequently appeared which distilled the main points.

Dublin City Council, which manages the island, has an Interpretative Centre at the island end of the causeway.

Species

The great attraction of the North Bull is that so many species can be seen so closely within the confines of a capital city, over 200 have been recorded. The variety of habitats provides opportunity for seeing virtually anything, even the strange discovery on the beach of the remains of both Bridled and Royal Terns within four months of each other back in the 1950s.

Off the Point and out to sea, divers, grebes, Common Scoters and seabirds which have come into Dublin Bay can be seen. On the sandy beach Knots, Ringed Plovers, Sanderlings, Curlews and godwits occur at the Point and near the Bull Wall, while White Wagtails and Northern Wheatears pass through in autumn and Snow Buntings occasionally feed by the high water mark.

The intertidal zone between the island and the shore is where the most spectacular sights are to be seen. Up to 2,500 Brent Geese, 1,300 Shelducks, 1,000 Eurasian Wigeons, 800 Common Teals, 100 Mallards, 150 Pintails, 120 Shovelers and small numbers of Red-breasted Mergansers are the main wildfowl species.

The geese feed in different areas depending on the time of year. In early November they feed on what remains of the *Zostera* beds at Sutton strand and on mats of *Enteromorpha* near Kilbarrack. From early December many move onto grassland around Dublin Bay. They feed on the football pitches in St Anne's Park, across the road from the Bull causeway, on the golf courses and on mown grass close to the road at Clontarf.

The Shelducks congregate at both sides of the causeway where they feed on the small snail *Hydrobia*. Eurasian Wigeons, which graze exclusively, concentrate off Raheny but can be found all along the intertidal flats. Common Teals, which have a more catholic diet, also gather at Raheny, but the largest numbers are found on the *Salicornia* flats. Pintails are found mainly between Raheny and the causeway, and Mallards and Shovelers both favour the outlets of the streams to the south of the causeway. All the common duck species can usually be seen at low tide from the causeway as they feed or roost on the mud on both sides. Depending on the light, they can be seen well from the road on the mainland or from the causeway.

Many rarer ducks have been seen including American Wigeon, Black Duck and Blue-winged and Green-winged Teals. Gadwalls have occurred on occasions.

Even larger numbers of waders winter, but they use the North Bull as a roosting area and spread out over much of Dublin Bay to feed. Only when the tide is flooding in do large numbers feed in the Bull channel. The roosts, however, are spectacular and include at peak 3,200 Oystercatchers (autumn), 300 Ringed Plovers (autumn), 350 Grey Plovers, 4,000 Knots, 7,000 Dunlins, 450 Black-tailed Godwits, 1,800 Bar-tailed Godwits, 1,000 Curlews, 1,600 Redshanks (autumn) and 250 Turnstones. Peak numbers of most species occur in winter, but some, as indicated, pass through in larger numbers. All these birds roost on the saltmarsh but many of them feed on the south side of Dublin Bay (see the account which follows) or off Clontarf.

Scarcer species such as Spotted Redshank, Ruff, Curlew Sandpiper and Little Stint are annual. Rarities include Buff-breasted Sandpiper, which are almost annual, and several other species of American wader. Avocets have been seen at the North Bull on a number of occasions although with less frequency in recent years. The Bull has a large wintering gull population, but tends not to be the best place for rarer species. In summer terns from the nearby colony in Dublin Port feed in the channels and a handful of pairs of Ringed Plovers nest on the shingle beach at the Point.

In autumn and winter the Alder Marsh and dunes are worth scouring. Several Short-eared Owls usually winter on the saltmarsh and in the vicinity of the golf courses. The southern end of the saltmarsh is usually the best place to look for them. Peregrines and Merlins are frequent in winter. Passerine migrants such as Northern Wheatears, infrequent Whinchats, and just occasionally something more exotic such as a Shore Lark or Great Grey Shrike have been seen.

Close to the Bull Wall a small party of Snow Buntings can usually be found on the beach in mid-winter.

The Bull Wall itself provides good views of divers and Red-breasted Mergansers in winter and the seaweed-covered boulders provide feeding for Turnstones at the tip. In summer it is a good place for watching terns.

Timing

The Bull is worth a visit at any time of the year. The best time for wildfowl and waders is from August to March, but interesting birds can turn up at any season and, in summer, there are usually feeding gulls, terns and Gannets on the seaward side.

Covering the entire North Bull takes most of a day, but to see the wildfowl and waders best try to ensure that part of your visit covers the period within three hours of high tide. The ducks are best watched from the road rather than the island as walking on the saltmarsh causes disturbance.

Access

To see most of the species in a short time, make your way to the causeway opposite St Anne's and walk along the path beside the road to both south and north. This path is flat and level and can be easily negotiated by wheelchair.

Having seen the ducks on either side of the causeway, walk across the causeway and scan the flats on either side. Many of the common wader species should be seen.

A thorough visit requires much more time. Ideally, the visit should start at Clontarf and combine a walk along the shoreline opposite the North Bull as far as Kilbarrack with a complete traverse of the saltmarsh and a visit to the Alder Marsh. In the evening, both Grey Herons and Little Egrets can be seen flying in to roost at St. Anne's.

CALENDAR

All year: Shelduck, Mallard, Grey Heron, Little Egret, Cormorant, Oystercatcher, Curlew.

Autumn: returning wildfowl and waders, including first Brent Geese. Migrant waders including Curlew Sandpiper and Little Stint. Possibility of migrant passerines.

Winter: Brent Goose, Eurasian Wigeon, Common Teal, Pintail, Shoveler, Red-throated and Great Northern Divers, large numbers of waders, especially Dunlin, Knot and Bar-tailed Godwit, small groups of Turnstones on the Bull Wall. One or two Black Brants and possibly a Dark-bellied Brent Goose. Short-eared Owl, Snow Bunting.

Spring: late wildfowl and waders. Brent Geese remain into early May. In May there is movement of Whimbrels, Ringed Plovers and Sanderling.

---

80 SOUTH DUBLIN BAY OSI Discovery map: sheet 50
O20 33; O25 20

Habitat

South Dublin Bay is a broad arc, which swings from the Poolbeg lighthouse at the mouth of Dublin port around Sandymount and Merrion strands and out to Dun Laoghaire. The habitat includes the shallow water of Dublin Bay, the extensive sand flats of the intertidal zone, the weedy edges of the piers and the small marsh at Booterstown.

The bay is very shallow; the 5–fathom line stretches north from Dun Laoghaire more or less directly to Howth Head. This depth provides feeding for divers, grebes and seaducks in winter and for terns in summer and autumn. The low tide mark runs from close to Blackrock north to the South Wall. A number of shallow pools mark the strand, the largest of which is known as the cockle lake. Cockles are in profusion across the sand. There is a large bed of *Zostera* which provides feeding for Brent Geese.

Both the South Wall and the West Pier, Dun Laoghaire project well out into Dublin Bay and provide vantage points for scanning the water for ducks.

Species

The shallow waters attract divers, grebes and ducks in winter. Great Northern and Red-throated Divers are regular, while Black-throated occurs in most but not in all winters. Great Crested Grebes are regular off both the South Wall and the West Pier. Slavonian has been seen and Red-necked has also been recorded, but very rarely. The commonest seaduck is Common Scoter and there are usually 25–50 between the South Wall and Dun Laoghaire. A few Red-breasted Mergansers and Common Goldeneyes and one or two Long-tailed Ducks are also usual.

Flocks of gulls feed around the piers and roost on the water. Among the commoner species are the occasional Iceland or Glaucous in winter and at almost any season there is the possibility of Mediterranean, Little or Ring-billed. All of these species are annual in Dublin Bay. The piers at Poolbeg or Dun Laoghaire and the sand at Merrion Gates, when the tide is rising, are among the best places to search.

On the strand there are 500–1,000 Brent Geese in late winter and a few Eurasian Wigeons, but the most numerous birds are waders. Flocks of Oystercatchers (up to 8,000), Bar-tailed Godwits (up to 1,000), Sanderling (up to 300), Ringed Plovers (up to 130), Redshanks (up to 1,200), Knots (up to 2,000) and Curlews (up to 500) feed on the beach, with smaller numbers of other species. At one time it was thought that these were all birds from the North Bull which move over here to feed, but it is now known that many of the waders feeding on the south side of Dublin Bay roost here as well.

The strand in late July and August is a quite spectacular place with large numbers of roosting terns. Towards dusk, thousands of terns, which have been feeding on the sandbanks several kilometres east of Dublin Bay, fly in to settle on the beach. Most of them are Common and Arctic Terns but Roseate Terns, presumably from Rockabill, can usually be distinguished by call and, in calm weather when the birds are approachable, by plumage tone as well. An occasional Black Tern turns up at this time of year in most years. The calling of the terns as they rise before a flooding tide is a wonderful sound on a clear night.

Behind the railway line at Booterstown is a small marsh which holds Common Teal and Common Snipe and, at high tide, small numbers of roosting waders.

The piers at both the South Wall and Dun Laoghaire have small populations of Purple Sandpipers as well as the ubiquitous Turnstones. The West Pier sometimes has Snow Buntings in late winter and occasional winter and late-autumn Black Redstarts.

Access

The entire south side of the bay is ringed by roads and can be viewed at many points. The DART rapid transit railway line stops at stations at Booterstown, Blackrock, Seapoint and Dun Laoghaire which provide immediate access to the shore and good points for placing a telescope.

A thorough search of the area would start with a drive out towards the South Wall, parking the car at Poolbeg and walking out to the lighthouse. Return, stopping the car at various points where birds are congregating, finally parking near Seapoint and walk out along the West Pier. On Sunday afternoons the pier is thronged with people taking the air or walking their dogs, but there are usually a number of birdwatchers among them. However it is not wheelchair accessible as the surface is rather uneven and the sea wall is quite high.

Timing

South Dublin Bay is interesting at any season, but is best from late July through to May. The South Wall and the West Pier are best at high tide, when the feeding divers, grebes and ducks come closest. The sandy beach is best a couple of hours before high tide, when the feeding waders and gulls are pushed close to the road.

CALENDAR

Autumn: Common Scoter, possibility of Little Gull, terns including Roseate Tern and occasionally Black Tern, waders.

Winter: Brent Goose. Eurasian Wigeon, Common Scoter, Common Goldeneye, Long-tailed Duck, Red-breasted Merganser, Red-throated and Great Northern Divers, Great Crested Grebe, Sanderling, Purple Sandpiper, gulls including likelihood of Mediterranean, Ring-billed, Iceland and Glaucous Gulls, Black Redstart, Snow Bunting.

Spring: late ducks, divers, grebes, waders, Whimbrel, arriving terns.

81 SKERRIES

OSI Discovery map: sheet 43
O25 60

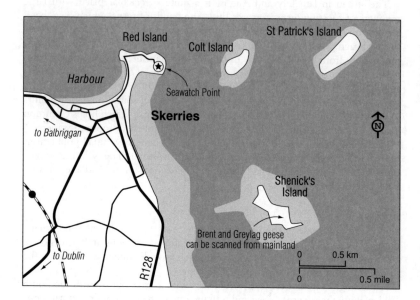

Habitat and Species

Skerries is a small coastal village with a largely stony shoreline and several small flat-topped islands offshore. The shoreline holds wintering Brent Geese (up to 200 in late winter), Eurasian Wigeons (up to 350), Oystercatchers, Ringed and Grey Plovers, Dunlins, Sanderlings, Redshanks and Curlews. On the islands a few Greylag Geese winter each year.

Large numbers of gulls winter on the shoreline. Up to 2,000 Great Black-backed Gulls congregate in September, but numbers are reduced in winter to 500–700. Both Iceland and Glaucous Gulls are regular.

This is a good seawatching spot. Good passage of Manx Shearwaters and Fulmars is recorded and small numbers of European Storm-petrels pass between July and October. Arctic, Great and Pomarine Skuas are seen each autumn and Long-tailed Skuas have been recorded in some years.

In summer there are breeding Shags, Cormorants and Great Black-backed, Lesser Black-backed and Herring Gulls on the islands. Roseate Terns breed on Rockabill Island about 6 km off the coast and can be seen from Skerries in summer when they fish along the coastline.

Access

Skerries is easily visited by car, train or bus. The harbour lies north of Rush and is reached by turning right off the main Dublin–Belfast road about 5 km north of Swords. Follow the signposts through Lusk to Skerries.

82 HOWTH HEAD

OSI Discovery map: sheet 50
O29 39

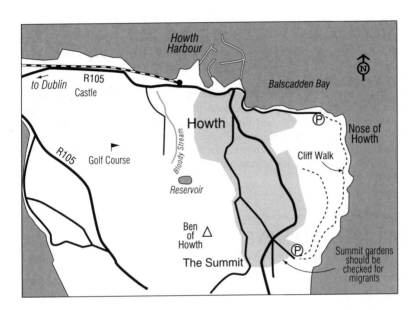

Habitat and Species

At the northern extremity of Dublin Bay the hilly promontory of Howth Head drops sharply to the sea at its north-east and eastern sides, the resulting cliffs providing nest sites for a growing seabird nesting colony. There are a number of gardens, many of which are not accessible, but some between Howth Harbour and Balscadden can be viewed.

There were only a few gulls, some Black Guillemots and a handful of pairs of Manx Shearwaters breeding here in the late 1940s. The shearwaters are unlikely to still nest, though nobody knows for certain, but there are now over 100 Fulmar nest sites, 1,700 Kittiwake nests, several hundred pairs of breeding Common Guillemots and Razorbills, a few pairs of Cormorants and Shags, several Black Guillemot nest sites and small numbers of gulls. Up to the early 1980s, there were about 1,000 pairs of Herring Gulls nesting here, but numbers have declined drastically. The breeding colony is easily seen. A small roof-nesting population in the village has not declined with the coastal population.

Seabird passage can be worthwhile. Manx Shearwaters often occur in good numbers and Arctic and Great Skuas are fairly frequent. European Storm-petrels are regular from July to October. Rarer species seen off Howth Head include Sooty Shearwater, Pomarine and Long-tailed Skua.

Passerine migrants certainly appear on the Head, but many of the best looking sites are in very private gardens. However, an area of hillside near Balscadden on the north-east side of the Head produced Radde's Warbler, Pallas's Warbler and a number of other rare migrants in October 1988, and local birdwatchers usually find migrant Ring Ouzels and Grasshopper Warblers here in early May without too much difficulty. Blackcaps, Garden Warblers, Whinchats and the occasional Common Redstart are regular in autumn.

Access

Howth Harbour is readily accessible by bus. The harbour itself should be looked at for interesting gulls. Then walk east along Balscadden Road and follow the track which leads along the top of the cliff. From this path, many of the nesting seabirds can be seen.

Seabird watching can be carried out from the Nose of Howth, but the cliffs are dangerous and great care should be taken if visiting them. Passerine migrants should be searched for in the trees and on the hillside around the north-east side of the head, in the gardens between the harbour and the car park at Balscadden, and in the gardens near the Baily lighthouse. Remember that all these gardens are private property and should not be entered without permission.

83 IRELAND'S EYE   OSI Discovery map: sheet 50
O28 41

Habitat and Species

Just to the north of Howth Head lies the small island of Ireland's Eye. The island has grassy slopes with steep cliffs on the north-east corner and a sheer stack offshore. There is a Martello tower at the north-west corner.

The island has an important seabird breeding colony. Its small Gannet colony is the most recent in Ireland. Breeding commenced in 1989, and by 2005 there were 300 nests. The most numerous nesting birds are Kittiwake (1,000 nests), Common Guillemot (over 2,000 pairs) and Razorbill (over 800 pairs). Fulmars, Cormorants, Shags and Black Guillemots also breed and there is a small colony of Great Black-backed, Lesser Black-backed and Herring Gulls. As elsewhere along the coast, the Herring Gull population has collapsed in recent years. There were over 1,000 nests in the early 1970s, but now there is only a handful. A very few Puffins nest here.

Shelduck, Oystercatcher, Ringed Plover and Common Whitethroat also breed on the island. Manx Shearwaters were believed to be nesting and were proved to do so in the early 1950s.

Access

The only way to visit Ireland's Eye is by boat. During the summer, trips operate for the public from Howth Harbour. To see the seabirds and particularly the Gannets well, ask the boatman to take the boat around the entire island.

84 BALDOYLE ESTUARY

OSI Discovery map: sheet 50
O24 41

Habitat and Species

Baldoyle is the smallest of the impressive chain of estuaries which stretches along the Dublin coast from Rogerstown to Dun Laoghaire, and it is also the one most damaged by the growth of *Spartina anglica*. The estuary is a narrow

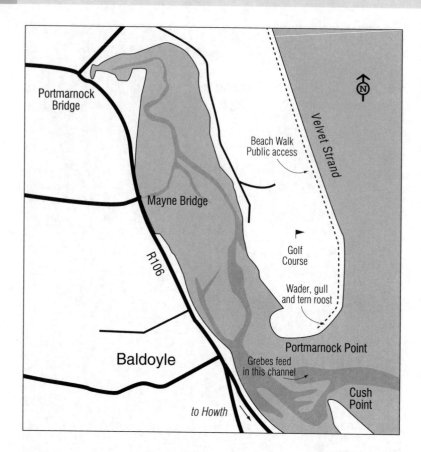

finger-like bay, sheltered from the sea by sand dunes which provide, as at Malahide and the North Bull, an excellent surface for golf links. The head of the estuary, near the village of Portmarnock, is like a field of *Spartina* and rather few birds are found.

In winter, surface-feeding ducks congregate around the freshwater stream which enters the estuary at Mayne Bridge. Small numbers of Shelducks, Eurasian Wigeons, Common Teals and Pintails are found. Further south in the estuary, Brent Geese and waders feed at low tide. The species are similar to those found at the nearby North Bull: Oystercatcher and Dunlin are the most numerous.

The beach on the seaward side of Portmarnock sand dunes holds good numbers of Sanderlings and large numbers of gulls. Offshore there are usually Red-throated and Great Northern Divers, Great Crested Grebes, Common Scoters and Red-breasted Mergansers. One or two Slavonian Grebes are usually here in winter. The inlet to the estuary at high tide is probably the best place on the Dublin coast for seeing this species.

A few pairs of Ringed Plovers nest at Portmarnock Point and Sandwich Terns use this area as a roost.

Access

The estuary can be watched easily from the road between Sutton and Portmarnock which runs along the west side of Baldoyle Bay. The strand can be walked from Portmarnock.

85 KNOCK LAKE

OSI Discovery map: sheet 43
O19 60

Habitat and Species

Although there are many fine saltwater wetlands in Co Dublin, there are few decent freshwater habitats and Knock Lake is about the best. The small lake is artificial and provides a water supply to the town of Balbriggan, but it is a well-watched site and has turned up many good birds over the years. It supports regular winter flocks (in small numbers) of diving ducks and Whooper Swans as well as Co Dublin's only regularly breeding Great Crested Grebes.

Access

Going north from Dublin on the M1, take the first exit for Balbriggan and continue towards Balbriggan for about 1 km. Turn left at the signpost for Bog of the Ring (itself an area of wet pasture that sometimes floods in winter), and then after a short distance take the right-hand fork. The lake is located about 500 m on the right-hand side of this road.

The lake can be viewed adequately from the road, but you can also enter through the gate and walk as far as the bird hide, which is accessible only to key holders but provides a vantage point to search all of the hidden corners of reedbed and shoreline.

WICKLOW

The landscape of Wicklow is dominated by the granite and slate of its mountains, contrasting sharply with the limestone lowlands of Dublin.

West and central Wicklow is mountainous and still has a considerable area of blanket bog. The highest mountain in Ireland outside Kerry is Lugnaquilla, but there are a number of other peaks jutting up from the spine of land over 300 m which runs down the centre of the county.

Some of the bog on these mountains has been drained and coniferous forests planted on it and the rough pasture and heath land farther down the hillsides. Below the rough pasture is permanent pasture with numerous hedges and small deciduous plantations. The whole area provides habitat for Ravens, Common Buzzards, Peregrines, European Stonechats, Chaffinches, Siskins, Linnets, Reed Buntings and, in summer, Whinchats and Grasshopper Warblers. The coniferous plantations at Cruagh Wood, Coronation Plantation and Lough Tay provide habitat for Common Crossbills which should be looked for between July and September.

There are a number of fine stands of deciduous woodland which provide breeding habitat for Goldcrests, Common Chiffchaffs, Blackcaps and a small number of Garden Warblers, Wood Warblers and Common Redstarts. Pied Flycatchers have bred on occasions in the past and should be looked for. A Red Kite introduction program commenced in 2006. All of the mountain streams support Dippers along their length and Goosanders are breeding along the more secluded stretches of the rivers. The oakwoods at the Vale of Clara and the Glen of the Downs, the mixed woods at the Devil's Glen, Shillelagh and Glendalough and the hazel woods at Glenasmole are examples of a relatively scarce Irish habitat and 2009 brought the exciting news that several pairs of Great Spotted Woodpeckers were found breeding in these woods.

The coast is mainly low-lying, but is broken by the promontories of Bray Head and Wicklow Head where seabirds nest. Behind the sandy and shingle beach, which runs from Greystones to Wicklow, is low-lying poorly drained pasture and reedbeds with several small pools at Kilcoole and Newcastle and a lagoon at Broad Lough. There is another small pond at Arklow, used in summer for boating, but interesting in winter for birds. The sandy beach from Wicklow town south extends on eventually to Wexford Harbour.

Wicklow has a large body of standing water at Blessington Reservoir in the north-west comer of the county near the Dublin border. Several other lakes in the mountains such as Lough Tay, Lough Dan, the Glendalough lakes and the Vartry Reservoir are deep and only occasionally good for wild swans or a few ducks, most especially Goosander.

86 KILCOOLE

OSI Discovery map: sheet 56
O31 07

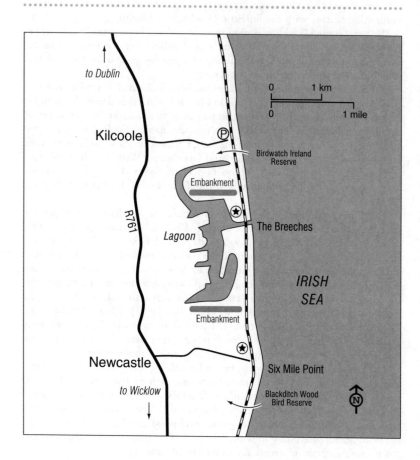

Habitat

Kilcoole marsh lies south of Greystones on the flat stretch of lowland lying behind the shingle bank stretching south to Wicklow Head. The railway line from Dublin to Wexford runs along the bank. It consists of a series of channels where small streams meander about the fields before converging and cutting through the shingle bank to the sea. The cut, known as the 'breeches', carries the tide in as well as providing an exit for the river. Hence the channels are muddy and estuarine in appearance. Scattered about the area are a number of small, brackish pools. In recent years embankments have been built to restrict the effect of flooding and sheep have grazed the grassland.

Species

In winter quite large numbers of wildfowl use this area. Up to 400 Greylag Geese, 800 Brent Geese and small numbers of Whooper Swans are perhaps the most spectacular. The largest numbers of Brent Geese are seen in March when they move onto grassland, having exhausted the easier pickings on the north Dublin estuaries, though they return to Dublin Bay each evening to roost. Some hundreds of Eurasian Wigeons, Common Teals and Mallards also winter. A few Pintails, Shovelers, Gadwalls and Shelducks also occur in most winters.

Wader numbers are lower than on the nearby north Dublin estuaries as would be expected. Curlews and Redshanks are much the most numerous species, but there is diversity. Ruffs, Little Stints, Spotted Redshanks and Green Sandpipers are probably annual. Rarities seen in recent years include White-rumped Sandpipers, Long-billed Dowitcher and Red-necked Phalarope. Ringed Plovers and Oystercatchers both breed.

Off the beach Red-throated Divers are scattered along the shore in winter. Little Gulls appear with more frequency and in greater numbers than anywhere else in Ireland. The largest numbers are usually in February and several hundred are seen in most years at Greystones, with smaller numbers farther south at Kilcoole.

In summer Little Terns and Ringed Plovers nest on the beach. The Little Tern colony has been very successful in most recent years, partly because of regular wardening and the construction of enclosures around the nests to protect them. In autumn sea passage can be sizeable. Large numbers of Manx Shearwaters pass and occasional Great and Arctic Skuas are among them.

Migrant passerines are often present on this coast in spring and autumn, especially Whinchats in autumn, and several species of bird of prey are regular. Common Buzzard, Kestrel and Merlin are the most regular in winter but Hen Harrier, Peregrine and Sparrowhawk are occasional, and Marsh Harrier sometimes appears in spring and autumn.

Access

Much the best way to see the birds of this coast is to walk south along the side of the railway track from Greystones. This gives opportunities to see birds at sea, on the beach and on the fields to the north of Kilcoole. Walk at least as far as the breaches before turning back and walking to Kilcoole railway station where a road leads up to Kilcoole village and a bus stop. Alternatively, the visitor can walk as far as Newcastle railway station where a similar road leads to a bus stop in Newcastle village.

For a quick inspection of the marsh, travel to Kilcoole village and turn left there for the strand. Park the car at the car park by the railway station and walk south along the side of the railway track. The marsh is private property and should not be entered upon.

Timing

Kilcoole is best in autumn and winter for wildfowl and waders. Early spring is the best time for Little Gulls and summer is obviously the time for nesting Little Terns. A calm day makes birdwatching easiest at Kilcoole. The state of tide makes very little difference.

87 BLACKDITCH BWI RESERVE

OSI Discovery map: sheet 56
O31 03

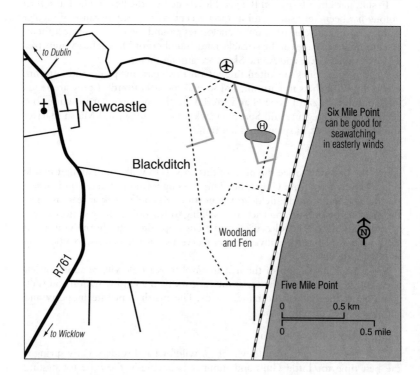

Habitat and Species

Blackditch is a new bird reserve in which BirdWatch Ireland have invested considerable effort in creating a fen-like freshwater marsh and outlying fields to attract wintering geese. The reserve has been developed to provide facilities for visitors such as hides and footpaths. The reserve can also be viewed from the coastal path which runs along the railway track. This area is mostly reedbed and birch, alder and willow woodland, and is recommended in summer when Sedge Warbler, Grasshopper Warbler and a variety of woodland species can be seen.

Access

The entrance to the reserve is reached by taking the Sea Road east from Newcastle village to the coast at Sixmilepoint. There is an entrance on the right-hand (south) side of this road. You can gain access to the southern part of the reserve by taking the coastal path south from Sixmilepoint along the railway track and entering the reserve midway along its eastern boundary. Facilities at the Reserve are still under development but it is hoped that improvements in the future will permit wheelchair access.

88 BROAD LOUGH

OSI Discovery map: sheet 56
T30 96

Habitat

Broad Lough lies about 10 km south of Kilcoole and is in a similar situation behind the shingle bank. However, it is a much broader expanse of water, though the edge is muddy and estuarine in appearance because of the tidal inflow at the southern end. The Vartry river reaches the sea through Broad Lough after flowing east from Ashford and the Devil's Glen. The lough is long, narrow and very shallow at the southern end; at its northern extremity it broadens out into a reed-fringed lake. Shooting is prohibited and the area is a BirdWatch Ireland reserve by arrangement with certain of the local landowners. The site is not wardened.

Species

This is an excellent site for wintering swans, geese and ducks. Mute Swans are the commonest swan species, but Whooper Swans occur most winters and Bewick's Swans are occasionally seen in hard weather. A flock of 300–350 Greylag Geese moves between this lough and Kilcoole to the north and appears to be expanding in size. Small numbers of Shelducks and larger numbers of Common Teals, Eurasian Wigeons and Mallards winter. Occasional parties of Greenland White-fronted Geese spend a few days but this is not a regular site.

The most common waders are Curlews and Redshanks, but most of the common species occur in small numbers in autumn and winter.

There is a fine roost of gulls and terns in autumn, and both Little and Mediterranean Gulls are regular.

This site would repay much more frequent observation in autumn as it seems ideal for passage migrants. It attracts migrating Ospreys, which usually spend a few days fishing in the lough, almost every year.

In summer Reed, Sedge and Grasshopper Warblers breed. Bearded Tits have bred here in the past. This is an ideal site for seeing Water Rails with their chicks in late June or July. Normally very elusive, the birds show well on calm mornings and evenings.

Access

Broad Lough is approached most readily from Wicklow town. Travel north along the seafront and out onto the grassy path which runs north along the edge of the sea. At the end of the path there is a turnstile on the left where the railway track can be crossed. The lough can be approached from here.

Timing

This is best from autumn through winter to spring. As with Kilcoole, the state of tide does not matter greatly.

CALENDAR

Autumn: early ducks, Little Egret, Osprey, waders including Dunlin, possibility of Little Stint, Ruff, Curlew, Redshank, Greenshank, Green Sandpiper.

Winter: occasional Whooper Swans, regular Greylag Goose, Eurasian Wigeon, Common Teal, possibility of Shoveler, Little Egret, Common Buzzard, Dunlin, Curlew, Redshank, Little Gull.

Spring: late ducks and waders, Little Gulls.

89 BRAY HEAD

OSI Discovery map: sheet 56
O28 17

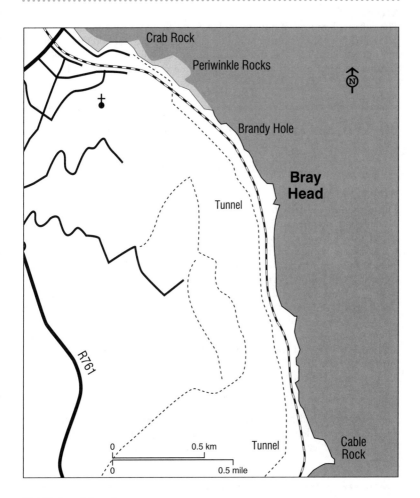

Habitat and Species

Bray Head has the only cliffs between Dublin Bay and Wicklow Head. A granite cliff rises from the sea for about 25 m to the Dublin to Wexford railway track which runs round the headland. Above the railway line, the cliff rises another 50–70 m to a public footpath. Above the path there are further cliffs.

The cliffs below the railway hold a colony of nesting seabirds of which the Black Guillemots are the most striking, being easily visible from the train as it passes the cliffs. About 80 pairs of Fulmars, a few Cormorants, Shags and Herring Gulls, over 500 pairs of Kittiwakes, 100 pairs of Razorbills, over 200 pairs of Common Guillemots and about 50 pairs of Black Guillemots breed.

Manx Shearwaters have been heard calling over the head in summer but have never been conclusively proven to breed. An interesting investigation would be a search for birds outside nesting burrows in summer. A Puffin was seen here in 1987, but breeding has not been proved. Ravens also nest on these cliffs.

Access
The cliffs are best viewed from the public footpath which runs around the headland, above the line of the railway. Direct access to the seabird cliffs is difficult and not advisable, both because it is dangerous and likely to cause unnecessary disturbance. Most of the birds can be seen quite well from the footpath.

90 WICKLOW HEAD
OSI Discovery map: sheet 56
T34 92

Habitat and Species
This is the most easterly projecting headland south of Co Down and, while it has cliffs with nesting seabirds, it is at least as important as a birdwatching site for its potential for seawatching and passerine migrants.

The nesting seabirds are rather similar to those at Bray Head to the north and include Fulmars, Shags, Herring Gulls, Great Black-backed Gulls, Kittiwakes, Common Guillemots, Razorbills and Black Guillemots. The colony is doing well, with most species increasing. Peregrines and Ravens also nest here.

The headland is an excellent seawatching site and the trees and hedges on the way out to the head provide cover which looks ideal for land migrants. There is more cover to the south of the head which could be good for holding birds after a fall. In recent years, Pied Flycatcher, Black Redstart and Yellow-browed Warbler have been seen in autumn and Wood Warbler and good numbers of Grasshopper Warblers in spring.

Access
The head is reached by driving south from Wicklow town on the main road for Wexford. Turn left down a narrow road about a kilometre after leaving the town. This road leads to the lighthouse at the tip of the head.

91 BLESSINGTON RESERVOIR
OSI Discovery map: sheet 56
N99 14; O1 10

Habitat and Species
The large reservoir at Blessington, which supplies much of the water for Dublin city, is an excellent site for Greylag Geese and ducks.

Between 700 and 900 Greylag Geese occur in winter, but numbers vary throughout the season, probably because there is movement to and from the nearby coast. Small numbers of Greenalnd White-fronted Geese and Whooper Swans occur as well. Eurasian Wigeon, Common Teal, Mallard, Pochard, Tufted Duck and Common Goldeneye all winter. Mallard and Tufted Duck nest, as does Common Sandpiper.

This lake holds a large winter flock of Lesser Black-backed Gulls. While the ducks are scattered around the lake, the geese tend to prefer the south-western end near Valleymount.

Access
The road provides access to most of the reservoir. Drive south-west from Dublin through Tallaght and on to Blessington. Follow the road around the reservoir, stopping when birds are seen.

92 GLENDALOUGH

OSI Discovery map: sheet 56
T11 96

Habitat and Species
Glendalough, with its monastic settlement and spectacular views of two lakes and high cliffs, is a famous Wicklow beauty spot and is much visited by tourists in summer. The birdwatcher will be attracted more by the deciduous wood-lands which provide nest sites for a wider diversity of species than can be found in most Irish counties. As well as Chaffinches, Common Chiffchaffs, Robins and Wrens, these woods hold Sparrowhawks, Blackcaps and a small scattering of Wood Warblers and occasional Common Redstarts. Above the woods, on the rocky slopes, one or two Ring Ouzels breed, but they are extremely difficult to

find. A visit in May or early June is essential for seeking these passerines, as they are best picked up on song – early morning is best. Wood Warblers can usually be found in the pines beside the car park.

Grasshopper Warblers breed by the lower lake and Goosanders breed around the upper lake. Dippers can be seen throughout the year on the stream between the two lakes. In winter there are sometimes Whooper Swans on the lakes.

Access

Take the road to Laragh, and follow the signposts to Glendalough, about 3 km west of the village. There is a large public car park and a number of walks through the woodland on the southern side of the lakes.

Wren

93 GLENMALURE

OSI Discovery map: sheet 56
TO6 94

**Boulders and scree
above car park should be checked
for Ring Ouzel**

Peregrines also found in this area

Youth Hostel

**Spruce forest
in this area
is good for
crossbill and siskin**

Baravore
Car Park

GLENMALUR

Ballinatunshoge

N

Clonkeen

to Rathdrum

0   0.5 km

0   0.5 mile

Habitat and Species

Much wilder than Glendalough, this Wicklow valley is long, rugged and
glaciated. There is a rocky hillside on the north-east side of the road which may
still hold Ring Ouzels. They are difficult to find, but can sometimes be picked
up by listening for their distinctive call. The Glenmalure river tumbles down
the valley and there are several patches of deciduous wood which hold
Blackcaps and, at times, Wood Warblers and Common Redstarts as well as the
commoner breeding birds.

Common Buzzards and Peregrines nest in this area and there is also the
possibility of Merlin and Hen Harrier. Kestrels are common. Red Grouse nest
on the open moor, though they are nowhere numerous.

Access

Drive south from Laragh on the road for Rathdrum. After 2 km take the turn
to the right which rises through Derrybawn wood (another good site for Wood
Warbler) onto open mountain. This is an old military road built to provide
access for the British army to rebel retreats. Follow the road until you reach the
cross roads at Drumgoff Bridge in Glenmalure. Turn right here and follow the
road up to the car park at Baravore. This is a good stopping place and one of
the best sites for finding Ring Ouzel. Peregrine, Raven, Siskin and Lesser
Redpoll can usually be seen (or heard) from the car park and Common
Crossbills can be found in the plantation opposite it.

94 ROUNDWOOD RESERVOIRS

OSI Discovery map: sheet 56
O19 03; O21 01

Habitat and Species

This is a large water-supply reservoir, one of several in the Wicklow mountains to supply water to Dublin. The open water and the surrounding woodlands all hold some interest for birders but this is a rather large area and the birds are thinly distributed. Winter is the best time to visit when there are small groups of ducks on the reservoir, Greylag Geese and Whooper Swans in the surrounding fields and, if you are lucky, Bramblings and Common Crossbills in the woods. The reservoirs also offer the opportunity to see one or two Goosanders from the small but increasing population in Co Wicklow.

Access

The best place to start is the bridge across the south reservoir immediately east of Roundwood village. This enables you to scan both sides of the bridge and the shoreline. The coniferous woods on both sides of the bridge can be good for Common Crossbills. Continue east past the bridge and take the first right then drive about 3 km to the southern end of the reservoir where the waterworks are located. You may drive across the dam and scan from there. Continue back towards Roundwood village along the west shore of the lake and check any stubble fields or beech woods for Brambling in winter.

Continue north from Roundwood on the R755 which goes along the west shore of the north reservoir. About 5 km north of Roundwood there is a right-hand turn which brings you to a causeway over the north reservoir. This is also a good point to scan the north reservoir. The area north of the causeway is quite shallow and muddy, particularly when water levels are low and is usually frequented by flocks of Northern Lapwings and Curlews.

WEXFORD

Wexford is one of the best birdwatching counties in Ireland, with a list of species recorded second only to that of Cork. Its location in the south-east of the country marks the first landfall for many spring migrants returning from Africa; its estuaries and lagoons are habitat for a diversity of wildfowl and wader species; the great reclaimed slob lands in Wexford Harbour are the best goose wintering area in the country; and the relatively short distance from Dublin means that it is well watched.

The eastern coastline is low-lying, with long sandy beaches backed by fine dune systems. The shallow waters here provide feeding for seaducks, divers and grebes. Wexford Harbour is the only estuary facing east, but the extensive mud-flats, with the reclaimed land on either side, make it one of the most important wetland habitats in Ireland. Carnsore Point, at the south-east corner of Ireland, is a good seawatching point. The south facing coastline has a spectacular choice of bird habitats.

The brackish lagoons of Lady's Island Lake and Tacumshin hold a rich diversity of wildfowl and waders. Farther west the muddy estuaries at The Cull and Bannow Bay are typical of the series of estuaries which stretch right along the south coast of Ireland to west Cork. Offshore, the Saltee Islands have over 50,000 breeding seabirds on the cliffs and Great Saltee is also one of the best migration watchpoints in the country. Hook Head, on the western edge of the county, does not have large seabird breeding colonies but rivals Saltee in the number of scarce passerine migrant species seen. It is also a good seawatching point.

Inland, the Blackstairs Mountains in the north-west of the county hold small numbers of Red Grouse. Farming is varied and the county has a great deal of tillage. Many wooded areas remain, however, and these are the habitat for the common woodland songbirds.

The slow-moving River Slaney flows through the middle of the county. In its lower reaches, extensive reedbeds hold nesting Sedge Warblers and, increasingly, Reed Warblers as well as Reed Buntings, Moorhens and Water Rails.

So, while Wexford is a very rich county ornithologically, the accounts which follow will concentrate on the major sites. This should not deter the visitor from exploring the many other parts of this wonderful county.

95 NORTH SLOB

OSI Discovery map: sheet 77
T07 24

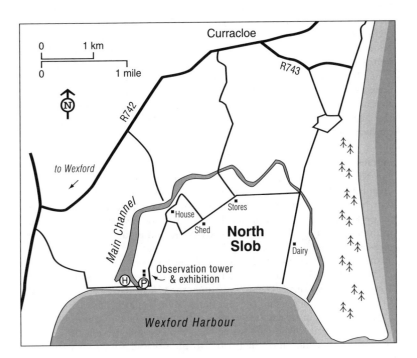

Habitat

The North Slob, on the north side of Wexford Harbour, consists of 1,000 ha of low-lying land reclaimed from the sea in the 1840s. A dyke constructed from just north of Raven Point at the entrance to Wexford Harbour to the shore near Wexford town enclosed a large area of intertidal mud and several islands. These islands remain as low undulations on the otherwise flat expanse of farmland. A wide channel runs through the west, north and east of the Slob and this collects much of the rainwater which drains off the land. Drainage ditches separate many of the fields and empty into larger channels. A pump station at the southern edge of the channel is operated by the North Slob Commissioners to ensure that surplus water is pumped into Wexford Harbour.

The land has been farmed since it was reclaimed and there are four groups of farm buildings, a dwelling house on Begerin Island, and a complex of buildings surrounding a reception area for the Wexford Wildfowl Reserve. Begerin Island has a cluster of deciduous trees and there are stands of conifers nearby. Otherwise, a small number of rows of hedges provide what cover there is on this flat landscape. A network of untarred roads provides access for farm vehicles and reserve workers to all the fields.

Up to the late 1940s, the land was largely pasture with a relatively small amount of tillage. In the early 1960s most of the North Slob was acquired by one landowner who drained the fields very effectively, making it possible to grow larger areas of cereal and tillage. In 1968, the Irish government and the Irish Wildbird Conservancy jointly purchased 100 ha and obtained a long lease of another 50 ha, and these lands were kept under pasture. A resident warden has been present since 1968 and the observation tower, hide and reception area were opened to the public in 1974. In 1990 a further 90 ha were purchased, again jointly by the government and BWI, thus enlarging the reserve substantially. The South Slob, which is located on the south side of Wexford Harbour, has similar habitat but is privately owned and not open to the public.

An extensive area of sand dunes borders the eastern edge of the North Slob, stretching from the Raven Point north to Curracloe and Ballinesker. These have been planted with conifers. Offshore the shallow seas provide rich feeding for divers, grebes and seaducks.

Species

The North Slob is famous for its geese. From October to April thousands of Greenland White-fronted Geese feed on the Slobs. In recent years the total on both North and South Slob has reached 7,000 birds, reduced somewhat from the peak numbers recorded in the 1990's. The birds are suffering competition on their breeding grounds from Canada Geese and productivity has been low in recent years.

Among the Greenland White-fronted Geese each winter are a small number of Pink-footed Geese and, in most winters, a blue- or white-morph Snow Goose and a few Canada Geese. Sometimes the Canada Geese are of one of the very small subspecies, indicative of a transatlantic origin rather than an escape from a collection in Ireland or a wanderer from the feral population in Britain. Brent Geese feed in the harbour and increasingly also use the fields on the southern side of the North Slob close to the sea wall. Other geese recorded include Greylag and Barnacle Geese (both regular in the past but now very rare), Russian White-fronted Goose (a few in most winters), Bean Goose (very rare) and Lesser White-fronted Goose (once).

The North Slob is one of the few remaining places in Ireland where Bewick's Swans winter regularly, while Whooper Swans seem to be increasing. Mute Swans are present throughout the year.

Most of the common duck species winter on the North Slob. Shelduck, Mallard, Common Teal, Gadwall, Eurasian Wigeon, Pintail, Shoveler, Scaup,

Tufted Duck, Pochard, Common Goldeneye and Red-breasted Merganser all occur on the North Slob, though Scaup and Red-breasted Merganser are best seen from the sea wall, looking south into Wexford Harbour. Over the years the North Slob has added five species to the Irish list: Lesser White-fronted Goose, Western Sandpiper, Isabelline Shrike, Paddyfield Warbler and Pine Bunting. Other rarities have included Black Duck, American Wigeon, Blue-winged and Green-winged Teals, Lesser Scaup and Ring-necked Duck, from North America.

Off Curracloe and Ballinesker there are large rafts of wintering Common Scoters. Velvet and Surf Scoters sometimes accompany them and a scattering of divers and grebes are usually interspersed among the ducks. Great Northern and Red-throated Divers and Great Crested and Slavonian Grebes occur each winter and there is always the possibility of one of the rarer grebes.

The North Slob has large wintering numbers of Northern Lapwings, European Golden Plovers and Curlews, and smaller numbers of Little Egrets, Black-tailed Godwits, Redshanks and Dunlins. The harbour area has Oystercatchers, Ringed and Grey Plovers, Turnstones, Bar-tailed Godwits, Redshanks, Spotted Redshanks, Greenshanks and Dunlins. Rare waders recorded on the North Slob include Upland and Baird's Sandpipers, Long-billed Dowitcher and Pectoral Sandpiper as well as the first Irish Western Sandpiper, on the small pool in front of the reception area, in autumn 1992.

Birds of prey quarter the slob regularly. Kestrels and Sparrowhawks occur throughout the year. Hen Harriers, Merlins, Peregrines and Short-eared Owls are regular in winter. Hobby, Common Buzzard, Marsh Harrier, Osprey and Montagu's Harrier have all been recorded.

The farm buildings are excellent sites for watching finches in winter. Greenfinches and Chaffinches are common and there are usually some Tree Sparrows and a few Bramblings among them.

Timing

The best time to visit the North Slob is from October to April when geese are present. A visit in August or September can sometimes coincide with migrant waders. The state of the tide does not make much difference, but it is important to avoid visiting the Slob on the morning of a shoot. There are organised shoots on the area of the North Slob outside the reserve at weekends: the entire Slob appears relatively birdless after the disturbance so check with the warden in advance. Most of the birds seek refuge on the South Slob at these times.

Access

The North Slob is approached from the road north from Wexford to Gorey. After crossing the bridge in Wexford town, drive for about 3 km to the first right turn. This is signposted for the Wexford Wildfowl Reserve and the turn is situated just before a garage on the right-hand side. Follow the narrow road for 1.5 km to the car park and reception area. There is an observation tower at the reception area from which much of the North Slob can be scanned. The Pat Walsh hide and the Pump House hide (wheelchair-accessible) provide viewing of the main channel; the harbour can be examined from the sea wall. Access to the rest of the North Slob is restricted.

To view the Curracloe area, return to the reception area and leave the Slob. Take the first turn to the right and follow the road around to Curracloe. The

Greenland White-fronted Geese

scoter flocks can be seen from the sand dunes by taking one of the right turns off the road which runs north along the edge of the dunes.

Contact details: Wexford Wildfowl Reserve, North Slob, Wexford (telephone 053 23129)

CALENDAR

All year: Mute Swan, Mallard, wildfowl collection (for those who must see geese out of season !), Great Crested Grebe, Little Egret, Kestrel, Sparrowhawk, Tree Sparrow.

Autumn: early geese, ducks, waders, possibility of Marsh Harrier, terns and possible Black Terns, some passerine migrants.

Winter: Whooper and Bewick's Swan, Greenland White-fronted, Pink-footed and Brent Geese, possibly Snow Goose and Canada Goose; Common and Velvet Scoters, divers and grebes at Curracloe; Peregrine, Merlin, Spotted Redshank, Ruff, Short-eared Owl, finches.

Spring: Whooper and Bewick's Swans, Greenland White-fronted Goose, Pink-footed Goose, Brent Goose; scoters, divers, grebes and at Curracloe; terns in Wexford Harbour.

Summer: Black-tailed Godwits summering; terns in Wexford Harbour.

Note: The map of the North Slob is redrawn from the Wexford Wildfowl Reserve map.

96 CURRACLOE

OSI Discovery map: sheet 77
T11 27

Habitat and Species

A large flock of Common Scoter winters off the coast from the North Slob, north to Curracloe. In calm conditions, this flock is worth checking for Velvet and Surf Scoters while Slavonian Grebes are regular and Red-necked Grebes are occasional.

Access

Take the R741 north from Wexford and after about 8 km turn right onto R742 (signposted) for Curracloe. Drive through Curracloe village to the beach car park and then climb the high sand-dunes to get a good vantage point to scan the sea. The south exit of the car park leads to a narrow twisting road which runs parallel to the sea behind the sand –dunes for about 2 km and arrives at the norththern perimeter of the North Slob. This area (Ballinesker) is also a good spot to scan the sea for scoters, grebes and divers.

97 ROSSLARE BACK STRAND

OSI Discovery map: sheet 77
T09 17

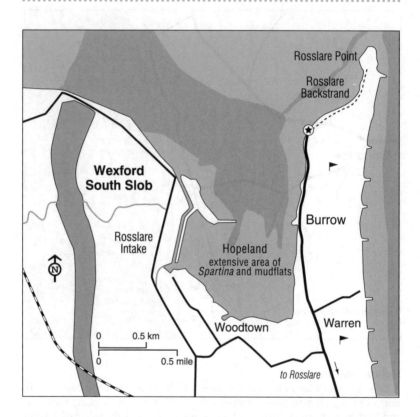

Habitat and Species

The south-east corner of Wexford Harbour, between the South Slob and Rosslare Point, is known as the Back Strand. The northern part of this area is intertidal mudflat, grading to sandy beach close to Rosslare Point. The southern part, known as Hopeland, was once reclaimed land like the Slobs, but the sea wall was breached in the 1930s and the area reverted to mudflat and saltmarsh. Much of this part of the Back Strand is infested with *Spartina*.

Many of the waders which feed in Wexford Harbour can be found here. Several hundred Oystercatchers, Ringed Plovers, Curlews, Black-tailed Godwits, Redshanks and Knots, and several thousand Dunlins, can be found here in autumn and winter. Scarcer species such as Curlew Sandpiper and Little Stint are seen in most autumns and some American species, such as White-rumped and Semipalmated Sandpipers, have been recorded. Ireland's first Terek Sandpiper was found here in 1996.

Wildfowl numbers are varied, but Brent Geese, Shelducks and Eurasian Wigeons usually feed here. In summer and autumn, terns are usually seen feeding in the area.

Access
Take the road north from Rosslare village past the golf links until Hopeland can be seen on the left. Walk on from here to Rosslare Point. Visits to Rosslare Point are best just after high tide when birds are starting to feed on the freshly exposed mud.

98 LADY'S ISLAND LAKE OSI Discovery map: sheet 77
T10 07

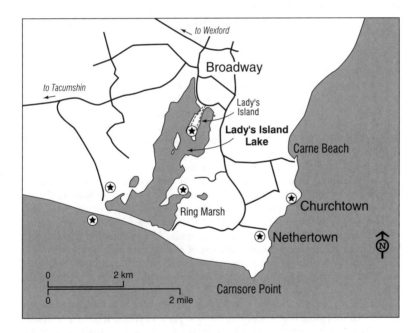

Habitat
Lady's Island Lake lies south of Rosslare, on the south coast of the county, just around the corner from Carnsore Point. The lake is about 4 km long and 2 km wide at its broadest. It is fed by a number of small streams and is impounded from the sea by a broad shingle bank. From time to time an exit channel is dug through this bank and the water level falls rapidly. Southerly gales quickly close the exit, but while it is open there can be a considerable expanse of sand and mud at the northern end of the lake providing good feeding for waders.

The lake is named after Lady's Island, a small island joined to the mainland by a broad causeway which has the ruins of a Norman castle on it. The island is a place of pilgrimage in August and prevention of flooding of the pilgrims' route around the island is the reason for cutting through the shingle bank at the southern end of the lake.

Off the west side of Lady's Island is a small, very low island named Scarageen which is completely covered by water when the level is at its highest. To the south is a larger island named Inish which is farmed.

The shoreline is stony and backed by low-lying farmland. The little village of Lady's Island is at the north end of the lake. The southern side is a shingle bank with sand dunes. In the south-east corner is an area of enormous granite boulders, many of which have been removed in recent years for building work in Rosslare.

Ring Marsh, a small lagoon and marsh, lies to the east of the lake. This lagoon has more cover than Lady's Island Lake itself and the *Phragmites* beds provide nest sites for ducks, Sedge and Reed Warblers.

At the south-west end of Lady's Island Lake there is a small isolated pool near the end of the road which has held Lesser Yellowlegs and Stone-curlew in the past. There is a farm nearby providing feeding for thrushes and finches in winter.

Species

In summer there is an important tern colony on Inish island. Sandwich Terns are the most numerous but Common, Arctic and Roseate also breed. Roseate Terns number about 70 pairs and, while Rockabill Island off the north Dublin coast has more birds, this is much the most accessible place to see the species in summer. The presence of a large tern colony can attract rare tern species and both Forster's and Elegant Terns have been recorded here as well as the American race of Black Tern. It is also an important breeding site for Black-headed Gulls and a few pairs of Mediterranean Gulls are also breeding.

Ring Marsh has breeding Great Crested and Little Grebes, Mallards, Shovelers, Tufted Ducks and Sedge and Reed Warblers. Little Grebes, Mallards, Gadwalls, Coots, Moorhens and a colony of Mute Swans nest on Lady's Island Lake itself.

The lake is an important wildfowl and wader area in autumn and winter, though numbers are not as high as at Tacumshin. All the common dabbling and diving duck species can be seen. Numbers of waders are usually low, but most of the common species occur. Curlew Sandpipers, Ruffs and Little Stints are recorded in most years. Many species of American wader have been seen over the years.

On the sea, off the south-western corner of the lake, Black-throated Divers are regular in spring. This is probably the best place in Wexford to have a reasonable chance of seeing this species. Red-throated and Great Northern Divers also occur. This corner also has a small pool with potential for vagrant waders.

Timing

Lady's Island is worth a visit at any time of the year. In spring and summer there are migrant and breeding terns; in autumn there is always the possibility of scarce migrant waders; and in winter wildfowl numbers can be high. Ring Marsh has potential as a breeding site for most species of ducks known to nest in Ireland and can also be interesting for wildfowl and waders throughout the remainder of the year.

The area is best visited in calm weather.

Access

Take the Rosslare road south from Wexford town and follow the signs for the ferry port at Rosslare Harbour. At Tagoat, about 4 km before Rosslare Harbour, take the second right turn, clearly marked for Lady's Island Lake, and drive the 4 km to the village which surrounds the large church at the north end of the lake. There is plenty of room to park a car at the causeway. A wide grassy path runs around Lady's Island and this is well worth walking. The entire north shore can be well watched from this area.

To get to the south-east corner of the lake and to Ring Marsh take the road east from the village and follow the signs for Carne Beach. At the Lobster Pot bar, about 2 km from Lady's Island, take the right turn indicated for Carnsore Point. This road deteriorates after a few kilometres and eventually reaches the south-east corner of the lake.

Ring Marsh can be reached by turning right about 2 km after the Lobster Pot and following the narrow road down to the sand dunes.

The south-west end is reached by turning left off the road to Tacumshin, about 5 km from Lady's Island, and following the narrow road down to the sea.

CALENDAR

All year: Mute Swan, Mallard, feral Greylag Goose, Little Egret.

Autumn: migrant waders including Greenshank, Curlew Sandpiper, Little Stint and possibility of American vagrants.

Winter: Whooper Swan, Eurasian Wigeon, Common Teal, Gadwall, Shoveler, Pintail, Pochard, Tufted Duck, Scaup, Common Goldeneye, Red-breasted Merganser, Coot, Oystercatcher, European Golden Plover, Northern Lapwing, Curlew, Redshank, Greenshank. Occasional Black-throated Diver on the sea. Small grebes have been seen as well.

Spring: late wildfowl and waders. Migrant terns including the possibility of Black Tern.

Summer: Shoveler, breeding Great Crested Grebe, Sandwich, Common, Arctic and Roseate Terns, Sedge and Reed Warblers.

98A NETHERTOWN

OSI Discovery map: sheet 77
T12 04

Habitat and Species

For a very small, rather unassuming beach, Nethertown has produced a wonderful selection of rare birds in recent times. It is located on the east coast of Wexford about 3 km north of Carnsore Point and can be 'done' very quickly from the rolled-down window of your car, as the road runs adjacent to the beach. Check the Dunlins and Sanderlings for vagrant Nearctic waders, or indeed even rarer species (a Red-necked Stint was found here in 2007). The offshore rocks are good in late summer and autumn for loafing terns and you can sometimes get quite good views of Common, Arctic and Roseate Terns alongside each other.

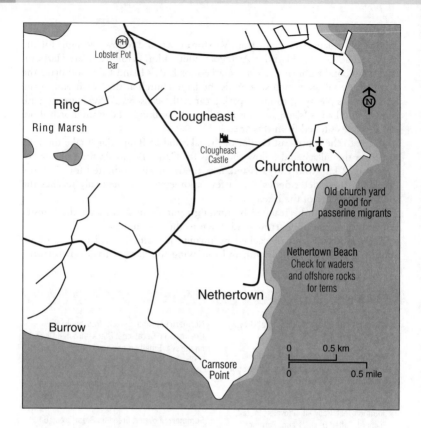

Access

Nethertown beach can be found by taking the road south from Lady's Island, take the right-hand fork at the Lobster Pot pub and after about 1.5kms tale a sharp left-hand turn down a very narrow road (this turning is easy to miss). The road reaches the beach after less than 1 km.

98B CARNSORE POINT   OSI Discovery map: sheet 77
                                                        T12 03

Habitat and Species

Carnsore Point is at the south-east corner of Ireland and well situated for watching seabird passage and passerine migration. The promontory is of granite and is low-lying with little cover.

Many seabirds breeding in the Irish Sea pass Carnsore, going to and from their feeding areas in the Atlantic. Skuas, including large numbers of Pomarine Skuas at times, occur among the Manx Shearwaters, Gannets and auks which stream past. Because the point has such a wide field of view, ranging from north-east to south-west, the glare of the sun can usually be avoided.

Diurnal migration is frequently evident in both spring and autumn. Large numbers of hirundines, Common Swifts, Skylarks, Meadow Pipits and White Wagtails can often be seen coming in from the sea or heading out, depending on the season. Although there is very little cover, warblers and flycatchers can sometimes be found on the stone walls or boulders. In recent years rarities seen here have included Honey Buzzard, Great Spotted Cuckoo, Marsh Warbler and Ireland's first Desert Wheatear.

Access
Carnsore Point is reached by following the road for the south-east corner of Lady's Island Lake (see above). Instead of turning right, take the lane to the south-east and drive through an area of bracken onto some low dunes and then east to the head. The car can be parked at the headland and you can seawatch from the car.

99 TACUMSHIN LAKE   OSI Discovery map: sheet 77
T03 07; T06 06

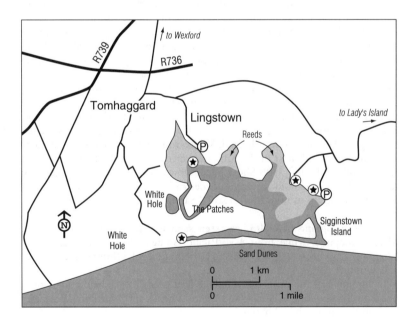

Habitat
Tacumshin is another lagoon only 2 km west of Lady's Island Lake. The water level is normally far lower than at Lady's Island, so this lagoon holds a much

greater diversity of wildfowl and, in particular, waders throughout the autumn, winter and spring. The lake is separated from the sea by a shingle bank and dune system. The lagoon is not tidal, but the water fluctuates considerably. Rainwater drains off the surrounding fields into the lagoon and evaporates in dry sunny days in summer.

Tacumshin is about 2 km from north to south and 5 km in length. There is one island at the eastern end, Sigginstown, and two at the western end, known as The Patches. The eastern island is farmed, but the two western islands are very low-lying and sandy, with *Salicornia* and other saltmarsh plants.

The south-eastern corner has a small area of saltmarsh and extensive reedbeds. The shoreline from Sigginstown around to the north-west corner has a number of reedbeds and stony beaches. The north-west corner at Lingstown has a large reedbed and a number of pools. The south-western corner has a subsidiary marsh known as The White Hole, which is separated from the main lake by a dyke and sluice.

The shingle bar at the southern edge of the lake has an extensive sand dune system, which has attracted its share of rare migrants.

Species

Tacumshin is a fine place for a visit at any time of the year. In summer there are Shelducks and Redshanks breeding on The Patches, Oystercatchers and Ringed Plovers nesting on the shingle bar and always the possibility of a vagrant wader. A large flock of moulting Mute Swans, one of the largest in Ireland, can be found here in late summer. Water Rails are a feature of Tacumshin, their squealing call being very striking to the visitor.

Autumn, however, is the peak time when birdwatchers can be found here daily. Duck numbers build up and Mallard, Common Teal, Shoveler, Gadwall, Pintail, Pochard and Tufted Duck can all be seen. Garganey is almost annual in autumn. Wader diversity is remarkable, but the area is so extensive that a thorough investigation is very difficult. As a result, the visitor should not be despondent if there are a number of birdwatchers in the area. Rare birds can turn up at any time of the day and are not always found by the earliest arrival. All the common species occur, but the Dunlin flocks should be searched thoroughly. Pectoral, Semipalmated, White-rumped and Baird's Sandpipers are near annual and most of the American species on the Irish list have been seen including the first Irish Short-billed Dowitcher. Tacumshin is legendary for its ability to hold multiple American waders; six White-rumped Sandpipers and up to nine Buff-breasted Sandpipers have been recorded in a day.

European vagrants have also been seen, such as Broad-billed Sandpiper and Marsh Sandpiper, while from Asia, Pacific Golden Plover and Sharp-tailed Sandpiper have been recorded. Marsh Harriers are regular through the summer and autumn.

In autumn large numbers of hirundines feed over the lake before migrating, occasionally attracting a Hobby, and White Wagtails and Northern Wheatears feed on the saltmarsh and beach.

In winter there are large numbers of ducks and regular winter flocks of Whooper Swans and Brent Geese. The geese and Eurasian Wigeons feed mainly on the saltmarsh on The Patches.

Early spring is probably the quietest time but Little Gulls often occur in small parties from March onwards. Later on, there is the possibility of Garganey, Marsh Harrier, Yellow Wagtail or perhaps a Little Ringed Plover.

The reality of Tacumshin is that the unexpected turns up repeatedly and at all seasons. The area is worth a visit at any time of the year.

Timing

Tacumshin is good for birds all year round. Calm conditions are best, as the waders can be approached closely when there is little wind.

The lake is most frequented by birdwatchers on weekends in September and October.

Access

A visit could start at The White Hole, working back around the lake to Sigginstown. Take the road from Wexford for Kilmore Quay. After about 12 km turn left at a sign for Tomhaggard. Bear right through the village and then turn left, after about 1 km, following the narrow road until a small parking area is reached. The White Hole can be covered from here, and then Tacumshin itself can be seen by walking eastwards until a good view of The Patches can be had.

To get a better view of the birds in the north-west corner return to Tomhaggard, and take the right turn in the village, then, after almost 1 km, take the right turn marked cuI de sac. This road leads down to the Lingstown Corner. A car can be parked and this corner of Tacumshin explored on foot. The edge of the main lagoon should be scanned and all the bays checked carefully. There are a number of pools holding birds and these all deserve scrutiny. Make your way to The Patches and walk across much of the area. Not just waders but wagtails, pipits and buntings use this part.

The eastern end can be viewed from a couple of spots. Drive back from the Lingstown corner but, instead of turning left from Tomhaggard, turn right and drive for about 5 km until a right turn comes into view, with the ruins of an old castle beside it. Turn right here and then, at the fork, turn right, following the road down to the shore. The shore to the west should be walked as the area opposite here, known as The Forgotten Corner, has held interesting birds in the past. Returning to the fork, turn right, rather than returning to the main road, and follow the narrow road to a small car park overlooking Sigginstown island. The eastern corner of the lake can be explored from here.

CALENDAR

All year: Mute Swan, feral Greylag Goose, Shelduck, Mallard, Little Egret, Moorhen, Water Rail, Oystercatcher, Ringed Plover.

Autumn: early wildfowl, including Eurasian Wigeon, Common Teal, Gadwall, Shoveler, Pintail. Marsh Harrier. Waders including Curlew Sandpiper, Little Stint, Ruff, Black-tailed Godwit, Spotted Redshank, American vagrants.

Winter: Whooper Swan, Brent Goose, ducks, Hen Harrier, waders.

Spring: terns, migrant waders, Little Gulls, other migrants.

Summer: breeding waders. Occasionally breeding terns. Breeding Reed Warblers at Tomhaggard end.

100 THE CULL

Habitat and Species

The Cull is a long, narrow estuary running from east to west parallel to the shore at Ballyteigue Bay.

The eastern part of the inlet has been reclaimed, but the western part, which extends for over 6 km and is less than 0.5 km wide, is a good wildfowl and wader site.

Ireland's largest flock of Bewick's Swans occur in winter, nearby at Killag, together with Whooper Swans and Brent Geese. Greenland White-fronted Geese are sometimes seen and small numbers of Mallards, Common Teals, Eurasian Wigeons, Shelducks and Red-breasted Mergansers winter. There are up to 1,000 waders in winter, but larger numbers in autumn. Passage species such as Common Sandpiper, Curlew Sandpiper, Little Stint and Ruff all occur occasionally. Rarities recorded here include Blue-winged Teal, Black-winged Stilt, Avocet, Western Sandpiper and Temminck's Stint.

Access

The best point for viewing The Cull is at Killag. From Kilmore Quay drive north for about 3 km to Killag. Turn left on the Duncormick road and drive for 2 km to Park. At Park, where the road turns sharp right, take the narrow lane to the left. This unsurfaced lane leads down to The Cull Bank where the pump-house can be seen. Most of the birds can be viewed from here.

101 SALTEE ISLANDS

OSI Discovery map: sheet 77
X95 97

Habitat

The two Saltee islands, Great Saltee and Little Saltee, lie between 4 and 6 km off the fishing village of Kilmore Quay. Little Saltee is about 1 km long and less than 0.5 km wide. It has no high cliffs and very little cover, and the island is no more than 30 m high. Great Saltee is a much larger island, being 2 km long and about 1 km wide at its broadest. The southern and western sides have steep cliffs, especially at the southern tip. The island slopes down to low boulder-clay cliffs overhanging the boulder beach which runs for much of the north-western shore. There are two houses on Great Saltee: an old stone farmhouse and a wooden bungalow. These are the property of the Neale family who own the island and made it a bird sanctuary. The family has erected a stone Throne near the mid-point of the island.

There are trees and the remnants of a garden around the old farmhouse and these provide cover for some passerine migrants. The island was farmed in the past but the fields are now overgrown with bracken and brambles.

Species

The seabird colony on Great Saltee is much the most impressive sight for any visitor to the island in summer, and probably the main reason why so many people take a boat trip across from Kilmore Quay. Over 25,000 pairs of birds of 12 species nest on the two Saltees. Only Cormorants breed on Little Saltee, but Manx Shearwaters, Fulmars, Gannets, Shags, Common Guillemots, Razorbills, Puffins, Kittiwakes and Great Black-backed, Lesser Black-backed and Herring Gulls all nest on Great Saltee and all, except the Manx Shearwaters, which come to land only at night, can be seen with ease.

The Gannet colony, concentrated at the high cliffs at the southern tip of the island, is expanding rapidly, and has recently spread onto the Makestone Rock close to the Throne. Breeding was first proved in 1929; by 1960 there were 60 nests, by 1970 165, by 1990 1,050 and by 2004 2,500. This rate of increase shows no sign of slowing, and there is still room for more nest sites. There are thousands of Common Guillemots, Razorbills and Kittiwakes and hundreds of Puffins. The auks and Kittiwakes breed on the cliffs or, in the case of the Puffins, above the cliffs around the southern and western sides of the island. Gulls breed on the bracken-covered fields and on the shoreline.

As well as seabirds, Shelducks, Mallards, Oystercatchers, Ringed Plovers, Common Snipes, Ravens and Choughs also breed. Very few passerines nest.

In spring and autumn, however, Saltee is a great migration watchpoint. There was a bird observatory here from 1950 to 1963, the first in Ireland, and pioneering studies were made. Nowadays, birdwatchers and bird ringers visit regularly in May and September, but there is not the intensive coverage there was in the past.

Great Saltee experiences much larger falls of migrants than any other Irish site. On a good day in spring hundreds of Willow Warblers feed in the bracken, Swallows and Cuckoos fly over, Common Redstarts and Whinchats show in ones and twos, and a rarity or two, such as a Hoopoe, Wryneck, Golden Oriole, Woodchat Shrike or Tawny Pipit, appears for a few hours. Both Black-eared Wheatear and Lesser Grey Shrike have been recorded here. In autumn these falls are not quite so spectacular, but there has been a long list of rarities including Greenish and Western Bonelli's Warblers, Olive-backed and Buff-bellied Pipits and Siberian Stonechat.

Seabird passage in autumn is not so good as off the headlands of Cork and Kerry but skuas and shearwaters can be seen when the wind is southerly or south-westerly.

Timing

The months of May to July are the best times to go to Great Saltee. In mid-May there is the chance of interesting migrant landbirds and from then on the seabirds can be seen. A calm day with bright sunshine is best, and make sure to bring a picnic.

In autumn, the days are shorter and there are few seabirds remaining. At this time of year, a visit ideally should cover several days so that there is a good chance of hitting a period of south-easterly winds which may bring a fall of migrants. Permission from the owner is required to stay overnight.

Access

The islands are privately owned but visitors are welcome to come on day trips. Provided the weather is fine, particularly if the wind is not from the north, it is usually possible to hire a boat at Kilmore Quay to take one out to Great Saltee, especially in summer (contact Declan Bates at 053 9129684). Little Saltee is difficult to land on and has far less diversity of birds, so visits are rare.

Arrangements should be made well in advance with the boatman if a trip is being planned and the visitor is travelling a considerable distance to Kilmore Quay.

Spotted Flycatcher

CALENDAR

All year: Cormorant, Shag, Great Black-backed Gull, Herring Gull, Peregrine, Oystercatcher, Raven, Chough, Meadow and Rock Pipits.

Autumn: warblers, Common Redstart, Pied and Spotted Flycatchers, scarce migrants.

Winter: the island has never been adequately watched in winter, but thrushes and finch flocks have been seen.

Spring: Willow Warbler, Common Chiffchaff, Northern Wheatear, other spring passerine migrants, returning seabirds.

Summer: nesting Fulmar, Gannet, Shag, Mallard, Northern Lapwing, Common Snipe, Common Guillemot, Razorbill, Puffin, Herring, Lesser Black-backed and Great Black-backed Gulls, Kittiwake.

102 HOOK HEAD

OSI Discovery map: sheet 77
T73 98

Habitat

Hook Head is a promontory at the eastern side of Waterford Harbour projecting far to the south. The only part of Wexford county which extends farther south is the island of Great Saltee. This position means that the headland is an excellent seawatching and passerine migration watchpoint.

The head comprises low-lying limestone. The main cover on the head is provided by dense hedgerows of blackthorn and bramble. There are also a few gardens centred around the clusters of houses at Churchtown and Slade. Otherwise, the overall impression is of a well farmed area with a number of small fields. About hall the area is tilled, most of the remainder being grazed by cattle. Slade has a fishing harbour and is dominated by the ruins of Slade Castle, the earliest part of which dates from the late 15th or early 16th century. At the tip of the headland is Hook Head lighthouse, a striking and ancient tower. There has been a tower here since the thirteenth century or earlier, and a lantern on the tower since the late 17th century.

Species

This is a headland for watching spring and autumn migration. The absence of high cliffs means that there are few suitable sites for breeding seabirds, and the breeding landbirds are those typical of south Wexford.

As a seawatching point, Hook has recorded large spring passages of Pomarine Skuas in May, as many as 191 being seen in a day. Maximum numbers of Manx Shearwaters and Gannets are also seen in spring. In autumn, in optimal south-westerly winds with mist or rain, the passage of Manx

Shearwaters, European Storm-petrels, Gannets, auks and Kittiwakes can be joined by Great and Arctic Skuas, Sooty Shearwaters and, occasionally, a Great Shearwater or Sabine's Gull.

On the land, this is the second-best spring migration site in Wexford (after nearby Great Saltee). On a good day in early or mid-May the head can have large numbers of Swallows, Common Swifts, Northern Wheatears and Willow Warblers and smaller numbers of Cuckoos, Turtle Doves, Common Redstarts, Blackcaps and Garden Warblers. Among the commoner birds are one or two rarities every year: Golden Oriole, Lesser Whitethroat, Subalpine Warbler and Woodchat Shrike are typical of the species which turn up.

In autumn, movement has been recorded from August to early November. Pied and Spotted Flycatchers, Whinchats and Blackcaps are all regular, and Icterine and Melodious Warblers, Lesser Whitethroat, Firecrest, Red-breasted Flycatcher and Red-backed Shrike have all appeared on several occasions. Major rarities recorded include Pallas's and Radde's Warblers from Siberia, Red-rumped Swallow and Lesser Grey Shrike from southern Europe and Upland Sandpiper, Bobolink, Blackpoll Warbler and Red-eyed Vireo from North America.

Choughs do not breed on the Head but a few are regular in late autumn and winter.

Timing

Hook Head is best in spring and autumn. For passerine-watching try to choose a day with light south-easterly winds. Seawatching is best, as elsewhere along the south coast, in south-westerlies with rain or mist. Birds are most active in the early morning.

Access

Hook Head is best approached from Wexford or New Ross by following the signposts for Fethard-on-Sea. In Fethard take the road south which is indicated for Churchtown and runs right to the lighthouse at the tip. The best area is from Slade south to the lighthouse and west to Churchtown. There is a small car park at the tip from where you can seawatch.

CALENDAR

All year: Cormorant, Shag, Herring Gull, Oystercatcher, Magpie, Hooded Crow, Jackdaw, Meadow Pipit, Rock Pipit, Pied Wagtail, Starling, House and Tree Sparrows.

Autumn: Manx and Sooty Shearwaters, European Storm-petrel, Gannet, Arctic and Great Skuas, Chough, scarce seabirds, warblers, Common Redstart, Pied and Spotted Flycatchers, scarce migrants.

Winter: Red-throated and Great Northern Divers, wintering European Golden Plovers, Northern Lapwing, Common Snipe, Curlew, Chough, thrushes and finches.

Spring: seabird passage, especially Pomarine Skua; Willow Warbler, Common Chiffchaff, Northern Wheatear, other spring passerine migrants.

103 BANNOW BAY

OSI Discovery map: sheet 77
S84 12; S82 09

Habitat

This broad and long bay lies at the western end of the county, close to Hook
Head. The bay is about 7 km from Wellingtonbridge, at the northern end, to
the sea and about 3 km wide at its broadest. The intertidal zone comprises very
extensive mudflats which hold large numbers of feeding wildfowl and waders.
The estuary is fed by the Owenduff and Corock rivers which meet at
Wellingtonbridge and by a number of smaller streams.

Species

Bannow Bay has rather small numbers of wildfowl. The main feature is its flock
of several hundred Brent Geese, but it also holds some hundreds of Shelducks

and Common Teals, up to 800 Eurasian Wigeons and smaller numbers of Pintails, Mallards, Common Goldeneyes and Red-breasted Mergansers.

Wader numbers are quite high, with several thousand Northern Lapwings and European Golden Plovers and over 1,000 Curlews, Redshanks and Dunlins recorded most years. There is a nice flock of 500–800 Black-tailed Godwits and small numbers of the scarcer species, such as Greenshank and Spotted Redshank, have been seen. Ruff, Sanderling and Curlew Sandpiper have been recorded.

Timing
This is of interest to the visitor principally from autumn through winter to the spring, the months August to March. Birdwatching is easiest two hours either side of high tide when the birds are forced close to the shore by the water level.

Access
Bannow Bay is a very difficult area to cover well as the mudflats are very extensive and the public road only runs along the edge of the bay at a handful of points. Try, therefore, to time a visit for high tide.

Most of the birds roost at three areas. The saltmarsh at Clonmines at the north end of the bay holds large numbers of waders and ducks. It can be viewed from the road between Wellingtonbridge and Duncormick just south of Wellingtonbridge.

The saltmarsh east of Bannow Island, in the south-east corner, is another wader roost and frequently holds most of the Brent Geese. It can be viewed by taking the road south along the east side of the bay leading to the south-east corner.

The west side of the bay and the channel in the middle can be seen best by taking the road which runs along the shoreline between Wellingtonbridge and Saltmills Just to the north-east of Saltmills the road provides excellent views.

CALENDAR

Autumn–winter–spring: Brent Goose, Shelduck, Eurasian Wigeon, Mallard, Pintail, Common Teal, Common Goldeneye, Red-breasted Merganser, Red-throated and Great Northern Divers, Little Egret, Oystercatcher, Ringed, European Golden and Grey Plovers, Northern Lapwing, Knot, Dunlin, Common Snipe, Curlew, Black-tailed and Bar-tailed Godwits, Spotted Redshank, Redshank, Greenshank, Turnstone.

---

104 CAHORE MARSHES   OSI Discovery map: sheet 77
T21 46

Habitat and Species
The marshes south of Cahore Point are mainly low-lying fields which flood in winter, rather than a permanent water-body, although there are some wide (and deep) drainage channels. For many years this area was ignored by birders in

favour of the much better-known sites in south Wexford, but recent observations have shown this area to be an important wetland site and being so close to the coast it has excellent rarity potential. Its main significance is as a refuge for a small satellite flock of Greenland White-fronted Geese which commute between here and the Wexford Slobs and also a herd of Whooper Swans with the occasional Bewick's, as well as other concentrations of wildfowl and Curlews, Northern Lapwings and European Golden Plovers.

Access

From Courtown, take the R742 south for about 10 km, passing the turnoff for Cahore in Ballygarret and turn left at Clonevin. This road takes you along the northern perimeter of the marshes. The lands are privately owned, so access is restricted and birding has to be conducted from the roadside. The road ends in a car park by the coast and you could park here and walk south along the dunes, and in the morning would have the advantage of elevation and the sun behind you to scan the marshes.

To approach from the southern end of the marshes, return to the R742, drive south for about 2.5 km and again turn left towards the coast. This road also ends in a car park by the coast. You can walk north along the sand dunes to scan the marshes.

Cahore Point itself is an underwatched coastal promontory which has potential for migrants and to scan the sea for divers, grebes and seaducks.

KILKENNY

The inland counties of south Leinster are very much understudied by bird-watchers, principally because few enthusiasts live in them and those that do find the lure of the nearby coast irresistible. Kilkenny is a large county with a variety of habitats but very few places where wildfowl congregate.

The best known wildfowl spot is Tibberoughney Bog in the south of the county on the edge of the River Suir. This is a large marsh with flooded areas of pasture. In winter the Greylag Geese, which feed at Coolfin in Waterford (see the separate account of that site), roost here. Whooper Swans and Eurasian Wigeons, Common Teals, Mallards and Tufted Ducks also occur. The area is best approached from the village of Tibberoughney, about 2 km south-east of Piltown.

There are excellent woodland sites in a number of locations, but especially in the river valleys. Jays, Barn Owls, Kestrels and Sparrowhawks are all quite widely distributed.

In winter, flocks of Northern Lapwings, European Golden Plovers, Redwings and Fieldfares are widespread.

CARLOW

Carlow is a much smaller county than Kilkenny to its west, but the birds are very similar. The only medium-sized body of standing water is an artificial pond at Oak Park, owned by the Agricultural Institute, where Common Teal, Mallard, Tufted Duck and Pochard can be seen.

There are Red Grouse on the tops of the Mount Leinster chain of mountains.

LAOIS

Laois is mainly a relatively low-lying agricultural county, but it does have the Slieve Bloom mountains on its northern border. This range holds Red Grouse and Hen Harriers; the best place to visit is The Cut, where the road runs across the summit.

There are a few wetlands. The 'Curragh' between Rathdowney and Durrow, a stretch of rough meadow along the River Erkina south of Ballacolla in the south of the county, holds a small wintering population of Greenland White-fronted Geese. These birds move about a little, generally in response to disturbance, and sometimes can be found on the flats beside the River Nore near Borris-in-Ossory or at Lough Annaghmore.

KILDARE

Kildare is a flat, low-lying county with the River Liffey, the River Barrow and the Grand Canal providing varied bird habitat. There are few notable bird-watching sites, but the county as a whole has the typical birds of the Irish mid-lands. The Curragh is a large, flat area where Northern Lapwings and European Golden Plovers winter in large numbers. Whinchats nest on the fringes of young plantations. Jays and Blackcaps can be found in the deciduous woods.

105 POLLARDSTOWN FEN

OSI Discovery map: sheet 55
N76 16

Habitat and Species

The Pollardstown Fen is fed by alkaline streams from the surrounding limestone plain and is a unique wetland in the midlands of Ireland, which are better known for acidic bogs. As such it supports a locally unique flora and is also quite good for birds. The fen is covered by extensive reedbeds and there are few open stretches of water; however, there is a patch of higher ground at the end of the entrance trail and walking the tracks affords some opportunity to see and (mostly) hear the reedbed species.

Apart from the usual breeding and winter aquatic species, this location should be checked for the occasional rarity. Indeed, with the ongoing colonisation of Ireland by Little Egret and Reed Warbler, both species should be borne in mind as well as Osprey and Marsh Harrier on passage. To further illustrate its potential a Savi's Warbler sang here for a week in 1989.

Access
The Fen is located about 3 km north-west of Newbridge. Take the R445 south from Newbridge (this is basically the continuation of the main street) for about 1 km following the signs for the Curragh Racecourse. Just before the entrance to the Racecourse Stand, turn right and then left after about 0.5 km, driving over a railway bridge and continue on this road for about 1.5 km where there is an entrance gate on the right-hand side leading to a footpath into the fen.

OFFALY

Offaly resembles the other inland counties of Leinster in a number of respects: it is low-lying apart from the Slieve Bloom mountains on its southern fringe, it has few large woods, it has very few bodies of standing water. But it has a huge advantage for the visiting birdwatcher in that its western edge is formed by the River Shannon and that several tributaries, including the Little Brosna, flow through the county.

The most northerly tributaries, the Rivers Brosna and Blackwater, which enter the Shannon at Shannon Harbour and a few kilometres to the north respectively, do not flood in winter and are not known to be of great importance for wildfowl. The Little Brosna, which looks on the map like a very similar river, has callows on either side which flood and provide wonderful habitat in winter and into spring.

The River Shannon between Athlone and Shannon Bridge has been described under the sites of Roscommon, but between Shannonbridge and Meelick on the borders of Offaly and Galway, there are a number of other areas where large numbers of wildfowl occur in winter and where Corncrakes and waders breed in summer.

106 LITTLE BROSNA

OSI Discovery map: sheet 53
N00 08

Habitat
The Little Brosna is a narrow, slow-flowing river which winds its way from the vicinity of Roscrea to Birr and then flows in a desultory fashion on to the Shannon just south of Meelick. The river in summer is popular among coarse fishermen and paths run alongside it. In autumn it floods and the surrounding meadows are inundated. Large areas of shallow water stretch for several kilometres on either side from above Newtown to the confluence with the Shannon.

The extent of flooding is variable, beginning in early autumn but with some areas remaining uncovered until late November. A system of surface drains prevents the callows, as they are known, from prolonged waterlogging.

Species
The Little Brosna is a spectacular place in late winter when thousands of Eurasian Wigeons throng the shallow waters. Among them are hundreds of Mallards, Common Teals, Pintails and Shovelers, as well as 100 or more Whooper Swans. This area has one of the largest flocks of Greenland White-fronted Geese in the country away from the Wexford Slobs. Up to 500 geese feed on the callows and on the surrounding bogs.

The sight of geese here, on callows which have flooded for millennia, is far more stirring than seeing them on the reclaimed fields of the Wexford Slobs.

The Greenland White-fronted Goose on the callows somehow seems a much wilder bird in a much more fitting habitat.

It is not just a good place for wildfowl. Wader numbers are even larger. Some of the largest concentrations of Northern Lapwings and European Golden Plovers in Ireland scatter over the callows and adjoining farmland. There are large numbers of Curlews and a flock of Black-tailed Godwits which peaks in late winter at up to 4,000 birds. Dunlin is also recorded in winter and over 1,000 can be seen at times. Redshanks, Greenshanks and, as would be expected, large numbers of Common Snipes are also to be found. Over 20,000 waders have been counted here.

The largest numbers of birds occur here in February and March, probably gathering to build up their fat reserves before returning to Iceland and other breeding grounds to the north.

Access

The entire length of the river from New Bridge, 6 km west of Birr, to Meelick on the Shannon and including Big Island and Friar's Island, is excellent for wildfowl and waders. Take the road from New Bridge along the north side of the Little Brosna and leave it where you can gain access to the callows at a sand and gravel quarry. Walk along the edge of the callows as far as Cloghan Castle, for here the largest number of birds normally occurs and they usually include the geese. It will take most of the day to work this area thoroughly

Large numbers of birds concentrate on Ashton's Callows, a south-eastern extension of the main callows (and in Tipperary), and can be observed from a BirdWatch Ireland hide which is reached by a track across a small bog south-west of New Bridge.

When both these parts have been fully checked, drive around to the Shannon at Lavagh and look across at Big Island and Friar's Island where large numbers of ducks often settle when there is shooting.

Timing

This is a late autumn, winter and spring site. Visit from September to April. If a large number of birds is your target, visit in February or March. Try to avoid weekends as there is shooting in sections, and this causes disturbance. Part of the callows is a statutory wildfowl sanctuary.

CALENDAR

Autumn–winter–early spring: Mute and Whooper Swans, Greenland White-fronted Goose, Eurasian Wigeon, Common Teal, Mallard, Shoveler, Pintail, European Golden Plover, Northern Lapwing, Dunlin, Black-tailed Godwit, Curlew, Redshank, Greenshank.

107 BULLOCK ISLAND
OSI Discovery map: sheet 53
N02 17

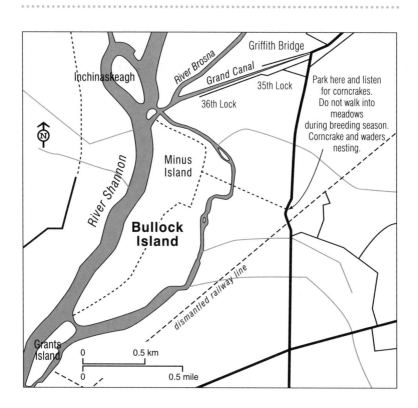

Habitat and Species

Bullock Island is an area of about 40 ha of traditional hay meadow south of Shannon Harbour on the east bank of the Shannon. It is separated from the mainland by a narrow creek on its western side. Access by tractors is over a small bridge. The island holds a number of pairs of breeding Corncrakes and a relatively high density of nesting Northern Lapwings, Common Snipes, Curlews and Redshanks. Duck species nesting in the area include Mallard, Common Teal and Shoveler.

In winter, much of the meadow floods and large numbers of Eurasian Wigeons and Common Teals feed on the island. In spring, Whimbrels stop off on migration.

Access

This is an area which should be approached with care as its main feature is breeding birds. Corncrakes can be heard easily but the other species are rather sensitive and, under no circumstances, should nests be sought out as this will cause quite unnecessary disturbance. The island is approached by turning west off the road south from Shannon Harbour.

BirdWatch Ireland has purchased some of the land on the island as a reserve for Corncrakes, and research into the biology of the species is being carried out here in summer. There is no warden present on the site, but information can be sought from the BirdWatch Ireland Midlands office, Crank House, located in nearby Banagher – tel: 05791 51676.

108 LOUGH BOORA PARKLANDS

OSI Discovery map: sheet 48
N18 20

Habitat and Species

Large tracts of the midlands of Ireland have been exploited for peat extraction, leaving behind what can look like an apocalyptic wasteland of black mud and acidic pools. However, nature does regenerate itself and with some careful management, cutaway bog can provide excellent undisturbed wildlife habitat. The Lough Boora Parklands project is an imaginative habitat restoration on tracts of cutaway bog and combines several habitats including wetland, pasture and new afforestation. The most significant species in the area is Grey Partridge. This is the last remaining population in Ireland of a species which has declined greatly due to agricultural intensification and specialisation. The area also supports breeding waders and other aquatic species as well as significant winter flocks of wildfowl and waders.

Access

There are four discontiguous areas between Tullamore and Birr, all of which present an interesting range of birds. Take the N52 west from Tullamore to Birr, after about 10 km turn right (north) at Blueball onto the R357 and continue for another 10 km until you reach a crossroads at Boora Church. Turn left at the crossroads to get to the main entrance and Boora Parklands Office, and the start of the Cycle Path road which provides access to the wetland areas and several small lakes one of which, Loch an Dóchais, has a wheelchair-accessible lakeside track.

Approximately 1 km south of the Parkland Office on the Cycle Path Road is a turn to the left towards the Model Plane Club. The fields on the left-hand (north) side of the road past the Model Plane Club is the best area for the Grey Partridges.

WESTMEATH

Westmeath is a county of lakes, popular for fishing in summer and autumn, and with good numbers of ducks in winter. The underlying geology is undulating carboniferous limestone and there are only a few hills of over 250 m. Most of the county is cattle farming country, though the farms tend to be smaller than those of Meath to the east.

The western edge of the county is bounded by Lough Ree and the River Shannon. Towards the Shannon there are large expanses of bogland.

For the birdwatcher, the principal interest is in the birds of the large lakes. These are close enough together to be visited in one day and hold quite different bird populations. Lough Ree, part of which falls within this county, has been dealt with under the accounts for Roscommon.

109 LOUGH DERRAVARAGH

OSI Discovery map: sheet 41
N40 66

Habitat

Derravaragh is a large limestone lake on the River Inny system which eventually drains into the Shannon. To the north-west of the lake is a large area of raised bog, but the long arm which runs to the south-east extends between oak-covered limestone ridges that slope steeply to the lake. Drainage of the Inny over the years has reduced the water level at Derravaragh and extensive areas of the lake bed are exposed at the north-west end. These sand and mud banks once provided feeding for regular migrant waders, but are now overgrown and less attractive to the birds.

Species

This is an excellent wildfowl site in autumn and winter. In August there is a large post-breeding congregation of Mallards, and Pochards begin to appear. In September they peak but then disperse rapidly, and from October Tufted Duck numbers increase. Peak numbers of several hundred occur and a large flock of Coots also occurs at this time. Mallard, Eurasian Wigeon, and Common Teal winter in relatively small numbers and other species, such as Shoveler and Pintail, can be seen as well. Whooper Swan is regular in winter, with a flock of over 100 being usual.

Derravaragh has potential as an inland wader site. The sandy and muddy shore in the north-west corner attracts a few passage migrants in both spring and autumn. All the usual passage migrants have been seen in the past, including Wood Sandpiper, Ruff, Little Stint and Curlew Sandpiper, and a number of American waders have also occurred, but numbers nowadays are much lower.

Skuas have been seen in autumn, and Sabine's Gull has been recorded. The lake is not watched with anything like the frequency of good wildfowl and wader spots on the coast and would repay regular visits.

Access

Lough Derravaragh lies to the north of Multyfarnham, a small town reached by turning right off the main road between Mullingar and Edgeworthstown. Follow the signpost for Multyfarnham about 9 km beyond Mullingar.

The north-west corner of the lake is approached by taking the road to the north-west from Multyfarnham, which curls around Derravaragh's western end. This narrow road crosses the Inny twice, once where it exits the lake, and again where it enters the lake. Turn right about 1 km after the first crossing of the Inny and follow the narrow road down to the lough. This point provides excellent viewing. Access to the northern corner is by following the road north-west from Multyfarnham, crossing the Inny river twice before reaching a junction. At the junction, turn right and then take the first right again (after about 2 km). This lane leads to the lake edge and provides access at several points. The south-western side can be reached from Multyfarnham by taking the road to the north-east bearing left at a fork after 1.5 km, then taking the first left-hand turn down to the lake.

Timing

This is a good lake to visit at any time from August through to May. Autumn and spring, especially August and September, are the best time to search for migrant waders. September to November usually have the highest duck numbers. Late winter could produce an unusual duck.

CALENDAR

Autumn: Pochard flocks, Redshank, Greenshank, Ruff, Wood Sandpiper, Curlew Sandpiper, possibly an American wader, possibility of skuas.

Winter: Whooper Swan, Tufted Duck and Coot flocks, Eurasian Wigeon, Common Teal, Mallard, Shoveler, flocks of Northern Lapwing and European Golden Plover.

Spring: migrant waders, late ducks.

110 LOUGH OWEL

OSI Discovery map: sheet 41
N41 58

Habitat and Species

Owel is another shallow lake on a limestone bed with marl deposits on the bottom. There are some reedbeds on the western side. The lake is the source of the water supply for the town of Mullingar and the water level fluctuates considerably. In late summer and early autumn it is often quite low and can be attractive for waders, especially around Church Island. This lake is a popular trout fishery.

Like most of the surrounding lakes, it has a sizeable population of Tufted Ducks, Pochards and Coots with up to 2,000 of each species occurring at times. The numbers of surface-feeding ducks are much higher than those of the other lakes, with Shoveler numbers being well over 100, one of the largest concentrations in the country. There are also small numbers of Common Teals, Eurasian Wigeons and Mallards.

Numbers can vary from day to day and it is probably best to see this lake as part of a complex with Derravaragh, Ennell, Iron and several smaller lakes. Depending on disturbance, birds move around from lake to lake.

The lake is well worth visiting in winter after storms; Great Northern Divers and Kittiwakes often occur and Long-tailed Duck (up to four), Smew and Red-crested Pochard have been seen.

Access

This lake lies on the left-hand side of the main road from Dublin to Sligo. Pass through Mullingar and the lake comes into view after about 5 km. The road is higher than the lake and provides a good vantage point to see most of the birds. Access is possible on the south-west side of Owel, by turning left at Bunbrosna, and taking the lane to the left after about 5 km. This route leads right down to the edge of the lake.

111 LOUGH IRON

OSI Discovery map: sheet 41
N34 62

Habitat and Species

Lough Iron is smaller than Lough Owel and situated about 3 km to the north-west. It has large wintering populations of Tufted Ducks and Pochards, but not so large as at Derravaragh or Owel. Over 1,000 Eurasian Wigeons and Common Teals and several hundred Mallards occur and, when there is disturbance at Lough Owel, substantial numbers of Shovelers visit the lake. Gadwall and Pintail are both regular in small numbers in winter. Like Derravaragh, this lake also has wintering Whooper Swans.

The principal feature of the lake for the birdwatcher is its wintering flock of Greenland White-fronted Geese which numbers over 400. The geese tend to feed on pasture fields on both the east and south sides of the lake. When disturbed, they fly out onto the water.

There are also large flocks of Northern Lapwings, European Golden Plovers and Curlews.

Access

Although there is a no-shooting order on some of the land around this lake, it is all on private property and public roads do not provide access directly to the shore. Permission should, therefore, be sought from landowners before venturing from the road to the edge. The lake lies less than 1 km south-west of the main road between Mullingar and Edgeworthstown.

112 LOUGH ENNELL

OSI Discovery map: sheet 48
N37 44; N41 46

Habitat and Species

Lough Ennell, like the other lakes in this area, is a shallow limestone lake. Drainage has led to the exposure of a wide, stony margin. The lake is highly eutrophic.

Lake Farm on the west side of the lake is a traditional wintering White-fronted Goose site, but the flock appears to have moved away in recent years, perhaps to Lough Iron. The lake itself has flocks of several hundred Pochards, Tufted Ducks and Coots.

Access

There are car parks and picnic sites located on each of the four shores of the lake and provide ample access to view the stretches of open water. It is best viewed from the south-west corner near Jonathan Swift Park and from the main Mullingar-Kilbeggan road on the north-east side, good access is available at Belvedere House and at Rochfort Demesne.

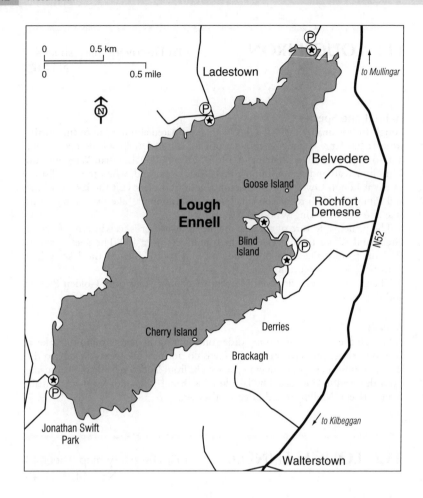

LONGFORD

Longford is another low-lying county like Westmeath with a number of lakes and its western edge bordered by Lough Ree and the River Shannon. The lakes here are even less often watched than those of Westmeath.

Lough Ree bas been dealt with under the accounts for Roscommon so, while one of the best sites in the county, it is not considered here to save duplication.

The two sites described appear to be minor, but more intensive watching might show them to be more varied than they seem

113 LOUGH KINALE AND DERRAGH LOUGH

OSI Discovery map: sheet 34
N39 81

Habitat and Species

This is a small lake adjacent to Lough Sheelin, famous for its trout fishing. Kinale also has trout but is not so popular as many of the other lakes in this region. The lake is surrounded by low-lying wet pasture and has large reedbeds around the margin.

The lake holds large numbers of Pochards, Tufted Ducks and Coots in winter. Great Crested Grebes breed in summer. It has rarely been visited by birdwatchers but looks an ideal place for unusual ducks.

Also worth checking is the adjacent Derragh Lough, to which many birds will fly if disturbed on Lough Kinale.

Access

Kinale is a small lake but rather difficult to work thoroughly because the road comes close at only one point and the reedbeds block views. The easiest way to see the birds is to take the first turn to the right on the Granard to Ballyjamesduff road (R194) towards Abbeylara (R396). Turn left in Abbeylara and drive north towards Ballyjamesduff, this road runs close to the western side of the lake.

Derragh Lough is reached by continuing straight through Abbeylara and taking the left-hand turn after about 1.5 km.

ULSTER

Cavan
114 Lough Oughter
115 Lough Sheelin

Monaghan

Donegal
116 Donegal Bay
117 Lough Swilly
118 Tory Island
119 Arranmore Island
120 Rocky Point
121 Malin Head
122 Trawbreaga Bay
123 Glenveagh National Park

Londonderry
124 Lough Foyle
125 Bann Estuary
126 Lough Beg
127 Lough Neagh: North-west Shore
128 Banagher Glen

Tyrone
129 Lough Neagh: West Shore
130 Grange
131 Annaghroe

Antrim
132 Rathlin Island
133 Fair Head

134 Craigagh Wood
135 Ramore Head
136 Shane's Castle
137 Belfast Lough: North Shore
138 Larne Lough
139 Portmore Lough

Down
140 Belfast Lough: South Shore
141 Strangford Lough
142 Copeland Bird Observatory
143 Dundrum Bay
144 Carlingford Lough: North Shore
145 Groomsport
146 Strand Lough And Killough Harbour
147 St John's Point
148 Tollymore Forest Park

Armagh
149 Lough Neagh: Oxford Island
150 Lurgan Park Lake
151 Craigavon Lakes
152 Reedy Flat

Fermanagh
153 Lower Lough Erne
154 Upper Lough Erne

ULSTER

CAVAN

Cavan is a county of numerous lakes but no coastline. It is far from Belfast and Dublin so tends not to be visited regularly by birdwatchers. However, the undulating drumlin landscape, with small lakes between the hills and a considerable extent of woodland on the rim of the lakes, provides habitat for a reasonable diversity of both breeding and wintering birds.

The centre of the county is dominated by the Lough Oughter system, formed by the broadening out of the River Erne among the drumlins. To the south and west are a number of smaller lakes, some of which are little more than ponds. As well as the Lough Oughter system, Lough Gowna and Lough Sheelin on the southern edge of the county appear likely to be of interest.

114 LOUGH OUGHTER   OSI Discovery map: sheet 27A
H34 06

Habitat and Species

Lough Oughter is a maze of islands and peninsulas separated by narrow channels and small lakes, all resulting from the submergence of drumlins. There are *Phragmites* beds on many parts of the system and the southern part is well wooded.

The area is better described as a lake system as it comprises a large number of interconnected lakes, many of which have their own names.

In summer this is an excellent area for breeding Great Crested and Little Grebes, Coots, Mallards and Tufted Ducks. It is very secluded so rarer species could occur as well.

In winter there are known to be large numbers of Whooper and Mute Swans while feral Canada Geese are increasingly seen. The lakes also hold between 100 and 200 Great Crested Grebes in winter.

The wooded areas in the south have nesting Blackcaps and should hold breeding Garden Warblers.

Access

The visitor is best advised to move around the entire area from Belturbet in the north to Killeshandra in the west and around to Butler's Bridge in the east.

115 LOUGH SHEELIN   OSI Discovery map: sheet 34
N45 83

Habitat and Species

Lough Sheelin is one of the larger lakes in Co Cavan and straddles the border with counties Meath and Westmeath. Most of the shoreline is in Co Cavan, but several of the better access points are in the neighbouring counties. As a result of regular winter wildfowl counts, this lake turns up some interesting winter rarities such as Great Northern Diver and Slavonian Grebe, as well as large numbers of both Tufted Ducks and Pochards. Although the lake is heavily polluted, this doesn't seem to have affected bird numbers, and it is one of only two sites in Ireland where Common Goldeneye has bred.

Access

The R194 road between Ballyjamesduff and Granard runs parallel to the western side of the lake and there are many side roads which run down to the shore. There are also good vantage points on the eastern shore, particularly at Derrysheridan in Co Meath and on the south-east shore near Finnea in Co Westmeath.

MONAGHAN

Monaghan is a small, landlocked county with a number of lakes. These tend to be smaller than those in Cavan and are certainly less known. Many of the lakes hold populations of ducks in winter and breeding Great Crested Grebes, Little Grebes and ducks in summer.

Lough Egish appears to be the best lake for birds with a large colony of breeding gulls and wintering Whooper Swans, Cormorants and both surface feeding and diving ducks.

DONEGAL

The most north-westerly county in Ireland, Donegal could be expected to attract a larger share of migrants from Iceland and Greenland than most other counties because of its position, and this is probably the case. Like so many of the western counties, however, Donegal has been relatively little watched and the untapped potential is clearly enormous.

The coastline of the county is very varied. Donegal Bay in the south is low lying as far west as Killybegs, but then the landscape takes on a wilder and more rugged aspect. The coast of west Donegal is a mixture of sheer cliffs, narrow bays and wet bogland. Few trees grow and exposed hedges show the impact of the strong winds. The north coast, from Sheep Haven around to Lough Foyle, is slightly more sheltered and includes a number of long narrow inlets.

Inland, much of Donegal is mountainous and boggy. Many of the hollows are filled with small lakes and a few of these hold breeding Red-throated Divers, the only place where they can be found in Ireland. Whooper Swan, Goosander and Snowy Owl have bred or attempted to breed in recent years but it is perhaps surprising that other rare northerly species have not been found breeding in the county as the county has ample habitat for Common Goldeneyes, Greenshanks, Redwings or Bramblings to nest.

116 DONEGAL BAY   OSI Discovery map: sheet 10, 11
G71 76; G87 69

Habitat
Donegal Bay is a very extensive area and comprises several quite distinct habitats. Taking the bay to mean, in its broadest terms, the entire area from Bundoran in the south round to Donegal town and west to Killybegs, incorporating Inver Bay, the most obvious habitat is the shallow waters off the coastline. These are ideal for seaducks and divers. Less obvious are the small strips of intertidal mudflat at Ballyshannon and below Donegal town which attract waders and some wildfowl.

Durnish Lough to the north of Rossnowlagh is unquestionably the best area for surface-feeding wildfowl. It is a shallow freshwater lake impounded by sand dunes. There are extensive reedbeds around the margin and the area is surrounded by marshy fields. This lake has been called Birra Lough in the past, but is correctly named Durnish.

The principal economic activities of this area are farming and fishing. The main fishing port is Killybegs. Ireland's largest trawlers are based here and the resulting activity attracts large numbers of gulls.

Species
The shoreline is excellent for divers and scoters. Great Northern and Red-throated Divers are numerous. Black-throated Divers, normally rare on the

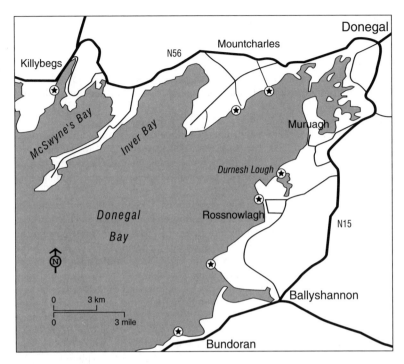

Irish coast, appear to be regular off Mountcharles, and up to 40 have been counted in recent years, Common Scoters are numerous, and up to 1,000 occur in the bay, though numbers fluctuate. Rossnowlagh is usually the best place for large numbers, the flocks should be checked carefully as both Surf Scoter and Velvet Scoter have been seen here. Indeed the records are so frequent that both species are probably annual here. Common Eiders, Red-breasted Mergansers and Long-tailed Ducks also winter in this bay. Indeed there have been records in August of enormous flocks of Red-breasted Mergansers – over 500 at a time – off Ballyshannon, and these are believed to be moulting birds.

This is one of the best places in the country for Long-tailed Ducks, and there have been several counts of over 50, though numbers vary from year to year.

Durnish Lough, a separate habitat within the bay complex, is the best place for swans. Up to 100 Whoopers and 100 Mute Swans are regular in winter, and small numbers of Bewick's are very occasional. Mallard, Common Teal, Eurasian Wigeon, Pochard and Tufted Duck can all be seen.

The small inlets and bays at the head of Donegal Bay have intertidal flats which support a small flock of Brent Geese and about 1,000 waders. Oystercatchers, Curlews, Redshanks and Dunlin are the most widespread, but Northern Lapwings, Turnstones and occasional Bar-tailed Godwits and Greenshanks should be seen on most winter visits.

The stony shores have small numbers of Purple Sandpipers and the sandier beaches have Ringed Plovers and Sanderlings.

Killybegs harbour is an essential port of call for the birdwatcher visiting this area. Glaucous and Iceland Gulls are virtually certain in winter and rarer gulls should be looked for such as Kumlien's and American Herring Gull, both of which have occurred in recent winters (the ultra-rare Thayer's Gull and Ross's Gull have also been recorded).

Timing

Donegal Bay is a winter site, best visited between September and early April. The state of tide matters little, but coverage of the bay will require a full day.

Access

The bay is relatively easily watched, though the distances involved in a thorough search are substantial. The coast road from Ballyshannon north to Ballintra provides several access points to the shore for scanning the diver and scoter parties. Bundoran town is a good place to see Brent Geese and Purple Sandpipers in winter.

Durnish Lough is accessible from several points. The southern end of the lake can be seen from the road between Rossnowlagh and Ballintra. The northern end can be approached by taking the first turn on the right after passing the lake on the road from Ballintra to Rossnowlagh (ignoring the lane through the reedbeds). Park at the first junction on the right, after about 1 km.

Inner Donegal Bay can be explored by following the main road from Laghy to Donegal and around to Mountcharles, taking turns off to the left where suitable habitat is seen. Just before Mountcharles, take the left turn which runs along the north-western edge of the bay. This area is good for Black-throated Divers.

The road from Mountcharles to Killybegs skirts the top of Inver Bay, McSwyne's Bay and Killybegs Harbour. These inlets can be explored easily by taking the byroads which run along the edges of the bays. Killybegs itself is a bustling, busy harbour and gulls surround the port.

CALENDAR

All year: Mute Swan, Common Eider, Red-breasted Merganser, Oystercatcher, Ringed Plover, Curlew.

Autumn–winter–spring: Red-throated, Great Northern and Black-throated Divers, Whooper Swan, Brent Goose, Mallard, Eurasian Wigeon, Common Teal, Pochard, Tufted Duck, Scaup, Common Scoter, possibility of Velvet and Surf Scoters, Long-tailed Duck, Dunlin, Sanderling, Purple Sandpiper, Redshank, Greenshank, Glaucous Gull, Iceland Gull, possible rarer gulls.

---

117 LOUGH SWILLY   OSI Discovery map: sheet 2, 6
C30 28; G36 21

Habitat

Lough Swilly is a long, deep sea lough with several areas of intertidal mudflats and a couple of brackish lagoons. The lough is about 50 km long and 4 km broad at its mid point. The upper part of the lough, from Letterkenny to

Buncrana in the east and Rathmullan in the west, is much the most interesting for birds. Farther out, the lough is too deep for most diving birds and the shoreline is rocky.

The Swilly estuary at the head of the lough is a small area of intertidal flats formed where the Swilly river meanders into the bay below the town of Letterkenny. The Leannan estuary is another area of mudflats to the east of the town of Rathmelton.

On the eastern side are the two lagoons. Inch Lake, much the most important for birds, was formed by blocking off with dykes the two ends of a channel between Inch Island and the mainland. The resulting lake is brackish with extensive marshes which flood in winter. The water level at Inch is controlled by a sluice.

On the seaward side of Inch Island the shallow waters provide feeding for divers and grebes. There is also a small area of mudflats on the north and east of the island providing feeding for Brent Geese.

Blanket Nook, the other lagoon, is a small inlet which was cut off from the bay by the construction of a dyke across its mouth. The inlet is bordered by wet fields and by mudflats at low tide.

Species

Lough Swilly has a wide diversity of wintering wildfowl and waders and an excellent breeding bird site at Inch Lough.

In summer, Inch has nesting Great Crested and Little Grebes and a breeding colony of up to 70 pairs of Mute Swans. There is only one other colony of swans known in Ireland (at Lady's Island Lake in Wexford) so the assembly on the small island in the south-west corner of the lake is particularly interesting. Shelduck, Mallard, Tufted Duck and Coot also nest, along with several hundred pairs of Black-headed Gulls, about 200 pairs of Sandwich Terns and smaller numbers of Common Terns. Dunlin has bred in the surrounding area.

In winter the shallow waters off Inch Island and Buncrana attract Red-throated and Great Northern Divers, and occasional Black-throated Divers. Great Crested Grebes, Little Grebes and a few Slavonian Grebes are all regular as well. Indeed, this is one of the few places in Ireland where Slavonian Grebes can be found with certainty.

The area is excellent for swans and geese. Whooper Swans usually make their Irish landfall in autumn, on their return from Iceland, in the area between Lough Swilly and Derry. Up to 2,000 can be seen in the huge reclaimed fields opposite Inch or at Big Isle near Manorcunningham from late October onwards. Numbers usually decline somewhat from early November, presumably as the birds fan out to winter throughout Ireland.

Several species of geese can be seen. Brent Geese can be found along the north-eastern coast of Inch Island on the creek opposite Fahan. Greylag Geese winter at Inch Lake, Blanket Nook and Big Isle. Greenland White-fronted Geese concentrate at Big Isle, sometimes appear at Inch, but are rarely seen at Blanket Nook. A few Pink-footed Geese are sometimes among the other geese, particularly during migration, and Bean Goose has been recorded. The geese, like the swans, are very volatile, moving around the south-east side of Lough Swilly, across to Port Lough near Roosky and to the River Foyle between Carrigans and Saint Johnstown on the west side, and south to Grange on the east side.

The lough has a rich diversity of wintering duck species also. In the shallow waters of Lough Swilly itself there is a scattering of Red-breasted Mergansers, but the best places are the lagoons and estuaries. Shelducks, Eurasian Wigeons, Common Teals, Mallards, Shovelers, Pintails, Tufted Ducks, Pochards, Scaups and Common Goldeneyes are all regular, and Inch Lake is the best place to see them. Gadwall is probably annual and rarities recorded at Inch have included American Wigeon, Ring-necked and Ferruginous Ducks and Lesser Scaup.

In absolute terms, Lough Swilly is not a great place for wader numbers, but it holds more birds than any other bay west of Lough Foyle in Londonderry. Oystercatchers, Northern Lapwings, European Golden Plovers, Curlews, Redshanks and Dunlins are widespread where there is suitable habitat. At Inch and Blanket Nook there is the possibility of scarcer species such as Ruff, Little Stint and Curlew Sandpiper. American Golden Plover, Pectoral Sandpiper and Semipalmated Sandpiper have all been recorded, so clearly the potential for other American waders exists. Inch also holds a small winter population of Black-tailed Godwits.

The entire area is good for birds of prey. Peregrine and Common Buzzard are regular visitors to the lough and Short-eared Owls have wintered in the vicinity of Inch Lake.

In winter there are large finch flocks at both Blanket Nook and Inch Lake and sometimes parties of Snow Buntings.

Timing

Inch is worth visiting at any time of year. Breeding grebes, ducks, gulls and terns are present in summer. Migrant waders and wildfowl are likely in spring and autumn and large numbers of wintering wildfowl are present in winter. Late October is the time to see the most spectacular numbers of Whooper Swans.

The other sites are best between September and April. The largest numbers of birds are present from November to March.

State of tide only matters at the Leannan and Swilly estuaries where low tide or a rising tide are best.

Access

The estuary of the Leannan is best watched from the main road between Rathmelton and Rathmullan.

The Swilly estuary can be viewed on the north-western side by taking the road from Letterkenny to Rathmelton and turning off to the right after 5 km. This road provides viewing at several points. On the south-eastern side, the road from Letterkenny to Manorcunningham runs along the southern side of extensive fields where Whooper Swans can be seen. Big Isle can be approached by taking the last left turn before the turn off to the left for Manorcunningham, but is best watched by telescope from the main road.

Blanket Nook is approached by turning left off the road from Newtown Cunningham to Buncrana, about 2 km after Newtown Cunningham. Follow the narrow road to Castle Hill and turn right, following the twisting road until the lake comes into view. At the lake, pass through the old railway embankment and walk along it. The lake itself can be approached by following a rough track across a bridge over a stream to the pumping station. Good views can be had from this point.

Inch is reached by turning left off the main road from Derry to Fahan just beyond Burnfoot. The road leads onto a causeway which provides an ideal viewing point for many of the wildfowl in winter. The embankment on the south-eastern side, which once held a railway line, can be walked if necessary. Many of the swans are usually in the fields on the southern side of the lake and can be seen from the road. The southern side of the lake can be approached by driving along the road which leads to an old ford across the lake.

The road across Inch Island is worth following, as good views of Brent Geese can usually be obtained by looking across towards Fahan.

CALENDAR

All year: Mute Swan, Shelduck, Mallard, Tufted Duck, Great Crested Grebe, Little Grebe, Coot, Oystercatcher, Ringed Plover, Northern Lapwing, possible Dunlin, Curlew, Redshank, Black-headed Gull, European Stonechat.

Summer: Sandwich and Common Terns.

Autumn: Whooper Swan, Brent, Greylag and Greenland White-fronted Geese, possibly Pink-footed Goose, Eurasian Wigeon, Common Teal, Pintail, Shoveler, Scaup, Pochard, Common Goldeneye, Red-throated and, Great Northern Divers, European Golden Plover, Curlew Sandpiper, Little Stint, Ruff, Greenshank, Turnstone, possible American waders.

Winter–spring: Whooper Swan, Brent, Greylag and Greenland White-fronted Geese, possible Pink-footed Goose, Eurasian Wigeon, Common Teal, Pintail, Shoveler, Scaup, Pochard, Common Goldeneye, Red-throated and Great Northern Divers, possible Black-throated Diver, Slavonian Grebe, European Golden and Grey Plovers, Greenshank, Turnstone.

118 TORY ISLAND

OSI Discovery map: sheet 1
B85 46

Habitat

Situated almost 12 km off the north coast of Donegal, Tory Island is one of the most, if not the most remote islands off the Irish Coast. Indeed, it is not unusual for the island to be cut off from the rest of the country for weeks on end during the winter. However, in recent years, the establishment of a regular ferry

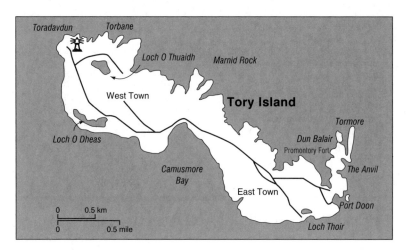

service has made the island much more accessible to birders, with less likelihood of being marooned during bad weather. Along with the regular ferry service, tourist facilities including a hotel (with restaurant) and guesthouses have now developed on the island. Birders have responded in kind and it is now a regular destination in autumn for rarity hunters. It is also a fascinating island to visit in summer as it has the largest population of Corncrakes in Ireland, and very unusually for Ireland, a sizeable population of Tree Sparrows which outnumber the House Sparrows.

Species
The island is very windswept and barren, so best sites for autumn passerines are any areas of vegetation near the villages of West Town, where the ferry disembarks, and East Town. The two small lakes at the north-west end of the island have produced several species of American wader and seawatching can be conducted from lighthouse on the north-west tip. Autumn migration can turn up anything, and it has built up a pretty good list of rarities for the short period of time for which birders have been visiting. It is the best place in Ireland for Lapland Bunting and this often shy and very flighty bird can almost be guaranteed on an autumn visit.

As befits its maritime status, Tory Island has good populations of breeding seabirds including Little and Arctic Terns and Puffins. Summer birding will also produce Chough, Common Eider, Peregrine, Raven and Corncrake. The Corncrakes can be heard from any of the areas of cultivation or indeed any rank cover and are particularly numerous in the fields around West town. They can remain quite late in the autumn and it is not unusual for an autumn twitcher to have to whoosh one out of the way while sprinting towards a Common Rosefinch or Barred Warbler!

Access
Ferries sail from Magheraroarty twice daily in summer and thrice weekly in winter, while there is a daily service year-round from Bunbeg. Call 074 9531320 for schedule information.

There is a small hotel and a few guesthouses on the island.

CALENDAR

All year: Common Eider, Fulmar, Gannet, Peregrine, Oystercatcher, Chough, Tree Sparrow.

Summer: Manx Shearwater, European Storm-petrel, Corncrake, Sandwich, Arctic and Little Terns, Common and Black Guillemots, Razorbill, Puffin, Northern Wheatear, European Stonechat, Sedge Warbler.

Autumn: Whooper Swan, Barnacle and Greylag Geese, possible Pink-footed Goose, Red-throated and Great Northern Divers, Sooty Shearwater, Leach's Storm-petrel, European Golden Plover, Dunlin, Curlew, Turnstone, possibly American waders, Arctic and Great Skuas, migrant warblers, Lapland and Snow Buntings.

119 ARRANMORE ISLAND OSI Discovery map: sheet 1
G68 16

Habitat and Species

Arranmore is an interesting island with lots of potential for attracting migrants, although be warned that this is quite a big island and very hilly – a Snowy Owl hid out in these hills for over a year in 1993–1994 and defied the efforts of many birders to find it! Arranmore is not too far offshore from Burtonport and served by a ferry which can take cars. The eastern side of the island is quite well-wooded by offshore island standards with many mature gardens in the area around the pier and also a small spruce plantation, whereas the western side is characterised by undulating hills covered by bog and moorland.

Its main claim to fame is that Ireland's first (and to date only) Semipalmated Plover was recorded on the small beach adjacent to the pier.

The lighthouse at the north-western tip of the island is a good vantage point for seawatching and the lighthouse garden is worth checking for migrants first thing each morning.

Access

There is a car ferry service from Burtonport all year round, with several sailings per day and increased frequency in summer. Call 074 9520532 for schedule information.

120 ROCKY POINT

OSI Discovery map: sheet 10
G48 83

Habitat and Species

The area bounded by Rocky Point and the villages of Glencolumbkille, Malinmore and Malinbeg has built up a solid reputation as a migration watch-point since the late 1980s. It combines the characteristic moorland and rough grazing of west coast headlands with pockets of vegetation around gullies and the gardens of houses which act as migrant traps. The sustained recording of migrants at this site has established a number of species which would more normally be associated with the south coast, as being regular Donegal migrants.

The distance between Glencolmcille and Malinbeg is about 8 km so a lone birder might prefer to focus on the area around Malinmore and the seawatching point at Rocky Point itself. This is the most westerly point in Donegal and one of its best seawatching sites. It is particularly good in north-westerly winds in September, producing good numbers of skuas and Leach's Storm-petrels.

Access

Take the R263 west from Glencolumbkille, checking roadside gardens and other likely-looking habitat. At the Malinmore crossroads, take a right and continue west to where the road ends and there is a track that leads out to Rocky Point by foot.

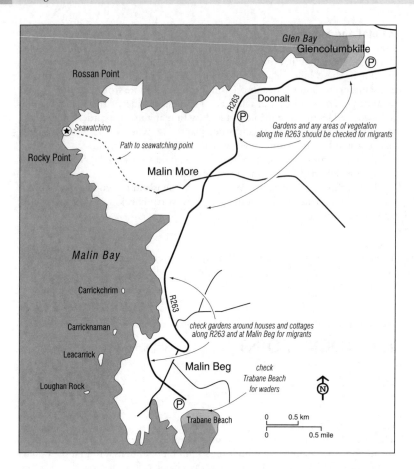

Glen Bay
Glencolumbkille
Ⓟ

Rossan Point

R263

Doonalt

Ⓟ

Gardens and any areas of vegetation along the R263 should be checked for migrants

⭐ Seawatching

Path to seawatching point

Rocky Point

Malin More

Malin Bay

Carrickchrim ○

R263

check gardens around houses and cottages along R263 and at Malin Beg for migrants

Carricknaman

Leacarrick

Malin Beg

check Trabane Beach for waders

Loughan Rock

Ⓟ

Ⓝ

Trabane Beach

0   0.5 km

0   0.5 mile

121 MALIN HEAD

OSI Discovery map: sheet 3
C40 59

Habitat and Species

Malin is the most northerly point on the mainland of Ireland – only the relatively inaccessible Inishtrahull Island is farther north. A Bird Observatory operated here in the 1960s for several years but it closed owing to shortage of manpower. The promontory is rugged and bleak with relatively little cover. Nevertheless, its location is ideal for attracting migrants in late autumn.

The Observatory records show that seawatching could be quite spectacular at times and Little Auks, Great and Sooty Shearwaters and skuas were seen. Whooper Swans, Greylag, Greenland White-fronted and Barnacle Geese, Fieldfares, Redwings and Lapland and Snow Buntings were all recorded in good numbers. Scarcer landbirds recorded included Hoopoe, Red-breasted Flycatcher and Yellow-browed Warbler.

Seawatching is still done at Malin and remains excellent in the right conditions of north-westerly winds. Leach's Storm-petrels, Sooty Shearwaters and Sabine's Gulls all turn up in these conditions in autumn. Visits in periods of south-easterly winds should produce a good variety of passerines.

Access
The road from Derry north to Carndonagh leads on to Malin and eventually right out to the head. The entire tip of the peninsula can hold birds. Seawatching is best from the cliffs just north of the signal tower.

Hoopoe

122 TRAWBREAGA BAY   OSI Discovery map: sheet 3
C46 50

Habitat and Species

Trawbreaga Bay is a muddy inlet lying between Malin village and the sea, but largely impounded by the Isle of Doagh, a wide area of sandhills and meadow. Common Eiders are common here in both summer and winter. Terns occasionally nest on the shingle bank on the north-west side of the Isle of Doagh along with Oystercatchers, Ringed Plovers and Common Gulls. Northern Lapwings nest on the meadow behind the dunes.

In winter Brent Geese feed on the mudflats of Trawbreaga Bay and Barnacle Geese on the Isle of Doagh meadows. The open water at the mouth of the bay usually has Long-tailed Ducks and divers as well as Common Eiders. In winter the mudflats hold Shelducks, Mallards, Eurasian Wigeons, Common Teals, Curlews, Oystercatchers and most of the common wader species. Spotted Redshanks and Curlew Sandpipers are probably near annual in autumn.

Access

The area is approached by driving north from Derry to Carndonagh and then north to Malin village. The estuary and the Isle of Doagh can be reached at a number of points.

Malin Bridge and the road along the north shore of Trawbreaga Bay are among the best vantage points for the estuary. The Isle of Doagh can be walked across if you leave your car at the beach at Pollan Bay about 1 km north of Ballyliffin.

123 GLENVEAGH NATIONAL PARK

OSI Discovery map: sheet 6
C04 23

Habitat and Species

The Glenveagh National Park was privately owned up to 1975 and comprises 9,600 ha in the mountainous centre of Donegal. Of this area, an enclosed deer forest covers 8,100 ha. Lough Veagh, nearly 5.5 km long, lies in the narrow valley which bisects the park. The imposing pseudo-Gothic castle on the shore of Lough Veagh was the home of the owner of this Irish example of the classic sporting estate. There are over 500 Red Deer in the park.

The mountains are granite and the slopes are drained by numerous streams which run into small lakes. Most of the park is covered by bog and moorland, but there are stands of sessile oak on the slopes and some planted woodland in the glen and around the castle.

The birds have been studied by staff of the Office of Public Works who operate the National Park and are very varied. The Park is now the site for an ambitious Golden Eagle re-introduction scheme – since 2001 more than 50 birds have been released and the first pair bred in 2007.

In summer, one or two pairs of Red-throated Divers and Goosanders nest on the lakes, along with small numbers of Common Gulls. Peregrines, Ravens and Ring Ouzels nest on the rockier slopes and cliffs. Red Grouse, Curlews,

Whinchats, Grasshopper Warblers and Northern Wheatears nest on the moorland, with a few European Golden Plovers on the plateaux. The woodland habitat holds as diverse a mixture of species as anywhere else in Ireland and has had Woodcock, Common Redstart, Wood Warbler and Common Crossbill recorded in summer in recent years.

In winter Snow Buntings frequent the more exposed parts. Fieldfares and Redwings are common lower down, particularly in early winter.

This must be a likely site for even more rare breeding birds. It has a range of habitats and is situated so far north that species like Whooper Swan, Black-throated Diver, Dotterel, Greenshank, Snow Bunting and Redwing might be hoped for.

Access
The national park is approached from Letterkenny by taking the road for Dunfanaghy and turning left at Termon, 3 km beyond Kilmacrenan. The entrance to the park is signposted on the left after another 9 km. There is a visitor centre at the entrance with impressive displays and, in summer, a mini-bus service between the centre and the castle. The park brochure has a 1:50,000 map with trails marked on it, and a booklet on the birds is available.

LONDONDERRY

The coast of County Londonderry is dominated by the huge intertidal mudflats of Lough Foyle, which run out to the open sea past Magilligan Point. Although the western side of the lough is in Donegal, virtually all the best birdwatching spots are in this county.

From Magilligan eastwards to Downhill is sandy beach backed by sand dunes, but at Downhill there are steep cliffs with breeding Fulmars. Beyond Downhill, along the coast, is the mouth of the Bann estuary and then a rocky stretch of coast around to Portrush.

The eastern side of the county is marked by the River Bann which runs from Lough Neagh through Lough Beg, and then along a broad flood plain to the sea north of Coleraine.

Inland, this is a hilly county with the Sperrin Mountains on the southern border with Tyrone the highest and most remote.

There are a number of wooded estates and country parks, some of which are open to the public, where woodlandbirds can be seen.

124 LOUGH FOYLE

OSNI Discoverer map: sheet 4, 7
C 48 23; C66 39

Habitat

This is the largest and broadest sea lough on the north coast. It runs for over 30 km from Derry to the open sea and is 12 km wide at its broadest, but little more than 1 km wide at its mouth. The north-west shore in Donegal is deep and there are virtually no mudflats exposed at low tide with the exception of a small section at Muff, just across the border from Derry.

The southern and eastern shores are very different with extensive intertidal flats backed by low-lying reclaimed land which was formerly famous for White-fronted Geese. Although there has been considerable drainage, the reclaimed farmland behind the embankment protecting it from inundation is still attractive to swans and smaller numbers of geese.

At the mouth, Magilligan Point is an 8–km long sandspit backed by extensive sand dunes.

Species

The most obvious birds in Lough Foyle are the enormous numbers of ducks and waders. This site holds over 1,000 Whooper Swans, over 5,000 Brent Geese, up to 1,000 Greylag Geese, peaks of over 10,000 Eurasian Wigeons, 2,000 Mallards, 2,000 Common Teals and small numbers of other duck species. They have been counted regularly for many years so the pattern of their occurrence is well known. The best time to see wildfowl in numbers is October when most are at their peak. The large numbers of Eurasian Wigeons are believed to be Icelandic birds making landfall before moving farther south to other sites. By mid-winter numbers of Eurasian Wigeons are much reduced.

Brent Geese have increased enormously in recent years, mirroring the increase in the Pale-bellied Brent population generally. Not all of those here are Pale-bellied, however, as there have been records of both American Black Brant and Dark-bellied Brent in most recent winters.

Out in the deeper waters near Magilligan Point, divers and grebes can be seen throughout late autumn and winter. Great Northern and Red-throated Divers are common with up to about ten of each being regular. Occasional Black-throated Divers turn up and they may well be annual here. Great Crested Grebes also occur, but Slavonian Grebes, which are annual visitors in small numbers, are most easily seen from Myroe where the River Roe enters the lough. As many as 100 have been seen here in winter.

Wader numbers are high but not so spectacular as the wildfowl flocks. Up to 5,000 European Golden Plovers, 4,000 Northern Lapwings, 2,000 Oystercatchers, 3,000 Curlews, 2,000 Bar-tailed Godwits and 5,000 Dunlins are the most numerous, but Redshanks, Grey Plovers, Greenshanks and Turnstones also winter. In autumn, scarcer migrant species turn up. Spotted Redshank is annual and Curlew Sandpiper and Little Stint near annual. At Magilligan Point there is a wintering flock of Sanderlings on the beach.

Off Magilligan passing seabirds, including skuas, can be seen in suitable weather conditions.

The stubble fields behind the embankment midway along the estuary are good for wintering finches and buntings, especially Snow Buntings and Twites.

1,000 Snow Buntings were once counted at Myroe, the largest flock ever recorded in Ireland, but this was quite exceptional. Up to 50 would be more usual. Lapland Buntings have been seen in some winters. These fields are regularly quartered by Peregrines, Merlins and Common Buzzards.

Finally, no winter or spring trip to Lough Foyle would be complete without a visit to Culmore Refuse Tip on the west shore of the lough, just north of Derry City. It is one of the few remaining open landfill sites in Ireland and, although its days are numbered, for now it remains an excellent site for large gulls in winter; Glaucous, Iceland, Kumlien's, American Herring and Yellow-legged Gulls are all regular, as well as hybrids, resulting in a real treasure trove for gull fanatics.

Timing

Without question the best time to visit the Foyle is from late autumn to early spring and the real optimum period is late October or early November. At this time, wildfowl numbers are at their highest and most of the winter visitors have arrived.

Most sections of the bay are best visited at or near high tide, when the water level forces waders and surface-feeding wildfowl onto the reclaimed land or its edge.

Access

From Derry eastwards on the Limavady road, access is possible at a number of points by turning left down minor roads.

Donnybrewer was once a famous goose haunt but has been much reduced in importance by drainage. It still holds good numbers of ducks and is reached by turning left from the main Limavady road at the White Horse Inn, forking right after 500 m, taking the left turn after another 800 m and then continuing on for another 1.5 km to a level crossing by which cars can be parked.

Eglinton Station to the east of Donnybrewer is reached by turning left off the main road opposite the turn to Eglinton. Continue to the station and cross the railway line. Check the fields on either side for wild swans and geese.

Longfield Point to the east of Donnybrewer is reached by turning left at the turn marked for Eglinton Flying Club. Cars can be parked at the Point where the road terminates.

At Ballykelly, about 10 km east of Eglinton, the shore and an excellent high-tide roost at Ballykelly Marsh, can be reached by turning left at the Bridge House restaurant.

The Roe Estuary, where the river Roe finally turns westwards into Lough Foyle after meandering north from Limavady, is the next spot. In Limavady, take the B69 to the north, following the signposts for Downhill. After 3 km turn left for Limavady Junction railway station: at the T-junction reached after 3 km turn right and take the road to the estuary, ignoring the cul de sac sign on the way. Cars can be left at the end of the road and the estuary approached by crossing the railway line.

The north side of the Roe Estuary, Ball's Point, can be reached by driving north on the B69 until it joins the A2, then turning left along the A2. About 1.5 km from this junction, turn left just past a small school and follow the narrow road to the estuary.

Meadow Pipit

Magilligan Point at the north-eastern extremity of Lough Foyle is reached by taking the A2 road from Limavady to Downhill. The left turn for Magilligan is signposted about 12 km from Limavady. The narrow road should be followed for about 5 km, past the prison, to a car park. The army firing range behind the car park should be avoided and a red flag flies when the range is in use. This is one of the best parts of the lough for divers in winter and for terns and skuas in summer and autumn.

Culmore Refuse Tip is located just north of the village of Culmore on the Donegal border and is reached by taking the A2 north from Derry to Muff.

CALENDAR

Autumn–winter–spring: Whooper Swan, Brent, Greylag and Greenland White-fronted Geese, Eurasian Wigeon, Common Teal, Mallard, Pintail, Red-throated and Great Northern Divers, Great Crested and Slavonian Grebes, Peregrine, Merlin, Sparrowhawk, Kestrel, Oystercatcher, European Golden Plover, Northern Lapwing, Dunlin, Sanderling, Knot, Curlew, Redshank, Linnet, Greenfinch, Chaffinch, Snow Bunting, Twite, Skylark, Meadow Pipit.

Autumn: Little Stint, Curlew Sandpiper, Ruff, Spotted Redshank.

Summer: terns and gulls at Magilligan.

125 BANN ESTUARY

OSNI Discoverer map: sheet 4
C79 35

Habitat

The estuary of the Bann has a diversity of habitat which has made it one of the prime sites for rare waders in Northern Ireland. The River Bann flows into the

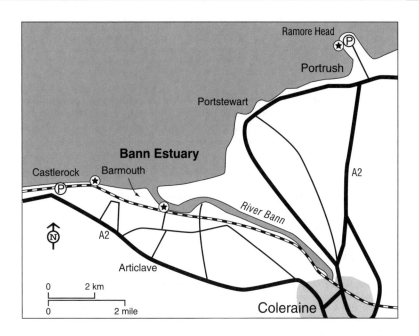

sea about 10 km west-north-west of Coleraine, broadening out into an estuary about 2 km before exiting at Castlerock strand.

The muddy estuary holds waders and ducks and is overlooked by a National Trust hide which provides an ideal viewing point when the tide is rising.

Castlerock strand is a popular sandy beach with a good dune system and a golf course. Near the mouth of the estuary is Barmouth Pier, a small pier which can be quite good for seawatching (though Ramore Head at Portrush in Antrim to the east is much better).

Species

The Bann is an excellent autumn migration watch point. On the sea, onshore north-westerlies bring seabirds such as skuas, Gannets and auks close to shore. On the edge of the mud, Knots, Dunlins, Whimbrels, Curlew Sandpipers and occasional Little Stints can often be seen. Sanderlings and Ringed Plovers are common on the beach. Rarities seen here include Collared Pratincole, Semipalmated Sandpiper, Long-billed Dowitcher, Wilson's Phalarope and Gull-billed and Forster's Terns.

Commoner waders such as Oystercatchers, Curlews and Redshanks are regular here from autumn through to spring.

Mallards, Common Teals, Eurasian Wigeons, Shelducks and Common Goldeneyes all winter on the estuary. At the mouth of the Bann, divers, Great Crested Grebes and Common Eiders are found from autumn through to the spring. The sand dunes frequently hold wintering Snow Buntings.

Timing

The Bann is best in September–October and in April–May. Autumn is very much the optimal time for a visit but spring migrant waders do turn up in some years. A winter visit can be productive – Ring-billed and Yellow-legged Gulls have been seen – but the numbers of wildfowl and waders are much lower than at the nearby Lough Foyle.

Access

Access to the estuary is from the A2 between Coleraine and Downhill. At Articlave turn right, after 1.5 km turn left at a T-junction, cross the bridge and turn right. Continue to the car park just before the railway crossing. Cross the railway on foot and continue to the estuary.

There is a National Trust hide at the edge of the water which may be used. If it is locked, call for the key at the nearest of the row of cottages facing the river.

Castlerock is reached by following the signposts beyond Articlave. This is a small seaside village with a car park at the shore. The beach and pier may be walked to from here.

CALENDAR

Autumn: Mallard, Common Teal, Eurasian Wigeon, Common Goldeneye, divers, Great Crested Grebe, Oystercatcher, Ringed and European Golden Plovers, Northern Lapwing, Knot, Dunlin, Sanderling, Curlew Sandpiper, Little Stint, Curlew, Spotted Redshank, Redshank, Greenshank, possibility of rare waders, skuas, terns, gulls.

Winter–spring: Divers, Great Crested Grebe, Mallard, Common Teal, Eurasian Wigeon, Common Goldeneye, Oystercatcher, Ringed and European Golden Plovers, Northern Lapwing, Dunlin, Sanderling, Curlew, Redshank, Greenshank, gulls.

---

126 LOUGH BEG

OSNI Discoverer map: sheet 14
H98 95

Habitat

Lough Beg is a shallow lake at the north-west comer of Lough Neagh formed by the broadening out of the River Bann 3 km after leaving the larger lake. It is one of the prime birdwatching sites in Northern Ireland because of its mix of habitats and its position on the Bann valley, which acts as a flyway between the north coast and Lough Neagh. The lough itself is approximately 5 km long and about 1.5 km wide at its broadest. The lough is generally shallow but a deeper, narrow channel runs through the middle. In summer the area of water is approximately 500 ha, but this can double with winter flooding.

Lough Beg was formerly much larger in extent. During the 1930s flood gates were erected where the Bann exits from Lough Neagh and these lowered the water level of Lough Beg. The southern end of the lough has the remnants of what were once thriving sand pits at Toome. These have long been abandoned and this part now comprises a mix of small islands and lagoons. The eastern side has reedbeds and some areas of mixed woodland, mainly alder and willow. A much more extensive woody section is in the north-west corner where Ballyscullion Estate has a variety of planted trees, mainly deciduous. Most of the remainder of the western side is rough grazing pasture which floods in winter.

The vicinity of the lough is extremely interesting botanically. Marsh orchids are common and two rare species, Irish ladies tresses orchid and butterfly orchid, occur here.

Species
With a species list approaching 200, this site has probably the longest list for anywhere in Ireland that does not directly adjoin the coast.

One of the reasons for the long list is the lough's attractiveness to passage waders in autumn. Small numbers of Black-tailed Godwits, Green, Wood and Common Sandpipers, Greenshanks, Knots, Little Stints, Curlew Sandpipers and Ruffs are annual. Pectoral Sandpipers occur in most years and other American species recorded include Long-billed Dowitcher, Greater and Lesser Yellowlegs, Stilt Sandpiper, Wilson's Phalarope, Baird's and White-rumped Sandpipers.

The wintering wildfowl and waders are among the highlights. Several hundred Whooper Swans are present from late October to April. In hard weather, numbers can rise rapidly. A few Greylag Geese can often be seen in winter, but other goose species are rare. The duck numbers, however, are very rewarding. Up to 2,000 Eurasian Wigeons, 1,200 Common Teals, 1,000 Mallards, 1,000 Pochards (though sometimes many more), 100 Common Goldeneyes and small numbers of Shovelers, Tufted Ducks and occasional Pintails and Red-breasted Mergansers can be found from October to March. Coots are also numerous in winter. Large numbers of Northern Lapwings and European Golden Plovers and smaller numbers of Curlews, Redshanks, Common Snipes and Dunlins can be seen from September to March.

Passage in spring is particularly exciting as returning migrants can be seen in May flying into the lough from the south and often moving on to the north without stopping. Whimbrels and Black-tailed Godwits are especially notable in spring at Lough Beg, and Garganeys have been found in many years.

In summer Great Crested Grebes nest in the southern part of the lough. Mallard, Common Teal, Shoveler, Tufted Duck, Red-breasted Merganser and Shelduck are the breeding duck species. Northern Lapwing, Common Snipe, Curlew, Redshank and (occasionally) Dunlin breed here. There are two colonies of Black-headed Gulls on islands.

In autumn the lough acts as a focal point for hirundines to assemble before commencing migration. Some thousands of Swallows and House and Sand Martins can be seen in August. Later on, in September and October, passage of Meadow Pipits, wagtails and Skylarks is noticeable.

The most frequent birds of prey are Kestrels, Peregrines, Sparrowhawks and, in winter, Merlins. Hen Harriers and Short-eared Owls are occasionally seen in winter, while the Lough is one of the most regular places in Ireland to see Ospreys on migration.

Timing

Lough Beg is worth visiting at any time of the year. In autumn, passage waders can be seen from August onwards. The main wildfowl arrival is from mid September and peak numbers are usually in December or January. Spring passage peaks in April and May, but can continue into June. A record of Broad-billed Sandpiper in June indicates how occasional rarities can turn up at the most unexpected time of the year.

In summer, there are lots of breeding birds and always the chance of something quite exotic.

Access

From Belfast, Lough Beg is approached by taking the M2 from Belfast and following the signposts for Toome. Toome is at the southern end of Lough Beg and access is best on the western side. From Toome drive west for Castledawson and turn right (following the signs for Bellaghy) after 3 km. Drive on for another 3 km until a crossroads is reached. Turn right here and then take the next right turn, following the narrow road down to a ruined farm at Annagh. The flood meadows can be crossed here and the lough approached.

Alternatively, do not take the last right turn, but continue on along the road across a narrow stream and park the car opposite Church Island, making sure to ask permission at the house adjacent to the road junction.

Reed Bunting

CALENDAR

All year: Mute Swan, Common Teal, Mallard, Shoveler, Tufted Duck, Pochard, Great Crested Grebe, Grey Heron, Kestrel, Sparrowhawk, Moorhen, Coot, Northern Lapwing, Common Snipe, Curlew, Redshank, Dunlin, Common, Black-headed, Herring, Lesser Black-backed and Great Black-backed Gulls, Kingfisher, Reed Bunting.

Autumn: Whooper Swan, Eurasian Wigeon, Pintail, European Golden and Grey Plovers, Curlew Sandpiper, Little Stint, Black-tailed

Godwit, Spotted Redshank, Greenshank, Green and Common Sandpipers, possible American waders, hirundines. Possibility of Hen Harrier or Osprey.

Winter: Whooper Swan, Eurasian Wigeon, Pintail, Hen Harrier, Merlin, Short-eared Owl, European Golden and Grey Plovers, Jack Snipe, Greenshank.

Spring: lingering winter wildfowl and waders, Garganey, Black-tailed Godwit, Whimbrel.

127 LOUGH NEAGH: NORTH-WEST SHORE

OSNI Discoverer map: sheet 14
H95 85

Habitat

Lough Neagh is the largest freshwater lake in Britain and Ireland, covering an area of 387 km2 and forming part of the borders of Cos. Tyrone, Antrim, Down

Blackbird

and Armagh as well as Londonderry. In this section, only the shoreline which falls within County Londonderry is dealt with, though some general features of the lake are considered.

The lake has a total shoreline of 125 km, of which 77% is exposed and mainly rocky. The lough is very shallow, with a mean depth of 8.9 m. It is rarely covered with ice in winter. Lough Neagh is very productive with an abundant invertebrate fauna. In addition, it is heavily polluted with nutrients, though its reputation in the 1970s as one of the most eutrophic water bodies in the world is no longer deserved.

The west shore is varied but has a great deal of alder wood on the edge. It is generally difficult to approach because few roads run close to the lake and most of the land adjoining the lough is privately owned.

Species

Lough Neagh differs greatly from Lough Beg, even though the lakes are almost adjoining, because it is much more exposed, slightly deeper and has very little muddy or sandy shore. As a result, Lough Neagh holds few waders and much smaller numbers of surface-feeding ducks. But it does hold far the largest concentrations of diving ducks in Britain and Ireland.

These concentrations have been counted since the 1960s in a mammoth series of monthly censuses conducted from the shoreline. In the recent past, peak counts of 24,000 Pochards, 22,000 Tufted Ducks, 4,000 Scaups and 7,000 Common Goldeneyes, as well as 7,000 Coots, have been made. Peak counts of surface-feeding ducks have included 3,000 Eurasian Wigeons, 100 Gadwalls, 1,700 Common Teals, 5,000 Mallards and 100 Shovelers. The Lough also supports the largest population of Ruddy Ducks in Ireland and post-breeding numbers reach about 100. Rarer species such as Red-crested Pochard, Smew, Ring-necked Duck and Lesser Scaup have also been seen, but these are not usually recorded on the west side.

The Lough Neagh shoreline also holds large numbers of Mute and Whooper Swans, but these are strung out all along the edge of the lake and the visitor will usually see quite small numbers of each.

The north-west corner of Lough Neagh, around Ballyronan Point, is one of the best places for seeing Scaup. Pochard, Tufted Ducks and Common Goldeneye are also off the shore in good numbers. The road south of Ballyronan, which runs along the shore for about 1.5 km, and the disused airfield close to Toomebridge usually provide views of Whooper and, occasionally, Bewick's Swans. Northern Lapwings and European Golden Plovers winter on fields in the area.

In summer, Great Crested Grebes, Shelducks, Mallards, Tufted Ducks, Moorhens and Coots breed near Ballyronan.

Timing
The best time for a visit is between September and April.

Access (see Map 129 Lough Neagh)
Ballyronan Point, some 10 km from Toome, is the best place to approach the north-west side of the Lough. Drive west from Toome on the road to Castledawson. After 3 km turn left for Ballyronan and follow the signposts to the village. Just before the village, the Marina can be seen on the left. Cars can be left at the car park here and the birds of the Lough viewed from the piers.

The woodland, which runs northwards along the shoreline, has paths marked in it. This alder scrub holds most common woodlandbirds.

CALENDAR

Winter: Whooper Swan, Eurasian Wigeon, Common Teal, Mallard, Scaup, Pochard, Tufted Duck, Common Goldeneye, Coot, European Golden Plover, Northern Lapwing, Curlew, Redshank.

Summer: Shelduck, Mallard, Tufted Duck, Great Crested Grebe, Moorhen, Coot. Sedge Warbler, Lesser Redpoll. .

---

128 BANAGHER GLEN　OSNI Discoverer map: sheet 7, OSNI Sperrins Activity Map 1:25000 C67 05

Habitat and Species
Banagher Glen cuts deeply into the northern slopes of the Sperrin Mountains and the steep sides of the valley are forested in deciduous woodland, some of which at least, is ancient oak woodland. The upper elevations are planted with spruce forest and this mixture of habitats supports a good variety of woodland species; both Wood Warbler and Common Redstart have been recorded here. Both species are rare breeding birds in Ireland and their presence in a woodland is a key indicator of a healthy biodiversity.

Three rivers converge within the glen and one of them, the Altnaheglish, is dammed creating the highest reservoir in Northern Ireland. The reservoir is not particularly good for birds but its existence provides some extra possibilities and there is open moorland to the north of the reservoir which is accessible by hiking trails.

Access

From Dungiven, take the B74 south towards Feeny. The entrance to the glen is signposted on the left-hand side of the road about 3 km from Dungiven.

There is a car park and information board at the entrance to the Glen, which is a National Nature Reserve and be prepared for a fairly steep hike up to the dam.

Bullfinch

TYRONE

Tyrone is a large inland county bordering the western shore of Lough Neagh between the Ballinderry and Blackwater rivers. The northern edge of the county is formed by the Sperrin Mountains; the south-eastern edge is bordered by the Blackwater; the south by moorlands and damp lake country on the fringe of the Lough Erne system, and the west by the Rivers Foyle and Finn.

The most obvious feature of the county is its extent of mountain and moorland and these habitats hold significant numbers of birds. The Sperrin Mountains have breeding Curlews while Peregrines and Ravens are widespread. In the wooded estates are Woodcocks, Long-eared Owls, Kestrels, Blackcaps, Jays and Siskins as well as the other common woodland breeders. The small lakes hold breeding Mallards and Tufted Ducks and wintering Pochards together with, in some cases, Whooper Swans.

129 LOUGH NEAGH: WEST SHORE

OSNI Discoverer map: sheet 14
H96 75

Habitat
As already described in the account of the north-west shore, which forms part of the border of County Londonderry, Lough Neagh is the largest freshwater lake in Britain and Ireland, covering an area of 38,700 ha.

In this section, only the part which falls within county Tyrone is dealt with, though a visit to the Tyrone shore should ideally be combined with a visit to the Londonderry shore and to Lough Beg. For more information on the lough in general, see the account of the north-west corner.

The west shore has a considerable extent of alder wood on the edge and is difficult to approach because few roads run close to the Lake and most of the land adjoining the lough is privately owned. Newport Trench and Ardboe Point are easily accessible, however, and provide good views over the lough.

Species
Small numbers of diving ducks can be seen off the pier at Newport Trench and from Ardboe Point. Tufted Ducks, Pochards, Common Goldeneyes and Scaups are usually present. Mallards, Eurasian Wigeons and Common Teals are also regular.

The abandoned Kinrush airfield nearby is a haunt of Whooper Swans, Northern Lapwings, European Golden Plovers, thrushes, Skylarks and finches. All the common gull species occur here in winter.

Timing
The best time for a visit is between September and April.

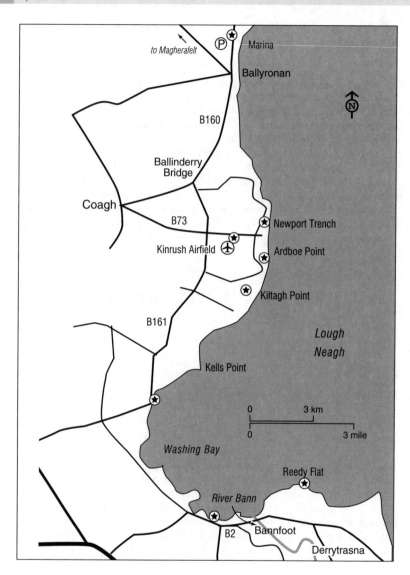

Access

Driving south from Toome, pass through Ballyronan (or check the area for wildfowl en route) and keep on the B160 for Coagh until a left turn is reached, just after crossing the Ballinderry river. Take the left turn and drive for 3 km to a crossroads. Turn left here, following the signs for Battery, and follow the road to the edge of the Lough. This is Newport Trench. The small pier provides a vantage point for scanning the lough.

To reach Ardboe Point, retrace your journey from Newport Trench and take the first left, after about 500 m, and follow the signs for Ardboe High Cross.

Mistle Thrush

The old graveyard, where the monument is situated, provides excellent views of the lough.

The abandoned Kinrush airfield can be reached from the road which leads down to Ardboe Point. Make sure to look at the tenth-century Ardboe High Cross in Ardboe graveyard.

CALENDAR

Winter: Whooper Swan, Eurasian Wigeon, Common Teal, Mallard, Scaup, Pochard, Tufted Duck, Common Goldeneye, Coot, European Golden Plover, Northern Lapwing, Curlew.

Summer: Shelduck, Mallard, Tufted Duck, Great Crested Grebe, Moorhen, Coot, Sedge Warbler.

130 GRANGE

OSNI Discoverer map: sheet 7
C35 07

Habitat and Species

Grange is on the east bank of the River Foyle midway between Strabane and Derry. The large, open fields are frequented at times by Whooper Swans and Greylag Geese in winter. These birds are part of the complex of sites which include Inch and Blanket Nook at Lough Swilly in Donegal.

Search fields either side of
Grange and Grangefoyle Roads
for Whooper Swan and
Greylag Goose flocks

River Foyle

DONEGAL

Grange Road

A5

Grangefoyle Road

0   0.5 km

0   0.5 mile

Access

The A5 from Strabane to Derry is the approach road for this site. Scan the fields to the left from a point about 10 km north of Strabane.

About 12 km north of Strabane, turn left along the narrow road which leads to Bready. The open fields can be viewed from the road.

131 ANNAGHROE   OSNI Discoverer map: sheet 19
                                          H73 45

Habitat and Species

The Blackwater river frequently floods near Caledon, and the resulting wet pastures attract a small flock of up to 50 Greenland White-fronted Geese and some Whooper Swans. Although fairly widespread in the Republic of Ireland, Greenland White-fronted Geese are hard to find in Northern Ireland. This flock uses the flooded fields at Annaghroe as one of several sites in a series of haunts used in the area, so the birds are not always present.

European Golden Plovers, Northern Lapwings, Common Snipes and Curlews are usually present in winter.

Access

From Armagh, drive west along the A28 to Caledon. After passing through Caledon, take the B45, sign posted for Monaghan, to the left. The road turns along the northern side of the Caledon estate before reaching the bridge over the Blackwater river and the border between Northern Ireland and the Republic. Look from the road to the west across the flooded meadows towards the ruined Annaghroe House.

ANTRIM

This county comprises the north-east corner of the country. The north and north-east coasts are spectacularly beautiful and the islands such as Muck, Carrick-a-Rede, Sheep, Skerries and Rathlin, provide breeding sites for seabirds in summer. The mainland coast from Portrush around to Larne is mostly a wall of cliff, but some sandy bays interrupt it at places like Whitepark Bay, Ballycastle and Murlough Bay. Much of the coast is owned by the National Trust, and the Ulster Way, a long-distance footpath of some 800 km, follows the edge of the sea from Portrush around to Glenarm before turning inland. The fit and enthusiastic birdwatcher can, therefore, walk most of this coast without much difficulty, though it will take three or four days.

The eastern coast of the county terminates at Larne Lough and Belfast Lough, both of which have significant intertidal mudflats with wildfowl and wader populations.

Inland, the principal feature of the county is the Antrim plateau where European Golden Plovers, Curlews and Red Grouse nest. This is a wild and bleak area but of immense value for breeding birds. There are some small lakes where Black-headed Gulls nest and small numbers of Redshanks also breed. The nesting waders are declining, however, and there are probably fewer than a dozen pairs of European Golden Plovers nesting now. It is an important county for breeding raptors, holding significant populations of Hen Harriers and Merlins and, increasingly, Goshawks in the coniferous plantations. Red Kites attempted to breed in the early 2000s.

The western edge of the county is formed largely by the River Bann and Lough Neagh. The Bann valley is an important migration route and has already been considered in the accounts of the Bann Estuary and Lough Beg (see under Londonderry). The Antrim side of Lough Neagh is accessible at a number of points.

132 RATHLIN ISLAND   OSNI Discoverer map: sheet 5
D17 51

Habitat

Rathlin is shaped like an inverted letter 'L'. A long arm runs from east to west and is surrounded by high cliffs where large numbers of seabirds breed. Another arm runs from north to south but is much lower as the ground falls away to sea level at the South Lighthouse at Rue Point.

The cliffs are a mixture of basalt and chalk. The southern cliffs are chalk, but from Bull Point at the western end around the entire northern coast, the cliffs and stacks are dark basalt. Inland, the most widespread habitat is moorland and rough pasture. There are several small lakes scattered around the island. Craigmacagan, midway along the southern arm, has an extensive reedbed.

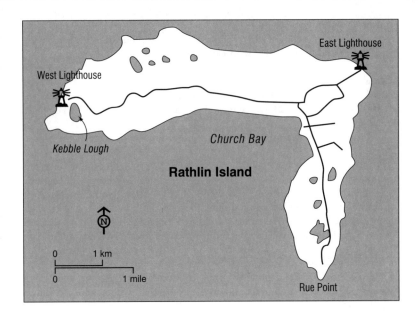

In summer the grasslands are carpeted with orchids: heath spotted, common spotted and early purple.

Species

The highlight of a visit to Rathlin for the birdwatcher must be the great numbers of seabirds. The main colonies are at the Kebble National Nature Reserve near the West Lighthouse and at the RSPB Rathlin Cliffs Reserve which runs along about 4 km of cliff. The most numerous birds are Common Guillemots and Razorbills of which there are about 90,000 and 20,000 birds respectively. Black Guillemots also nest, though in relatively miniscule numbers, with about 100 pairs. Perhaps 2,000 pairs of Puffins nest. Fulmars are quite common with about 2,000 nest sites. A small colony of Manx Shearwaters numbers several hundred birds. Great Black-backed and Lesser Black-backed Gulls and Kittiwakes (up to 10,000 nests) breed on the cliffs and both Common and Black-headed Gulls nest on the lakes.

These numbers are really spectacular, but among the seabirds are up to ten pairs of Common Buzzards and several pairs of Peregrines and Ravens. Golden Eagles have been seen on occasion. Choughs ceased to breed on the island in 1989, but one pair returned to successfully breed in 2007 and again in 2008.

On the land, Common Eiders nest on the southern arm leading out to Rue Point. Skylarks, Northern Wheatears, European Stonechats, Sedge Warblers, Meadow and Rock Pipits, Linnets, Reed Buntings and one or two pairs or Whinchats also breed. Twites breed in some years. The wet areas hold breeding Mallards, Tufted Ducks, Moorhens and Coots. Nesting waders include Oystercatchers and Ringed Plovers on the shingle beaches, Northern Lapwings on the rougher grazing land, and Common Snipes on the marshy areas.

Timing

Rathlin is best in summer when the weather is fine and the birds are on the cliffs. The period from mid–May to early July is optimal.

Access

Boats leave Ballycastle regularly during the summer, but advance booking is advisable. Caledonian McBrayne www.calmac.co.uk (tel: 028 20769299) operates the M.V. *Canna.*

Accommodation is available in several guesthouses, but there is no official campground.

The island bus operators will take visitors to the West Lighthouse, about 8 km from the harbour at Church Bay. A bus saves time, but the walk provides a much better feel for the island and good views of cliffs where Common Buzzards should be seen. At the West Lighthouse, most of the breeding seabird species can be seen, but Black Guillemots should be looked for below the chalk cliffs Access to the Lighthouse platform is only by escort with the RSPB warden, Liam McFaul (telephone 028 20763948). Development is in progress to improve access for disabled visitors – please contact the reserve for more information.

The road to Rue Point provides access to moorland on the way out where Twites are a possibility and eventually to the Point itself where Common Eiders and Oystercatchers nest.

An excellent booklet on the island, its geology, fauna and flora is available for purchase.

Starlings

CALENDAR

Summer: Shelduck, Mallard, Tufted Duck, Common Eider, Little Grebe, Fulmar, Manx Shearwater (visible from the boat to and from the island), Gannet (also visible from the boat), Shag, Common Buzzard, Peregrine, Kestrel, Coot, Oystercatcher, Ringed Plover, Northern Lapwing, Common Snipe, Redshank, Common, Black-headed, Herring, Lesser Black-backed and Great Black-backed Gulls, Kittiwake, Razorbill, Common and Black Guillemots, Puffin, Rock Dove, Skylark, Raven, Hooded Crow, Northern Wheatear, European Stonechat, Whinchat, Sedge Warbler, Meadow and Rock Pipits, Linnet, Reed Bunting, occasional Twite.

133 FAIR HEAD

OSNI Discoverer map: sheet 5
D17 43

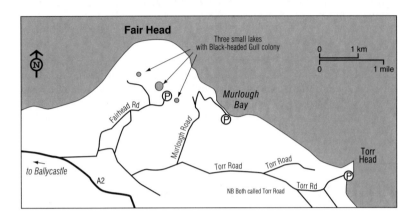

Habitat and Species

Fair Head is a magnificent headland with sheer basalt cliffs rising nearly 200 m from the sea. It is famous among ornithologists as the site where a pair of Golden Eagles bred in the 1950s.

Nowadays, the largest raptors to be found here are Common Buzzards, which are quite numerous, and Peregrines, but Sparrowhawks and Kestrels are

Cuckoo

both common. Rock Doves, Cuckoos, Meadow Pipits, European Stonechats, Northern Wheatears and Ravens can also be seen on the top of the head which has a surface of heather and rough pasture. There are also three small lakes which hold Tufted Ducks and Black-headed Gulls.

Just around the corner to the east is Murlough Bay where Oystercatchers, Curlews and Redshanks can be seen on the shore and Fulmars, Gannets, Common Eiders, gulls and auks on the sea.

Access

One of the great scenic sights of Northern Ireland, Fair Head is on the north Antrim coast, about 8 km to the east of Ballycastle. From Ballycastle, drive east for Cushendun. After 4 km turn left, following the signs for Fair Head and Murlough. There are well signposted car parks at both locations.

The top of the cliff has marked paths. The enthusiastic walker can follow trails around the head and back to Ballycastle.

134 CRAIGAGH WOOD OSNI Discoverer map: sheet 5,
OSNI Glens of Antrim Map 1:25000
D 18 30

Habitat and Species

Craigagh Wood is a woodland area in the Glens of Antrim which has the best track record of breeding Wood Warbler in Northern Ireland, as well as the usual bird communities of Irish deciduous woodland. The woods lie along either side of the Glendun river valley. As you ascend the valley, the deciduous woodland gives way to coniferous woodland and a careful lookout should be kept for Goshawk which is slowly increasing in this part of Ireland. Tree-nesting Hen Harriers also occur here. When you finally emerge from the coniferous belt, the terrain opens out into blanket bogland. This is the Antrim Plateau. Merlin, Red Grouse and European Golden Plover all breed here, but at very low densities.

Access

Take the A2 north from Cushendall to Cushendun, and continue north past the turnoff for Cushendun (Knocknacarry Road). Turn left after 1 km onto Glendun Road, continue along this road for about 4 km as it ascends the valley, stopping at suitable spots.

135 RAMORE HEAD
OSNI Discoverer map: sheet 4
C85 41

Habitat and Species

Ramore Head is at the tip of the promontory which extends to the north from the town of Portrush. The low cliffs are basaltic and grass-topped, but the principal feature for the birdwatcher is the head's suitability for autumn seawatching.

In north-westerly winds a great diversity of birds can be seen. Red-throated and Great Northern Divers, Fulmars, Manx and Sooty Shearwaters, European and Leach's Storm-petrels, Gannets and the three common skua species are regular. Sabine's Gulls and Balearic Shearwaters are annual and Macaronesian Shearwater has once been recorded. Long-tailed Skuas have been annual in recent years, Mediterranean, Little, Glaucous and Iceland Gulls occur in some years and Ross's has been seen.

As well as seabirds, Barnacle Geese can be seen on the Skerries Islands off-shore and Common Eiders, Purple Sandpipers and Turnstones on the rocks below.

Access

Follow the traffic through Portrush to the harbour. Continue onwards, fork right, then turn left at the top of the hill and continue to the car park at Lansdown. Park the car and walk to the coastguard look-out on the cliff.

136 SHANE'S CASTLE
OSNI Discoverer map: sheet 14
J13 86

Habitat

Shane's Castle Park is located on the estate of the O'Neills and co-exists with a steam railway which attracts large numbers of visitors. The castle is ruined but is surrounded by fine mixed woodland. The entire estate is a popular place for outings from Belfast, only 29 km away.

The park is bordered on the west side by Lough Neagh and is one of the prime access points for viewing the wintering wildfowl there.

Species

From the battlements of the old castle large flocks of wildfowl can be seen in winter and this is probably as good a place as any to see a representative selection of the birds of Lough Neagh. Great rafts of Tufted Ducks and Pochards, together with Eurasian Wigeons, Mallards, Common Teals, Scaups and Common Goldeneyes and, at times, Gadwalls, Pintails and Red-breasted Mergansers. Rarer ducks seen here include American Wigeon, Red-crested Pochard, Goosander and Smew. These are mainly winter species but in summer Great Crested Grebes nest and their fabulous courtship display can be seen in April and May. Whooper Swans can also be seen very occasionally along this shoreline.

Large numbers of gulls roost off Shane's Castle in winter. Little and Ring-billed Gulls have been recorded among the commoner species.

The wooded area is good for small birds. Use the well marked nature trails. In summer Blackcaps and Woodcocks nest but all the common woodlandbirds, such as Common Chiffchaffs, Spotted Flycatchers, Treecreepers and Long-tailed Tits, breed as well.

The reedbeds which fringe the lake shore hold breeding Sedge Warblers and Reed Buntings. The Milburn stream has Grey Wagtails, Dippers, Kingfishers and Moorhens.

This is a good place to see mammals. Fallow Deer, Badgers, Otters and Pine Martens all occur here.

Timing

In winter the numbers of wildfowl on the lough are at their highest and the chances of a rarity greatest. Summer, however, provides views of nesting Great Crested Grebes and woodlandbirds.

Access

Shane's Castle is reached from Belfast by heading west on the M2 and leaving the motorway at the A26 exit where the main signs indicate the exit for Ballymena and Coleraine. The first left turn at the roundabout is sign posted for Shane's Castle. Take the road towards Antrim and turn right after 5 km along the road for Randalstown. The entrance to the reserve is 1 km along this road on the left.

There is an admittance fee payable at Shane's Castle. The reserve is open to the public on certain days between Easter and mid-September from mid-day to 7 pm. At other times the gateman should be contacted in advance (telephone 028 94428216).

However, year-round access to the woodland and lakeshore can be found at Rea's Wood situated south west of Antrim town on the Dublin Road; park behind the DeerPark Hotel.

Long-tailed Tits

CALENDAR

All year: Mute Swan, Common Teal, Mallard, Tufted Duck, Pochard, Great Crested Grebe, Moorhen, Coot, Black-headed, Common Gull, Herring and Great Black-backed Gulls, Dipper, Kingfisher, Grey Wagtail, Goldcrest, Long-tailed Tit, Lesser Redpoll, Reed Bunting.

Winter: Whooper Swan, Eurasian Wigeon, Gadwall, Pintail, Scaup, Common Goldeneye. Possibility of rare ducks, Northern Lapwing, Curlew, Redwing, Fieldfare, Siskin.

Summer: Blackcap, Sedge Warbler, Common Chiffchaff, Willow Warbler.

137 BELFAST LOUGH: NORTH SHORE

OSNI Discoverer map: sheet 15
J35 78; J42 87

Habitat and Species

The north coast of Belfast Lough from Newtownabbey to Carrickfergus has a number of viewing points for seeing the ducks and grebes wintering on the sheltered waters of the lough and the waders using the rather limited intertidal mudflats. As the breeding population of Great Crested Grebes has expanded in recent years on Lough Neagh, so the winter numbers on Belfast Lough have increased and close to 1,000 are now counted each year. Occasional Slavonian Grebes occur among them.

Large numbers of Tufted Ducks, Common Goldeneyes and Red-breasted Mergansers flock on the open water and a few Scaups occur. Although the numbers of Common Goldeneyes at 200–300 are far less than the thousands which occur on Lough Neagh, this is still a very important wintering site for the species. Common Eiders, Long-tailed Ducks and Common Scoters are more often found at the mouth of Carrickfergus Harbour.

The waders of the intertidal zone include Oystercatchers, Ringed and European Golden Plovers, Northern Lapwings, Curlews, Bar-tailed Godwits, Redshanks, Greenshanks, Dunlins, Purple Sandpipers and Turnstones.

All the common gull species occur throughout much of the year and Iceland, Glaucous, Ring-billed, Little and Mediterranean Gulls have been seen.

Access (see map 140 Belfast Lough)

From Belfast take the M2 and then the M5 for Carrickfergus. At the roundabout at the end of the M5 take the right-hand turn for Hazelbank Park. Park the car and walk along the path which runs along the shore to Macedon Point and beyond.

The A2 leads on to Whiteabbey, Loughshore Park and Carrickfergus. The lough can be scanned with a telescope from several points along here.

Carrickfergus has an impressive Norman castle, well worthy of inspection, even if your priority is birds. About 2 km before the town, there is a car park on the left of the dual carriageway with a long pipeline running out to sea from the shore on the other side of the road. This is a good place for gulls.

At Carrickfergus itself, the bay can be scanned from the harbour. Fisherman's Quay, about 1 km beyond the Castle, is an excellent vantage point for seaducks.

138 LARNE LOUGH

OSNI Discoverer map: sheet 9
D42 00

Habitat and Species

Larne Lough is a sheltered sea lough impounded behind the long arm of Islandmagee with mudflats, saltmarsh and some reedbeds. Whooper Swans, Brent Geese, Eurasian Wigeons, Common Teals and Mallards winter here and occasional rare waders turn up in autumn. Great Crested Grebes winter in small numbers.

In summer Swan Island, an RSPB reserve, is an important tern colony with breeding Arctic, Common, Sandwich and, occasionally, a few pairs of Roseate Terns. Red-breasted Mergansers and Black-headed Gulls also nest on the island, and in recent years a pair of Mediterranean Gulls has attempted to breed.

Access

Larne Lough can be seen well from the A2 road. Leave Belfast on the M2 and head north onto the M5 and then the A2. The southern end of the lough is 25 km from Belfast.

Suitable places for viewing the lough include Ballycarry causeway at the southern end, laybys on the A2 and the village of Glynn.

Access to Swan Island is prohibited at all times. However, the feeding terns can be seen well from the shore of the lough.

139 PORTMORE LOUGH RSPB RESERVE

OSNI Discoverer map: sheet 20
J11 69

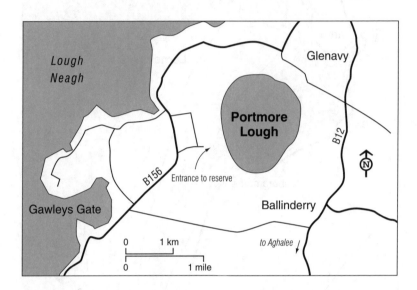

Habitat and Species

Portmore Lough is located about 1 km from the eastern shore of Lough Neagh. It is an RSPB Reserve open at all times except Christmas Day and supports important communities of breeding birds as well as being a wintering site for wildfowl. Its breeding duck list is one of the best in Ireland; it is one of the few places where both Shovelers and Ruddy Ducks breed, and much important work has been carried out to improve wet meadows for breeding Northern Lapwings and Redshanks. Breeding birds also include Tree Sparrow and what are probably the most northerly breeding Reed Warblers in Ireland. The surrounding pastures are good for wintering Whooper Swan and Greylag Geese with occasional Pink-footed Geese.

Access

To get to Portmore, take the A26 north from the M1 at Moira and then take the second turn left (Soldierstown Road) to Aghalee. In Aghalee village, the reserve is signposted. Make a right in Aghalee onto the Ballycairn Road and travel about 5 km to Gawley's Gate where you turn right and after about 1.5 km, the reserve entrance is signposted on the right. Although the main trails are not wheelchair-accessible, a 500 m all-weather path suitable for wheelchairs extends from the car park to a grassed picnic area. The information shelter has a picnic table suitable for wheelchairs giving a good view across the reserve.

DOWN

Co Down has two of the finest Irish wetland sites; the great sea loughs of Belfast Lough and Strangford Lough. The coastline is low-lying, even though the Mourne Mountains come close to part of it, and has several promontories which are good for seabirds. The Copeland Islands, lying off the north of the Ards Peninsula, include the oldest extant bird observatory in the country and the longest studied seabird colony. The Ards Peninsula, the arm which encloses Strangford Lough, has fishing ports, such as Portavogie which attract gulls and occasional rarities, and a rocky shoreline which has been found by regular censuses to be extremely important for waders.

The largest inlets by far are Belfast and Strangford Loughs. Both are well watched and have fine bird populations. But Killough Harbour and Dundrum Bay, slightly further south, and Carlingford Lough, which divides Down in Northern Ireland from Louth in the Republic, should not be overlooked as good birding sites where the unexpected can at times turn up.

While the north-eastern, eastern and southern boundaries of the county are entirely coastal, the western side follows the Newry Canal for much of its length. This county and Fermanagh, far to the west, are the only two of Northern Ireland's counties which do not share portion of Lough Neagh.

Inland, the county has a number of small reed-fringed lakes, many of which hold small numbers of both breeding and wintering wildfowl, and the south-eastern corner is dominated by the Mourne Mountains. The Mournes are not particularly rich in birds, but their wildness and the presence of Ravens, Peregrines and, in summer, a few pairs of Ring Ouzels, are attractions for the visitor who wants to leave the coast.

140 BELFAST LOUGH: SOUTH SHORE
OSNI Discoverer map: sheet 15
J37 78; J50 83

Habitat
Belfast Lough is a large and rather broad sea lough with the heavily industrialised city of Belfast at its head. The northern shore is in Antrim and is dealt with under that county. The southern shore still has quite extensive mudflats, though these have been steadily reduced by land reclamation over the past 150 years. Because of industrial encroachment, the Lough cannot be reached by the birdwatcher all along this shore. Instead, only certain points can be visited.

Working from Belfast city centre out along the coastline are a number of sites where the birds can be seen. Victoria Park is right at the head of the lough and has a small lake which is dry in winter and acts as a roost for waders. The park adjoins Belfast Lough and is separated from the intertidal flats by an embankment. The area has many sports pitches and is thronged with people at weekends.

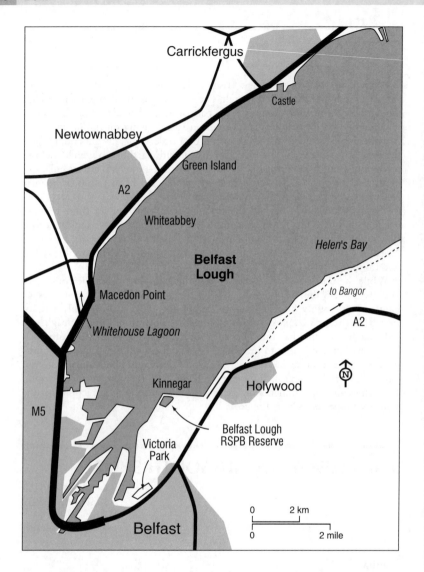

Some 5 km north-east of Belfast is the Belfast Lough RSPB Reserve, where extensive sand and mudflats are backed by a brackish lagoon, patches of scrub, rough pasture and a sewage works. This is a rich and relatively undisturbed patchwork of habitats right on the edge of industrialised Belfast. The lagoon, situated between an oil terminal and the Lough, is an important roosting site for the birds which feed on the muddy estuary at low tide.

Continuing land claim at the lough culminating in plans to drain three brackish lagoons led to a campaign to save at least one of them and the mud-flats. This has resulted in the establishment of the Belfast Lough RSPB Reserve and agreement not just to restore degraded habitat but to create new wildlife habitat as well.

Farther on, from Holywood, the shoreline is more accessible to the bird-watcher as it runs out to Cultra, Helen's Bay and, eventually, Bangor at the mouth of Belfast Lough. The shoreline is a mixture of rocky, sandy and muddy coast. A coastal path runs from Holywood to Bangor and the surrounding land includes grassland and scrub with some wooded areas.

Species

The south side of the lough has Great Crested Grebes, divers, Scaups, Common Goldeneyes, Red-breasted Mergansers, Common Scoters, Common Eiders and a few Long-tailed Ducks much like the northern side. The mouth of the lough tends to be best for most seaducks though they can be seen at any point.

Large numbers of Shelducks, Eurasian Wigeons, Common Teals and Mallards winter, with smaller numbers of Shovelers and Pochards. The lagoon at Belfast Lough RSPB Reserve is the best place to see them. This is also the best place for large wader flocks which in recent years have included peaks of 5,000 Oystercatchers and 2,000 Redshanks in autumn and 3,000 Northern Lapwings, 1,000 Curlews and 1,000 Dunlins in winter. Victoria Park is also a good spot for each of these wader species at high tide. For birds which prefer rockier shores, such as Turnstones and Purple Sandpipers, the best places are near the mouth of the lough.

The lough is an excellent place for seeing scarcer migrant wildfowl and waders. Green-winged and Blue-winged Teals have been seen at the RSPB reserve in winter, Black-winged Stilt in spring and Little Ringed Plover and several species of American wader in autumn. Garganey is annual in spring and Curlew Sandpiper, Little Stint, Ruff and Spotted Redshank are regular autumn migrants.

In autumn and winter Peregrines hunt the area regularly. Large numbers of gulls are present for most of the year and scarcer species such as Ring-billed, Iceland, Glaucous and Mediterranean are annual, with as many as six Ring-billed Gulls recorded at the Belfast Lough RSPB Reverve at times. In spring, summer and autumn, terns and skuas visit the Lough. They are usually better seen from near the mouth of the lough but Black and White-winged Black Terns have been seen at the RSPB reserve.

The unkempt vicinity of the Belfast Harbour Estate is not only attractive for birds in autumn, winter and spring. Its diversity of habitat also provides nesting sites for Shelducks, Mallard, Coots, Moorhens, Northern Lapwings, Ringed Plovers, Common and Arctic Terns, Common Snipes and Black-headed Gulls as well as one or two Shovelers.

Further out along the shore of the lough, most common woodlandbirds can be seen from the path between Holywood and Bangor.

Timing

The wonderful point about Belfast Lough is that rewarding visits can be made at any time of the year. In autumn and winter, wildfowl and waders are most numerous; in spring there is obvious passage migration and by the summer breeding birds are on their territories. Rarities are more likely in autumn than at other seasons, but Black-winged Stilt was seen in May and White-winged Black Tern in June and July, so, a visit always holds out the real possibility of the unexpected.

As with most estuarine areas, a visit within three hours either side of high tide is best.

Access

Working from Belfast out along the coast, each of the sites dealt with is reached as follows.

Victoria Park lies between the Sydenham Bypass and Belfast Lough, but is approached by following the signs from Holywood Road to Connsbrook Avenue. Turn left off Connsbrook Avenue down Park Avenue and drive to the right and under the Sydenham Bypass to Victoria Park. The park can also be reached by parking at Inverary Drive and crossing over the footbridge.

The outer part of Belfast Lough is far more accessible. A footpath runs the 17 km from Holywood to Bangor and can be accessed at a number of points. At Holywood, the path commences on the shore opposite the Army Depot near Kinnegar, but it can be reached by turning left at Cultra, Sea Park, or Helen's Bay. The path terminates at Pickie Pool at Bangor.

Kinnegar and Belfast Lough RSPB Reserve are reached by taking the A2 from Belfast for Holywood and Bangor. At the first set of traffic lights, turn left and follow the road (Dee Street) to the Harbour security checkpoint which is usually open. Turn right after the checkpoint and drive along the shore for about 2 km to the entrance of Belfast Lough RSPB Reserve on the left-hand side of the road. The observation room here is wheelchair-accessible, as is one of the viewpoints.

CALENDAR

All year: Mute Swan, Shelduck, Common Teal, Mallard, Shoveler, Common Eider, Red-breasted Merganser, Great Crested Grebe, Cormorant, Shag, Moorhen, Coot, Peregrine, Kestrel, Sparrowhawk, Common Buzzard, Oystercatcher, Northern Lapwing, Curlew, Common Snipe, Redshank, Turnstone, Black-headed, Common, Herring, Lesser Black-backed and Great Black-backed Gulls, European Stonechat, Linnet.

Autumn: Eurasian Wigeon, Common Teal, Common Goldeneye, Scaup, Long-tailed Duck, Common Scoter, divers, European Golden and Grey Plovers, Knot, Dunlin, Curlew Sandpiper, Little Stint, Purple Sandpiper, Ruff, Black-tailed and Bar-tailed Godwits, Spotted Redshank, Greenshank, Common Sandpiper, vagrant waders from North America, Ring-billed Gull, Mediterranean Gull.

Winter: Brent Goose, Eurasian Wigeon, Common Teal, Common Goldeneye, Scaup, Long-tailed Duck, Common Scoter, divers, European Golden and Grey Plovers, Dunlin, Purple Sandpiper, Jack Snipe, Bar-tailed Godwit, Greenshank, occasional Ruff, Glaucous Gull, Iceland Gull, Ring-billed Gull.

Spring: late-staying wildfowl and waders. Annual Garganey. Whimbrel and Common Sandpiper, Terns. Possibility of exotic vagrants.

Summer: breeding wildfowl and terns.

141 STRANGFORD LOUGH

OSNI Discoverer map: sheet 21,
OSNI Strangford Lough Map 1:25000
J48 72; J58 5

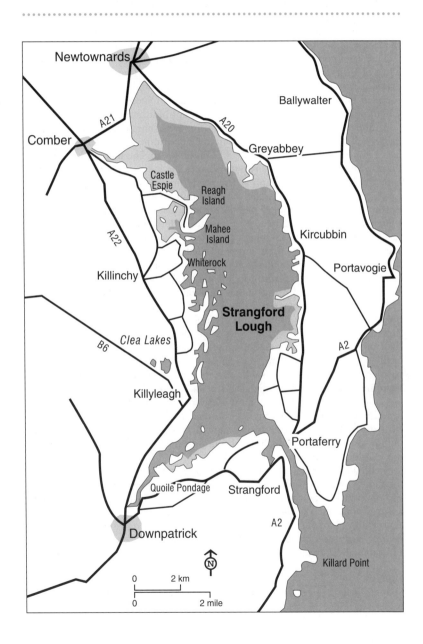

Habitat

Strangford is an enormous sea lough encompassing a range of habitats. Much of it has been managed by the National Trust for many years and wildfowl and wader counts have been carried out for almost 50 years so quite a lot is known of the distribution of its birds.

Strangford is more than 30 km long and has an area in excess of 15,000 ha. The lough varies in depth but, at its deepest, reaches 60 m. It connects with the Irish Sea at the 'Narrows', between Portaferry and the village of Strangford, where the exit channel is 30 m deep and only 800 m wide. The main body of the lough is much broader, varying up to 8 km from side to side.

There are more than 120 islands in the lough and many more reefs and rocks. Most of them are on the west side. Most of the islands are partly submerged drumlins, created by glaciers which deposited soil and gravel in a mosaic of rounded hills. The shoreline is extremely indented and extends for about 240 km, more than a third of the entire coastline of Northern Ireland.

Although the sea and the islands are important for some bird species, the really vital habitat for the birdwatcher is the enormous area of intertidal mud-flats, estimated to cover 40% of the area of the lough. The intertidal zone at the Narrows comprises rocky shore. Further into the lough there are shores where large boulders lie on sand and coarse mud. This habitat is widespread on the east side of the lough and on the west side south of Killyleagh. From Greyabbey north, however, fine-grained mudflats extend across the northern end of the Lough and around to Mahee Island on the western side.

The northern end of Strangford has large areas of eel-grass *Zostera*, which provide rich feeding for Brent Geese on their arrival from the Canadian Arctic. The mudflats surrounding the shallow bays at this end have a green appearance in early autumn as the plants develop, but by the end of November they have been so heavily grazed by geese that the mudflats revert to their usual hue.

Above the tideline there are areas of saltmarsh in the north-west corner of the lough, especially at the Comber river estuary near Castle Espie. Behind the shoreline, the land is low-lying with drumlins to the north and west. Most of the land to the north is farmed intensively for cereals and vegetables and many of the old hedges and ditches in the fields between Newtownards and Comber have been removed. Farther south, there are smaller fields and, around the exit from the lough, the fields are smaller still and divided by dry stone walls. There are some areas of scrubland and a scattering of woodland clumps.

Around the edge of the lough are a number of small marshes and freshwater lakes surrounded by reeds, willows and alders. These small lakes provide feeding for some wildfowl, which fly to and from the mudflats on the lough when the tides rise or they are disturbed. The Quoile Pondage, a freshwater lagoon formed by the impounding of the River Quoile by a barrage in 1957, is much the most important freshwater habitat on the fringe of the lough. The estuary was once backed by the flood meadows of the Downpatrick Marshes, famous for geese and ducks in the first half of the century, but now largely drained and almost devoid of wildfowl. Despite the Quoile Pondage now being almost entirely freshwater, there are still flood meadows which attract Greylag Geese and Eurasian Wigeons. This particular area is a National Nature Reserve.

Species

Strangford holds peak numbers of nearly 25,000 wildfowl and about 45,000 waders, making it one of the most important wetlands in the country. Its particular attraction is that many of these birds can be seen within 20 km of Belfast.

The dominant feature of Strangford's wintering wildfowl is its great flocks of Brent Geese. The first birds arrive from northern Canada in late August and flocks pile in during September and October to reach an October peak of 10,000–12,000 birds. They feed voraciously and, having grazed the *Zostera*, many move on to sites further south and the remainder turn to other food such as green algae *Enteromorpha*. Some birds move on quite quickly, so the lough is a vitally important staging point for the species. Among the Pale-bellied Brent Geese are, nearly always, one or two Black Brants, which usually winter on the Pacific coast of North America. The same individuals appear to return annually to Strangford, and Greyabbey is probably the best place to start a search for them. Dark-bellied Brents have been recorded as well, and there are indications that birds with mixed Pale-bellied Brent/Black Brant parentage are also occurring.

Most of the other geese to be seen at the lough are feral. Greylag, Barnacle and Canada Geese have all been released here. A few wild Greenland White-fronts sometimes occur and occasional Pink-footed Geese have been seen. The common swan of the lough is the Mute Swan, but a small number of Whooper Swans do winter. The stubble fields between Strabo and Comber are good places to look for them.

Strangford was once famous for its huge wintering flocks of Eurasian Wigeons. As recently as the 1970s there were over 20,000, but nowadays the peak is only 2,000. This was thought to be due to competitive pressure from the increasing Brent Geese, but subsequent research has shown it to be due to declining food supplies specific to Eurasian Wigeons.

Shelducks and Mallards occur in similar numbers to Eurasian Wigeons, Common Teals in somewhat smaller numbers and there are a few hundred each of Pintails, Shovelers, Pochards, Tufted Ducks, Common Goldeneyes and Red-breasted Mergansers. Gadwalls and Scaups also occur in small numbers. Up to 20 Slavonian Grebes and a few Black-throated Divers winter as well.

Wader numbers are very impressive. The lough is internationally important for its Knot and Redshank numbers. Up to 10,000 Oystercatchers, 9,000 European Golden Plovers, 10,000 Northern Lapwings, 10,000 Knots, 8,000 Dunlins, 1,000 Bar-tailed Godwits, 2,000 Curlews and 3,000 Redshanks occur each autumn and winter. All the other common wader species occur as well. Passage migrants, such as Ruffs and Spotted Redshanks, sometimes appear on the lagoons at the Castle Espie Conservation Centre or the river nearby and at the Quoile Pondage.

The southern end of the lough holds substantial numbers of Turnstones on the rocky shores. Smaller numbers of Purple Sandpipers can be found among them.

In summer, the lough is an important breeding area for wildfowl, waders and terns. A few pairs of feral Greylag, Barnacle and Canada Geese breed, mainly on islands. Shelduck, Mallard, Gadwall, Tufted Duck, Red-breasted Merganser and one or two Common Eiders nest on the lough. The breeding waders include Oystercatcher, Ringed Plover, Northern Lapwing and a couple of pairs of Redshanks.

Large numbers of gulls and terns nest on the islands of the lough. Over 5,000 pairs of Black-headed Gulls, 160 pairs of Common Gulls, 80 pairs of Lesser Black-backed Gulls, 50 pairs of Great Black-backs and 300 pairs of Herring

Gulls breed. The most numerous terns are Sandwich with about 1,000 nesting pairs; about 600 pairs of Common and 400 pairs of Arctic Terns nest as well. Roseate Terns once bred here, but now only occur as rare nonbreeding visitors. Cormorants, Black Guillemots and Herons also breed.

Although the area of the lough is enormous and the birds widely distributed, most of them can be seen at a small number of sites where viewing conditions are excellent. The Wildfowl and Wetlands Trust has a reserve at Castle Espie and the Department of the Environment (NI) has a reserve at the Quoile Pondage. Both these sites have visitor centres.

Quoile Pondage is an excellent breeding area for a number of species including Great Crested Grebe, Grey Heron, Shelduck, Mallard, Gadwall and Tufted Duck. Terns feed here in summer. In winter, the Pondage has hundreds of Greylag Geese, mostly feral, Mallards, Eurasian Wigeons, Common Teals, Tufted Ducks, Pochards and Common Goldeneyes. Smaller numbers of Gadwalls, Pintails, Shovelers and Scaups also occur and it is at this site that Ireland's first Barrow's Goldeneye overwintered in successive winters from 2005 to 2008. Wader numbers are not very large, but diversity is high. Spotted Redshanks are regular and Wood and Green Sandpipers occasional in autumn. The islands where the gulls and terns nest are, for obvious reasons, closed to the public, though Swan Island, close to the quay at Strangford village, provides excellent viewing opportunities because of its proximity to the mainland.

The lough is so extensive that parts of it attract seabirds. Gannets feed in the Narrows at the southern end and Manx Shearwaters, Fulmars and occasional European Storm-petrels can be seen in the same area. Razorbills and Common Guillemots feed in the lough at all times of the year.

Around the edge of the lough, the shoreline hedge and gorse scrub provide excellent habitat for European Stonechats, Linnets, Twites, Reed Buntings and Tree Sparrows. Birds of prey quarter the saltmarshes and Short-eared Owls are regular.

Timing

Strangford is at its best for wildfowl in September and October when the Brent Geese peak. Wader diversity is probably at its highest at the same time. Peak numbers are later for some species.

The best time for visiting is within three hours of high tide when the birds are within relatively close range of the shore.

The breeding terns and gulls can best be seen from May to July, though the Sandwich Terns arrive earlier.

Access

There are numerous access points as the road system runs around the entire Lough. Bob Brown's book on Strangford, *Strangford Lough – The Wildlife of an Irish Sea Lough* (available online at www.strangfordlough.com), includes a gazetteer which takes a tour around the complete shoreline and also a tour by boat through the centre of the lough. This account must necessarily concentrate on the most prominent access points. On the western side the following are among the best places to see a variety of species.

Island Hill is close to Comber, the starting point for a tour of the west side of Strangford. From Comber take the road for Newtownards (the A21). After 1.5 km take the right turn onto Ringcreevy Road. This links with Island Hill

Road and terminates at the shore, where there is a public car park. This section of the lough is excellent for Brent Geese and for wintering waders.

Castle Espie is a Wildfowl and Wetlands Trust reserve and has an impressive wildfowl collection, an art gallery, a restaurant and shop, an education room and woodland walks. Leave Comber on the A22 heading south for Killyleagh. After less than 500 m turn left at the signpost for Mahee Island. Follow the road for about 4 km until you see the signpost to the reserve on the left. Drive in and park. There are lagoons here where scarce waders such as Ruffs and Spotted Redshanks are sometimes seen in autumn. These lagoons are the remnants of limestone and clay quarries. To see the wildfowl on the mudflats, walk from the Centre buildings towards the shore or take the lane down to the shore immediately before the Reserve (on the Comber side). The Montgomery Hide is situated on the edge of the lough and provides good views of Brent Geese, Shelducks, Eurasian Wigeons and waders. It really is essential to be here within two hours of high tide as otherwise the birds are very distant. The reserve is open during daylight hours throughout the year, except at Christmas, and there is a modest entrance fee (tel: 028 9187 4146).

Island Reagh is another access point to the mudflats. Continue on beyond Castle Espie in the direction of Mahee Island. At Ballydrain turn left onto Ringneill Road and follow the signs for Nendrum. The road crosses a causeway onto Island Reagh. About 1 km after the causeway, a small car park is reached. A National Trust hide has facilities for the disabled. This section of mudflats has fewer Brent Geese but is good for Pintails, Shovelers and Black-tailed Godwits.

Whiterock Bay is further south. Take the A22 road from Comber for Killyleagh and turn left at Balloo, following the signpost to Whiterock. This is a popular sailing centre but it holds Brent Geese, Common Teals and waders on the mudflats opposite the saltmarsh north of the yacht club. The marsh itself is a good place to get excellent views of Common Snipes. Farther out, near Hen Island, Common Goldeneyes and occasional Slavonian Grebes feed in winter.

Quoile Pondage National Nature Reserve, a reserve operated by the Environment Agency of the Department of the Environment, is at the southern end of the west side of the lough. Follow the A22 through Killyleagh and on to the Quoile Bridge. Turn left over the bridge and then left again, following the signs for Strangford. The Quoile Countryside Centre is well signposted and has an exhibition centre illustrating how the area has been changed by the barrage. Access to most of the reserve is restricted to prevent disturbance. Visitors should contact the warden for advice on open access areas for viewing the birds. There is a hide at Castle Island which overlooks the largest concentrations of birds. The reserve is open throughout the year and admission is free (for the visitor centre tel: 028 4461 5520).

On the east side of the lough are a number of additional points where access is straightforward. Tidebank is on the southern side of Newtownards. Leave Newtownards on the A20 for Portaferry. Just outside the town, there is a small car park where the road meets the shore of the lough. Look for the square sewage pumping station building on the right; the parking area is just beyond the entrance. From here it is possible to walk along the embankment and see flocks of Brent Geese and waders.

The Maltings at Ballyreagh is about 1 km further along the A20. There is a layby which gives good views of massive flocks of European Golden Plovers and Knots as well as the other common wader species. Brent Geese also congregate here, and Whooper Swans can sometimes be seen.

The old Gasworks are farther on along the A20 towards Greyabbey. There is a National Trust car park on the right-hand side about 300 m beyond the entrance to Mount Stewart. The gasworks at one stage manufactured gas for the estate, but now provide an excellent vantage point for scanning the mudflats with binoculars and telescopes. The offshore islands can be seen well from this point.

Greyabbey is a small village on the A20 about 12 km south-east of Newtownards. The car park on the right-hand side, just beyond the village, overlooks the lough. This part of Strangford does not attract so many birds as the mudflats to the north, but it has held one or two Black Brant in the recent past.

Between Greyabbey and Kircubbin, farther south again, the coastline is good for Slavonian Grebes, and both Black-throated Diver and Red-necked Grebe have been reported in recent years. Access is difficult along much of the shore. The best viewing point is from the shoreline at Kircubbin.

CALENDAR

All year: Mute Swan, Greylag, Barnacle and Canada Geese, Shelduck, Mallard, Gadwall, Shoveler, Tufted Duck, Pochard, Common Eider, Red-breasted Merganser, Great Crested and Little Grebes, Cormorant, Grey Heron, Coot, Moorhen, Common Buzzard, Kestrel, Oystercatcher, Ringed Plover, Northern Lapwing, Common Snipe, Curlew, Redshank, gulls, Black Guillemot.

Winter: Whooper Swan, Brent Goose, Eurasian Wigeon, Common Teal, Pintail, Scaup, Common Goldeneye, Little Egret, Peregrine, European Golden and Grey Plovers,

Knot, Dunlin, Purple Sandpiper, Black-tailed and Bar-tailed Godwits, Common and Jack Snipes, Greenshank.

Summer: Common Sandpiper, Common, Arctic and Sandwich Terns, possibility of Roseate Tern.

Autumn: wintering wildfowl and waders, plus Whimbrel, Common Sandpiper, Spotted Redshank, Ruff, possible Little Stint, terns.

Spring: wintering wildfowl and waders, plus Whimbrel, Common Sandpiper and terns.

Note: The map for Castle Espie is redrawn from The Wildfowl and Wetlands Trust reserve map; the map for Quoile Pondage Nature Reserve is redrawn from the Department of the Environment's reserve map.

---

142 COPELAND BIRD OBSERVATORY

OSNI Discoverer map: sheet 15
J59 85

Habitat

The Bird Observatory on Lighthouse Island, one of the three islands of the Copeland group, is the oldest in Ireland, having been founded in 1954. The islands are located off the north coast of Down, about 7 km from Donaghadee. John's Island is small, oval-shaped and quite high, with small cliffs on its east side and gentle slopes on the other sides. The area is only 16 ha and the highest point is 30 m above sea level. The island is covered with grass, but there are elders, willows and sycamores in sheltered parts. The observatory itself is based in the old lighthouse buildings, which have been restored to provide accommodation and ringing facilities. (The new lighthouse is located on the neighbouring Mew Island).

Species

The Copeland Islands group have a breeding colony of some 4,500 pairs of Manx Shearwaters; this has been the subject of a ringing study for nearly 60 years. Birds first ringed several decades ago are still occasionally retrapped, so some are clearly very long-lived. The most distant recoveries have been of several birds in South America. There are also breeding Great Black-backed, Lesser Black-backed, Herring and Common Gulls and small numbers of Fulmars and Black Guillemots. The neighbouring Big Copeland Island holds Ireland's largest Arctic Tern colony, and Mediterranean Gull has also bred there. A few pairs of Common Eiders, Red-breasted Mergansers, Oystercatchers, Water Rails and Stock Doves also nest. European Storm-petrels are caught and ringed at night in late summer, but do not breed on the island.

Passerine migration in spring and autumn is not as varied as in south coast counties, and rarities are much less frequent. However, good numbers of Northern Wheatears, Willow Warblers, Common Chiffchaffs and Goldcrests are recorded together with small numbers of Whinchats, Common Redstarts and other warbler species. Numbers of migrants in spring are usually higher than in autumn.

Rare birds do turn up, however, and the island has had such extreme rarities as White's Thrush, Scarlet Tanager and Fox Sparrow.

Timing
As the island is uninhabited, visits must be made by prior arrangement with the observatory bookings secretary, and are easiest if a party of regular visitors is joined. The islands are manned most weekends between April and October and there are day visits in June.

Access
The island is private and access is by prior arrangement with the Bookings Secretary, Neville McKee, 67 Temple Rise, Templepatrick, Antrim BT39 OAG (tel: 028 9443 3068; email: neville.mckee@btinternet.com). The boat leaves from Donaghadee.

CALENDAR

Summer: Manx Shearwater, European Storm-petrel, Fulmar, Common Eider, Water Rail, gulls, terns, Black Guillemot.

Spring: Northern Wheatear, Willow Warbler, Common Chiffchaff, Grasshopper Warbler, Blackcap, Garden Warbler, Common Whitethroat, Goldcrest, Common Redstart, Spotted Flycatcher, Meadow and Tree Pipits.

Autumn: Great and Arctic Skuas, Sedge Warbler, Common Chiffchaff, Willow Warbler, Common Whitethroat, Blackcap, Goldcrest, Spotted Flycatcher, Meadow Pipit, Skylark, possibility of Pied Flycatcher, Common Redstart and Tree Pipit.

Note: The map for the site is redrawn from the Copeland Bird Observatory Report map.

---

143 DUNDRUM BAY   OSNI Discoverer map: sheet 21
J41 37

Habitat
Dundrum Bay comprises the inner bay and Murlough National Nature Reserve, an area of heath and dune between the estuarine inner bay and the sea. The inner bay is an extremely sheltered estuary with extensive intertidal mudflats.

The nature reserve is vegetated with heath in the north, grassland in the centre and dense sea buckthorn in the south. The seaward side of the Reserve is bounded with sand dunes backing onto a long sandy beach.

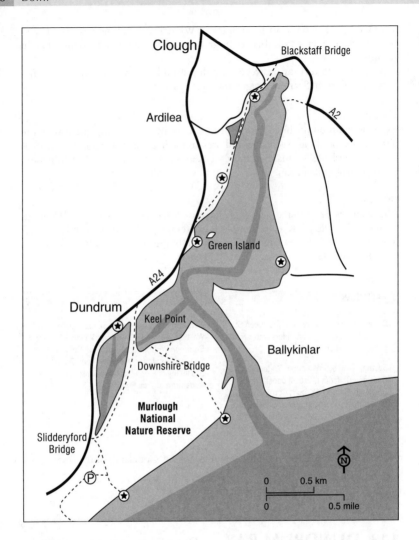

Species

The inner bay holds good numbers of Shelducks, Eurasian Wigeons, Mallards, Common Teals, Common Goldeneyes and Red-breasted Mergansers, together with several thousand waders. Outside the bay, large rafts of Common Scoters winter off Newcastle beach. Occasional Velvet Scoters are usually among them, and Surf Scoters have been found. Great Northern and Red-throated Divers, Great Crested Grebes, Common Goldeneyes, Scaups and one or two Long-tailed Ducks also winter in the outer bay.

The entire area holds up to 9,000 waders in winter, mostly on the mudflats of the inner bay. This section is an excellent place for autumn passage waders, especially Spotted Redshanks, Curlew Sandpipers and Little Stints.

The sand dune system holds a varied population of breeding birds including Cuckoo, European Stonechat, Grasshopper Warbler and Blackcap.

Timing

Autumn is the best time for passage waders, winter for wildfowl and larger flocks of waders on the inner bay and seaducks and grebes off the beach. In summer, the sand dune system has its breeding birds.

Access

Dundrum is 40 km south of Belfast and about 5 km north of Newcastle. The inner bay is accessible by road at a number of points along its north–west shore. Blackstaff Bridge on the A2 between Clough and Ardglass is at the northern head of the estuary. From here the National Trust Coastal Footpath runs along the edge of the estuary to Green Island where the A24 road is picked up again near Dundrum village. The A24 runs south from Dundrum and provides views of the southern arm of the inner bay. Murlough Nature Reserve can be reached by turning left off the A24 at Slidderyford Bridge or by turning into the National Trust car park about 1 km further on along the same road. There is a small entrance charge.

The warden can be contacted at the reserve (telephone 028 4375 1467).

CALENDAR

All year: Mute Swan, Shelduck, Mallard, Red-breasted Merganser, Grey Heron, Kestrel, Sparrowhawk, Common Buzzard, Oystercatcher, Ringed Plover, Collared Dove, Long-eared Owl, Skylark, Meadow Pipit, Kingfisher, Goldfinch, Linnet, Reed Bunting.

Autumn: possibility of Little Egret, passage waders including Curlew Sandpiper, Little Stint, Black-tailed Godwit, Whimbrel, Spotted Redshank, Greenshank, chance of Nearctic waders.

Winter: Whooper Swan, Brent Goose, Eurasian Wigeon, Common Teal, Common Goldeneye, Long-tailed Duck, Common Scoter, possibility of Velvet and Surf Scoters, Red-throated and Great Northern Divers, Great Crested Grebe, European Golden and Grey Plovers, Northern Lapwing, Dunlin, Curlew, Redshank, Redwing, Fieldfare, Twite.

Summer: Sand Martin, Northern Wheatear, Grasshopper Warbler, Common Whitethroat, Blackcap, Spotted Flycatcher.

Note: The map for this site is redrawn from the National Trust Nature Reserve map.

---

144 CARLINGFORD LOUGH: NORTH SHORE

OSNI Discoverer map: sheet 29,
OSNI Mournes Activity Map 1:25000
J17 18; J25 12

Habitat and Species

Carlingford is a long and deep sea lough which straddles the border between Northern Ireland and the Republic. The southern side, which is backed by the Carlingford Mountains on the Cooley peninsula, is dealt with under the accounts

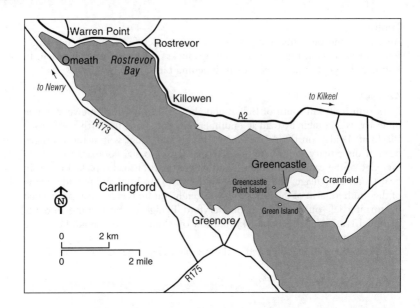

for Louth in the province of Leinster. The northern side, which concerns us here, has the more extensive mudflats and important seabird breeding islands, and is also backed by mountains, in this case the Mournes. With mountains on both sides, a tour of the lough shore is a very attractive scenic drive.

The lough has flocks of several hundred seaduck, mostly Scaups but also Common Goldeneyes, Red-breasted Mergansers and a few Long-tailed Ducks. Great Crested Grebes and both Red-throated and Great Northern Divers also occur, and one or two Slavonian Grebes usually winter. On the mudflats Brent Geese, Shelducks, Eurasian Wigeons, Common Teals, Mallards and the common wader species can all be seen in winter.

In summer, Green Island and Greencastle Point Islands, have breeding Common, Arctic and Sandwich Terns. These islands are closed to visitors but the terns can be seen well from the shore.

Access
Carlingford is a long lough. The best spots are near the mouth at Greencastle Point and near the head at Rostrevor Bay. Greencastle is best for terns in summer, but Rostrevor Bay is better for Scaup and the possibility of Slavonian Grebe and Long-tailed Duck.

Greencastle is approached from Kilkeel by following the road south towards Cranfield, turning right after 4 km and following the signs for Greencastle. Rostrevor is a village on the A2 midway between Kilkeel and Newry.

145 GROOMSPORT

OSNI Discoverer map: sheet 15
J53 84

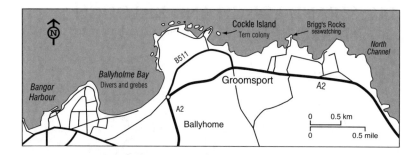

Habitat and Species

A small village on the coast about 5 km north-east of Bangor, Groomsport has a harbour, muddy and rocky shoreline and a small island offshore which provide a range of habitats. In addition, the location of the village at the mouth of Belfast Lough provides views of seabirds moving in and out of the lough as well as; along the coast. A birdwatcher who spent just over a year and a half in the village, Tony Marr, compiled a list of 139 species seen in the area in that period. The list included rarities such as Red-necked Grebe, Sabine's Gull and White-winged Black and Forster's Terns; since then it has hosted Ireland's second Sooty Tern. The records probably reflect as much the regularity of observation as the excellence of the habitats, but they show the potential of many similar places around the Irish coastline.

Cockle Island, the grassy island in the harbour, has breeding Ringed Plovers and Arctic Terns while Mediterranean Gulls have shown signs of breeding in recent years.

Dunnock

Access
Groomsport is reached by taking the B511 out or Bangor for Groomsport. Cars can be parked at the harbour.

146 STRAND LOUGH AND KILLOUGH HARBOUR

OSNI Discover map: sheet 21
J53 37

Habitat and Species
Strand Lough is a small freshwater lough which drains into a narrow muddy creek at the head of the open expanse of Killough Harbour. The lake has quite extensive reedbeds where Little Grebes, Mallards, Moorhens, Water Rails, Coots, Sedge Warblers and Reed Buntings nest. In winter Eurasian Wigeons, Common Teals, Mallards, Pochards, Tufted Ducks and Common Goldeneyes can all be seen and there are occasional visits by Whooper Swans, Pintails and Shovelers. Wader numbers are low but diversity is high and Ruffs are regular. Green and Wood Sandpipers turn up occasionally in autumn. Rarities recorded here include Lesser Yellowlegs, Long-billed Dowitcher and White-winged Black Tern.

Killough Harbour is an open muddy bay with good numbers of Mute Swans, Shelducks, Mallards and Eurasian Wigeons, and at times a party of Brent Geese. The common estuarine wader species can all be seen and occasional Glaucous Gulls turn up among the other gull species.

Access

Killough Harbour can be viewed from the A2 between Ardglass and Killough. The road runs around the harbour to Killough village, where there is a car park to the left of the main street and close to the pier.

Strand Lough is best watched from Killough Bridge on the road between Ardglass and Killough. Parking by the roadside is not easy and care should be exercised.

147 ST JOHN'S POINT   OSNI Discoverer map: sheet 21
J52 33

Habitat and Species

This is a rocky headland that projects southwards into the Irish Sea, giving excellent views of the sea. It is a popular seawatching point and can be attractive for passerine migrants. It tends to be better in autumn than spring.

Divers, Manx Shearwaters, occasional Sooty and Balearic Shearwaters, European Storm-petrels, Fulmars, Great, Arctic and Pomarine Skuas and terns all pass. Northern Wheatears, warblers and hirundines can be seen in suitable conditions. For both seabirds and passerines, the best conditions are in south-easterly winds.

Access

The headland is reached by driving south from Ardglass through Killough. At the end of Killough village, follow the signposts to the lighthouse and park at the point.

148 TOLLYMORE FOREST PARK
OSNI Discoverer map: sheet 29,
OSNI Mournes Activity Map 1:25000
J35 32

Habitat and Species

The Mourne Mountains are extensively forested with commercial spruce forestry but Tollymore Forest is a mixed deciduous and conifer forest at foothills of the Mourne Mountains and close to Newcastle on the coast. The Shimna River flows through the forest and it is the only breeding site for a feral population of Mandarin Ducks. The forest itself supports healthy populations of all of the Irish woodland species and has also attracted a number of rarer species

Tollymore Forest Park

such as Red Kite, Great Spotted Woodpecker and Hawfinch, while Wood Warbler has bred.

There is an entrance fee to the park, but there are good visitor facilities including an extensive trail system through the forest. The Lake and Ponds Trail which originates at the car park leads to the main lake where the Mandarins can usually be seen. However, only one of the trails, the Blue Path would be accessible for wheelchairs.

Access
From Newcastle, take the B180 towards Bryansford (this is well-signposted from the Town Centre); the Park Entrance is on the left-hand side of this road, about 3 km from Newcastle.

ARMAGH

This inland county is small and largely agricultural, with gardens and scattered wooded estates providing cover for breeding passerines. Although there is no direct access to the sea, the northern boundary is the next best thing to coastal, being formed by the lake edge of the southern shore of Lough Neagh.

The north-western boundary of the county is formed by the slow-moving River Blackwater, which holds breeding wildfowl and Common Snipes along its margins. The centre of the county is hilly. The eastern edge is marked by the Newry Canal, which joins Lough Neagh to Newry and eventually the sea at Carlingford Lough. The south is an area of small farms and villages adjoining the counties of Monaghan and Louth in the Republic.

149 LOUGH NEAGH: OXFORD ISLAND

OSNI Discoverer map: sheet 20
J06 61

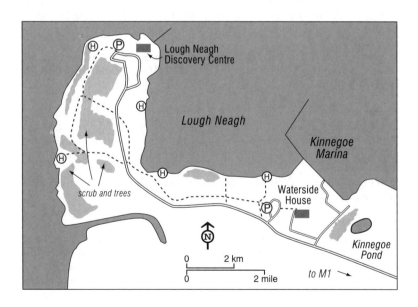

Habitat

The south-east corner of Lough Neagh is one of the best sections of the lake for diversity of wintering birds. Like much of the rest of the lough shoreline, the edge is backed by pasture and scrub of willow and alder. The peninsula, not really an island, projects out into Lough Neagh and is owned and managed by

Craigavon Borough Council and is a National Nature Reserve. On either side are shallow, reed-fringed bays, full of ducks in winter.

There are hides on each side of the peninsula from which most of the birds can be seen.

Species

Large numbers of diving ducks and smaller numbers of surface-feeding ducks and wild swans winter in the area. Whooper and a few Bewick's Swans are found on the fields nearby, but the principal features for the birdwatcher are the flocks of Pochards, Tufted Ducks and Common Goldeneyes, together with parties of Great Crested Grebes, Common Teals, Mallards, Scaups and Ruddy Ducks which feed around the peninsula. Rarer species occur among these ducks each winter. In recent years, Red-crested Pochards, Ring-necked Duck and Smew have been annual and Ferruginous Duck and Goosander have occurred. The first Irish record of Lesser Scaup is of a bird which returned annually for several winters in the 1980s and early 1990s. An unusual feature of this site is the number of seabirds that have been seen here during severe gales on the coast; its position on a peninsula jutting into the large lake has produced a list of seabirds that includes Sooty Shearwater, Leach's Storm-petrel, European Storm-petrel and regular occurrences of Manx Shearwater, Kittiwake and skuas.

In summer the reedbeds and offshore islands support over 150 pairs of Great Crested Grebes and smaller numbers of Mallards and Tufted Ducks as well as a handful of pairs of Gadwalls, Pochards and Ruddy Ducks. Black-headed Gulls and Common Terns nest on the small islands visible from the peninsula.

The scrub around the edge of the peninsula attracts a variety of breeding and wintering passerines. Reed Buntings, Grasshopper Warblers and Sedge Warblers nest, while flocks of thrushes and finches winter.

Timing

Oxford Island is at its best in winter between November and April when the chances of scarcer ducks species are highest. However, in summer the nesting grebes and ducks are an attraction as well. Autumn is the best time for migrant terns and waders.

Being so close to Craigavon, the area gets very crowded on Saturday and Sunday afternoons.

Access

The reserve is located close to the M1 about 7 km from Lurgan. Driving along the M1 from Belfast, turn off at junction 10 and take the third exit at the roundabout. The signposts point the way to Oxford Island. The Lough Neagh Discovery Centre is located at the reserve and comprises an exhibition centre, cafe and shop. The permanent exhibition includes graphic and multi-media displays covering most aspects of Lough Neagh from its history to its wildlife. Birdwatching trips by boat are also available. There are five hides and a network of paths runs around the Reserve.

For information, contact The Lough Neagh Discovery Centre, Oxford Island National Nature Reserve, Craigavon, Co Armagh, BT66 6NJ (tel: 028 38322205).

Note: The map for this site is redrawn from Craigavon Borough Council's map of the reserve.

150 LURGAN PARK LAKE

OSNI Discoverer map: sheet 20
J08 58

Habitat and Species

The public park in the centre of Lurgan has a broad reed-fringed lake, which holds a good variety of species of ducks and has held rarities. Because it is located so close to Lough Neagh and to the Craigavon Lakes, many ducks move between the three areas. If a rare duck has been found at Oxford Island, it may well turn up again at Lurgan Park or the Craigavon Lakes.

The commonest wintering ducks are Mallard, Tufted Duck and Pochard, together with smaller numbers of Common Teals, Shovelers and Ruddy Ducks. The last species breeds at Lough Neagh and up to 30 winter at Lurgan Park. The species began to colonise Northern Ireland from Britain in the 1970s. Rarities recorded here include Ring-necked Ducks, Ferruginous Ducks and Laughing Gull. Ring-billed Gull has also been recorded regularly.

A few pairs of Great Crested and Little Grebes, Moorhens and Coots nest on the lake.

Access
Coming from Belfast on the M1, turn off at junction 10 and follow the signs for Lurgan. Drive into the centre of the town and turn left down Windsor Avenue. Park your car at the entrance to the park.

151 CRAIGAVON LAKES

OSNI Discoverer map: sheet 20
J05 58

Habitat and Species
These lakes share with Lurgan Park Lake the advantage of being close to Lough Neagh. There are two artificial lakes, with three islands, and they have a shallow edge backed by open grassy areas and some scrub.

The lakes have similar wildfowl species to Oxford Island and Lurgan Park Lake: Pochard, Tufted Duck and Common Goldeneye are most common and Mallard also occurs. Smews and Goosanders are annual, though they move between here and Oxford Island, and Ring-necked Duck, Red-crested Pochard and Ferruginous Duck have been seen in recent years. Flocks of European Golden Plovers and Northern Lapwings are regular in winter on the open ground near the lakes.

Little Grebes, Mallard, Tufted Ducks, Coots and Moorhens nest on the lakes.

Access
Coming from Belfast on the M1, these lakes are approached from the same exit as are Oxford Island and Lurgan Park. Turn off at junction 10 and take the A76 towards Craigavon. Turn right after 1 km, following the sign for the Craigavon Centre. Take the right turn at the T-junction reached in 1.5 km and at the next roundabout follow the signs for Tannaghmore Gardens. There is a car park here and a footpath leads to the northern lake.

The southern and larger lake is reached by driving on along the A76 into Lurgan and turning right onto the A3 for Portadown. Cross the next two roundabouts, following the signs for the Craigavon Centre, and at the third roundabout take the right exit to Craigavon Lakes. There is a car park at the lake. This lake is popular for watersports at weekends.

152 REEDY FLAT

OSNI Discoverer map: sheet 19
H98 64

Habitat and Species

One of the frustrating aspects of birding around Lough Neagh is the lack of access by public road down to the lakeshore that is not obscured by dense reedbeds or willow scrub. However, the Reedy Flat is an area of lakeshore just west of Oxford Island where a road runs parallel to the lake from which there are several access roads to the shore and this exposes a section of shoreline and open water. The open meadows between the road and the shore are good for swans, Curlew and Northern Lapwing, and the open terrain affords better scanning of the lake for ducks and grebes without your views being obstructed by vegetation.

Access

From Oxford Island Nature Reserve, take the B2 west to Derrytrasna. Continue through Derrytrasna towards Bannfoot and after about 0.5 km turn right (Derrycrow Road). This road reaches the lakeshore after about 1 km and runs alongside for about 2 km.

FERMANAGH

A county of lakes and woodland, Fermanagh is relatively underwatched by birdwatchers, probably because of its distance from Belfast, where most birders live. Yet as well as its lakes and woods, Fermanagh also holds traditional pastures and damp meadows, which provide breeding areas for waders such as Northern Lapwing and Common Snipe.

Upper and Lower Lough Erne split the county into two halves and are the most prominent birdwatching sites in the county. Yet there are a number of other lakes holding wildfowl in winter, and a number of forest parks which are open to the public and hold a good number of breeding bird species. Fermanagh is probably the centre of the Irish Garden Warbler breeding population.

This is another county without direct access to the sea, so seabird numbers are low, but terns and gulls breed on Lough Erne.

153 LOWER LOUGH ERNE

OSNI Discoverer map: sheet 17, 27
H00 60; H24 48

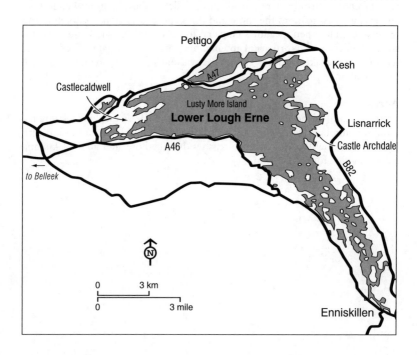

Habitat

This is a broad, open, triangular lough downstream of Enniskillen and very different in character to the Upper Lough. The water levels are controlled by the Ballyshannon Hydroelectric Scheme, so they fluctuate. Levels in winter are lower than in summer. The edge of the lough has been colonised by scrub, which provides breeding habitat for a number of breeding birds, and there are woodland areas at Castle Archdale on the east shore, Lough Navar on the west side and Castlecaldwell in the north-west corner, which support a number of passerine species in both summer and winter.

Species

The Lower Lough has fewer wildfowl in winter than the more sheltered Upper Lough, but it does have Great Crested and Little Grebes, Whooper Swans, Mallards, Common Teals, Tufted Ducks, Pochards and Common Goldeneyes.

For many years this was the centre of the Irish Common Scoter breeding population and over 100 pairs nested, mostly at Castlecaldwell, but in recent years they have become extinct as a breeding species. Competition with Roach for food and the impact of predatory Mink on nesting females have been suggested as reasons for the decline.

One can never predict which species may occur at an inland lake like this. Both Velvet and Surf Scoters, for example, have been seen on Lower Lough Erne in summer, though breeding has not been suspected.

Great Crested Grebe, Mallard, Common Teal, Tufted Duck and Red-breasted Merganser all breed on Lower Lough Erne. The scrub around the fringe of the lake is very attractive for warblers in summer: Sedge, Grasshopper and Willow Warblers, Common Chiffchaff, Blackcap and Garden Warbler all nest. This area is the headquarters of the Irish Garden Warbler breeding population. Common Crossbills have bred at Castlecaldwell and Siskins and Lesser Redpolls also breed.

On the shoreline a scattering of Northern Lapwings, Common Snipe, Curlews and Redshanks breed, and a tiny handful of Dunlins.

Great Black-backed, Lesser Black-backed and Black-headed Gulls as well as Sandwich and Common Terns nest on the islands. Yellow-legged, Iceland and Little Gulls have all been reported at this inland site.

Timing

Summer is much the best time to see gulls, terns and Garden Warblers, the specialities of Lower Lough Erne.

Access

The shore of Lower Lough Erne is ringed by a road which runs close to the water's edge for most of its length.

Castlecaldwell is an RSPB Reserve in the north-west corner of the lough and has wooded islands, two of which may be visited by boat. The old estate is owned by the Forest Service but operated by the RSPB under a management agreement. Access is off the main road from Kesh to Belleek and is sign posted from both small towns. It is about 8 km from Belleek and the warden can be contacted on 028 38322205.

Castle Archdale is another old estate and includes a group of islands on the east side of the laugh. It also has nesting wildfowl and Garden Warblers. Leave

Magpie

Enniskillen on the Pettigoe road and turn left onto the B82 about 6 km beyond the town. The country park is on the left-hand side about 5 km along this road. This is a National Nature Reserve. The warden can be contacted at, Castle Archdale Country Park, Lisnarick, Irvinestown, Co Fermanagh (tel: 028 6862 1588).

CALENDAR

Summer: Mallard, Common Teal, Tufted Duck, Red-breasted Merganser, Great Crested and Little Grebes, Coot, Moorhen, Northern Lapwing, Curlew, Common Snipe, Redshank, Dunlin, Black-headed, Common, Herring, Lesser Black-backed and Great Black-backed Gulls, Sandwich and Common Terns, Blackcap, Garden Warbler.

Winter: Whooper Swan, Eurasian Wigeon, Mallard, Common Teal, Tufted Duck, Pochard, Common Goldeneye, Red-breasted Merganser, Great Crested Grebe, European Golden Plover, Northern Lapwing, Curlew.

154 UPPER LOUGH ERNE

OSNI Discoverer map: sheet 27, 27A

H26 40; H41 23

Habitat and Species

This is a much more complex habitat than the Lower Lough. It is a continuation of the Lough Oughter system in Co Cavan, and the mixture of drumlins, small bays and lagoons and extensive reedbeds is very similar. The shore is shallow and sheltered and very attractive for wintering wildfowl.

Winter wildfowl counts have shown that Upper Lough Erne holds over 400 Great Crested Grebes, over 400 Mute Swans and about 800 Whooper Swans in winter. These totals are very impressive, and these species are accompanied by large flocks of Eurasian Wigeons, Common Teals and Mallards, and smaller numbers of feral Canada Geese, Tufted Ducks, Pochards and Common Goldeneyes.

Some of the islands hold heronries and Cormorants are common non-breeding visitors. Moorhens and Coots are widespread in both winter and summer.

The marshy land around the lough is an important habitat for nesting waders. Northern Lapwings, Common Snipes, Curlews and Redshanks all breed, although numbers have declined significantly in recent years.

Access

The Upper Lough has a very indented shoreline, which is difficult to reach. A number of small roads lead down to the edge of many of the bays and the visitor should use the 1:50,000 map to check out which to follow. The main road between Lisnaskea and Derrylin crosses the lough and provides good viewing.

Kilmore Lough and Moorlough on the east side of the lough are accessible from Lisnaskea and have a good cross-section of the birds of the area.

SELECTED BIBLIOGRAPHY

The author wishes to thank the authors and organisations for a source of information from the following publications.

BOOKS

Belfast RSPB Members' Group, 1989. 2nd Ed. *Birds Around Belfast*, RSPB, Belfast.

Belfast RSPB Members' Group, 1985. *Birds Beyond Belfast*, RSPB, Belfast.

Carruthers, T., 1993. *The Birds of Killarney National Park*. Stationery Office, Dublin.

Carruthers, T., 1998. *Kerry – a Natural History*. The Collins Press.

Colhoun, K., 2001. *Irish Wetland Bird Survey, 1998–99*. BirdWatch Ireland, Dublin.

Crowe, O., 2005. *Ireland's Wetlands and their Waterbirds: Status and Distribution*. BirdWatch Ireland, Dublin.

D'Arcy, G., 1978. *Birds at Lough Beg*. Blackstaff Press, Belfast.

Dempsey, E., 2008. *Birdwatching in Ireland*. Gill & Macmillan, Dublin.

Dempsey, E., & O'Clery, M., 2007. *Finding Birds in Ireland – The Complete Guide*. Gill & Macmillan, Dublin.

Gibbons, D. W., Reid, J. B. & Chapman, R. A., 1993. *The New Atlas of Breeding Birds in Britain and Ireland*. T & A.D. Poyser, Berkhamstead.

Heery, S., 1993. *The Shannon Floodlands – a Natural History*. Tír Eolas, Galway.

Hutchinson, C., 1989. *Birds in Ireland*. T & A. D. Poyser, Berkhamstead.

Irish Rare Birds Committee, 1998. *Checklist of the Birds of Ireland*. BirdWatch Ireland, Dublin.

Lack, P., 1986. *The Atlas of Wintering Birds in Britain and Ireland*. T & A.D. Poyser, Berkhamstead.

Lovatt, J. K., 2006. *Birds in Cavan*. BirdWatch Ireland, Dublin.

Lysaght, L., 2002. *Atlas of Breeding Birds of the Burren and Aran Islands*. BirdWatch Ireland, Dublin.

MacLochlainn, C., 2003. *Toraigh – Tory Island, a remote and historic outpost*. Comharchumann Thoraí Teoranta, Tory.

McElheron, A., 2005. *Merlins of the Wicklow Mountains*. Columba Press, Dublin.

Mitchell, P. I., Newton, S., Ratcliffe, N. & Dunn, T. E., 2004. *Seabird Populations of Britain and Ireland*. Christopher Helm, London.

Murphy, J. N., Cooney, A., Rattigan, J., Lynch, T., 2003. *The Shannon Airport Lagoon – a Unique Irish Habitat*. BirdWatch Ireland, Dublin.

Ní Lamhna, É., 2008. *Wild Dublin*. O'Brien Press, Dublin.

Roche, R. & Merne, O., 1977. *Saltees: Islands of Birds and Legends*. O'Brien Press, Dublin.

Sharrock, J. T. R., 1972. *The Natural History of Cape Clear Island*. T & A.D. Poyser, Berkhamsted.

Sheppard, R., 1993. *Ireland's Wetland Wealth*. Irish Wildbird Conservancy, Dublin.

BIRD REPORTS

Irish Birds: the major Irish ornithological journal, published annually by BirdWatch Ireland.

Irish Rare Bird Report: published annually online at www.irbc.ie and in *Irish Birds*, the annual journal of BirdWatch Ireland.

Rare Irish Breeding Birds: published annually in *Irish Birds,* the annual journal of BirdWatch Ireland.

Irish Ringing Report: published annually in *Irish Birds,* the annual journal of BirdWatch Ireland.

Irish Wetland Bird Survey: published annually in *Irish Birds,* the annual journal of BirdWatch Ireland.

Scarce Migrants in Ireland Report: published annually in *Irish Birds,* the annual journal of BirdWatch Ireland.

Northern Ireland Bird Report: published almost annually by The Northern Ireland Birdwatchers Association.

Irish East Coast Bird Report: Published annually by BirdWatch Ireland.

Cork Bird Report: published every few years by local birders.

Copeland Bird Report: published annually by Copeland Bird Observatory.

The Dingle Peninsula Bird Report: published every few years by the West Kerry Branch of BirdWatch Ireland.

Mid-Shannon Bird Repor: published every few years by BirdWatch Ireland.

WEBSITES

www.birdwatchireland.ie BirdWatch Ireland
BirdWatch Ireland (BWI) is the largest independent conservation organisation in Ireland.

www.birdweb.net BirdWeb
Website of the South Dublin branch of BirdWatch Ireland.

www.bwifingal.ie BWI Fingal
North Dublin branch of BirdWatch Ireland.

www.clarebirdwatching.com Clare Birdwatching
Website for the Clare branch of BWI.

www.birdwatchgalway.org BWI Galway
Website of the Galway branch of BWI.

www.birdwatchtipp.com BWI Tipperary
Website of the Tipperary branch of BWI. Local sites, events and information.

www.spd.dcu.ie/tolka BWI Tolka
Website from Dublin's Tolka Valley branch.

www.sligobirding.com BWI Sligo
Sligo BWI website.

www.castlebar.ie/clubs/mayo-birdwatch/BWIMayo
Mayo branch of BWI.

www.goldeneagle.ie/ Irish Golden Eagle Project
Golden Eagle reintroduction programme.

http://listserv.heanet.ie/lists/ibn-l.html IrishBirdNet (IBN)
Archived emails from the Irish BirdNet email group.

www.birdsireland.com/Birdsireland.com
Web site of the Birds of Ireland News Service, Ireland's rare bird news providers.

www.irishbirding.com Irish Birding
Birding news website with information on latest sightings etc.

www.geographia.com/northern-ireland/ukibrd01.htm   Birdwatching   in
    N. Ireland
NI Tourist Board website with information on birding in Northern Ireland.

www.irbc.ie Irish Rare Birds Committee
Website of rare bird recording body for the Republic of Ireland, includes a
    checklist of Ireland's Birds.

www.waterfordwildlife.com Waterford Wildlife
General natural history information for Co Waterford.

http://countynaturetrust.tripod.com/ County Nature Trust
Cork-based NGO dealing with wildlife conservation.

www.louthnaturetrust.org Louth Nature Trust
Louth-based NGO dealing with wildlife conservation.

www.habitas.org.uk/cbo Copeland Bird Observatory
Website of the Copeland Bird Observatory.

www.waterfordbirds.com WaterfordBirds
County website with recent reports, archives, county list, photos and site guide.

www.nioc.co.uk Northern Ireland Ornithologists Club

http://niraptorstudygroup.co.uk – Northern Ireland Raptor Study Group

http://iwt.ie Irish Wildlife Trust
Wildlife Conservation NGO.

www.strangfordlough.org Strangford Lough Information Network
Information site with maps, images and data on breeding birds and wintering
    birds.

www.ulsterwildlifetrust.org Ulster Wildlife Trust
Nature conservation NGO.

www.wexfordnaturalists.com/ Wexford Naturalist's Field Club
Wexford Naturalist's website with useful information on Wexford's birds.

www.npws.ie National Parks and Wildlife Service
Government environmental and conservation body.

CODE OF CONDUCT
FOR BIRDWATCHERS

Today's birdwatchers are a poweful force for nature conservation. The number of those of us interested in birds rises continually and it is vital that we take seriously our responsibility to avoid any harm to birds.

We must present a responsible image to non-birdwatchers who may be affected by our activities and particularly those on whose sympathy and support the future of birds may rest. There are ten points to bear in mind:

The welfare of birds must come first.
Habitat must be protected.
Keep disturbance to birds and their habitat to a minimum.
If you find a rare bird, think carefully about whom you should tell.
Do not harass migrants.
Abide by the bird protection laws at all times.
Respect the rights of landowners.
Respect the rights of other people in the countryside.
Make your records available to the local bird recorder.
Behave abroad as you would when birdwatching at home.

This is a shortened version of *The Birdwatcher's Code of Conduct* (RSPB).

INDEX OF SPECIES
BY SITE NUMBER

INDEX OF SITES
BY PAGE NUMBERS